GEORGE ELIOT

Also in the Virago/Pantheon Pioneers Series:

GEORGE ELIOT

JENNIFER UGLOW

· VIRAGO ·
PANTHEON
PIONEERS

Library of Congress Cataloging-in-Publication Data

Uglow, Jennifer S.
George Eliot.
Bibliography: p.
Includes index.
1. Eliot, George, 1919–1880.   2. Novelists, English—
19th century—Biography.   3. Women in literature.
4. Feminism and literature—Great Britain—History—19th
century.   I. Title.
PR4681.U35   1987   823′.8 [B]   87-43049
ISBN 0-394-53704-1
ISBN 0-394-75359-3 (pbk.)

Manufactured in the United States of America

Virago/Pantheon Pioneers

First American Edition

For my mother, Lorita, and in memory of my father
Brian Crowther, since they both–in different ways–taught me
how to read.

CONTENTS

ACKNOWLEDGEMENTS

My debts as a reader are innumerable, and I have tried to acknowledge at least some of them in the notes and the select bibliography. Here I should simply like to say how grateful I am to all the friends who have shared their reading of George Eliot with me and helped me clarify my ideas — especially Ursula Fanthorpe and Dorothy Bednarowska, best of teachers, and, more recently, Hermione Lee, Chris Cherry, Christine Carswell, Ursula Owen and, above all, Steve Uglow.

I should also like to thank Kathleen Adams of the George Eliot fellowship for her great help in tracking down one or two elusive photographs. The illustrations are reproduced by kind permission of the following: Mrs A.S. Womersley for the photograph of George Eliot, 1854; The National Portrait Gallery for the drawing of George Eliot, 1872 and the photograph of John Walter Cross; The British Library for the dedication to *Adam Bede* and the text of *Daniel Deronda*; Courtesy of the Trustees of the British Museum, Department of Prints and Drawings, for the drawing of George Henry Lewes; Coventry City Libraries for the photographs of Charles Bray and Herbert Spencer; Nuneaton Museum and Art Gallery for the portraits of Robert Evans, Cara Bray and Sarah Hennell; The Mistress and Fellows of Girton College for the portrait of Barbara Bodichon; the BBC Hulton Picture Library for the photograph of The Priory.

A NOTE ON THE TEXTS

The page references to the novels refer to the Penguin editions. Chapter numbers are also given for ease of reference to other editions. Other page references and abbreviations are as follows:

Poems   *The Legend of Jubal and Other Poems* (Blackwood, Edinburgh, 1874)

Impressions   *Impressions of Theophrastus Such* (Blackwood, Edinburgh, 1879)

Essays   *Essays of George Eliot*, ed. T. Pinney (London, Routledge & Kegan Paul, 1963)

Letters   *The George Eliot Letters*, ed. G.S. Haight (New Haven and London, Yale University Press, 1954–6, 1978)

CHRONOLOGY

1819	*22 November*: Mary Ann(e) Evans born at South Farm, Arbury, Warwickshire, daughter of Robert Evans, agent to the Newdigate family and manager of their Warwickshire estates, and his second wife Christiana Pearson. She was their third child after Christiana (1814) and Isaac (1816), and there were two older children by Robert Evans's first marriage, Robert (1802) and Fanny (1805). *29 November*: baptised at Chilvers Coton church.
1820	Her family move to Griff House, Chilvers Coton.
1824	Mary Ann and her elder brother Isaac go to dame school; then Isaac is sent to school at Foleshill and Mary Ann to Miss Latham's boarding school at Attleborough. Very unhappy.
1828	She moves to Mrs Wallington's school at Nuneaton. Maria Lewis is her teacher.
1832	She goes to the Miss Franklins' school, Warwick Row, Coventry.
1836	*3 February*: her mother, Christiana, dies. She leaves school.
1837	*30 May*: her elder sister Chrissey marries and she takes over as housekeeper to her father. Continues her lessons with tutors from Coventry.
1838	Visits London with Isaac.

1840	Her first published work, a poem, is published in the *Christian Observer*.
1841	*17 March*: Robert Evans and Mary Ann move to Bird Grove, 21 Foleshill, Coventry. In June Isaac marries Sarah Rawlins and takes over Griff. *November*: she meets Charles and Cara Bray at Rosehill.
1842	*2 January*: refuses to go to church with her father. No reconciliation until she attends church again in May. In the summer she becomes friends with Sara Hennell.
1843	*November*: visits Dr Brabant at Devizes.
1844	*January*: begins her translation of Strauss's *Das Leben Jesu*.
1845	*March*: proposed to by an unnamed picture-restorer. G.H. Lewes publishes *Biographical History of Philosophy*.
1846	*15 June*: publication of *The Life of Jesus, Critically Examined*. Her essays, 'Poetry and Prose from the Notebook of an Eccentric' published in the *Coventry Herald*.
1848	*July*: Mary Ann meets Emerson.
1849	*31 May*: Robert Evans dies. *12 June*: Mary Ann goes to Europe with the Brays but remains at Geneva on her own, staying with the painter François D'Albert Durade and his wife. Changes her name to 'Marianne', then 'Marian'.
1850	*March*: returns to Rosehill, visits Griff. *October*: John Chapman and Mackay come to Coventry and she reviews Mackay's *Progress of the Intellect* for *The Westminster Review* (January 1851); visits London.
1851	*8 January*: moves in as lodger with John Chapman and family at 142 Strand. Disputes with his wife and mistress make her return to Rosehill in March. In September she returns, as assistant editor of *The Westminster Review*. *October*: meets G.H. Lewes in a bookshop.
1852	Intense friendship with Herbert Spencer ends in

August. *June*: Bessie Rayner Parkes introduces her to Barbara Leigh Smith. *October*: she goes to stay with Combes, the phrenologist, and then Harriet Martineau.

1853   *October*: leaves Chapman's and moves to 21 Cambridge Street. Growing closeness to Lewes. Begins translation of Feuerbach's *Das Wesen des Christenthums*. Publication of Lewes's essays, *Comte's Philosophy of the Sciences*.

1854   *July*: her Feuerbach translation, *The Essence of Christianity*, is published, and on 20 July Marian leaves for Germany with G.H. Lewes. In Germany, where Lewes works on his *Life of Goethe*, she writes articles for *The Westminster Review* and begins a translation of Spinoza's *Ethics*. *1 November*: Lewes's *The Life and Work of Goethe* published.

1855   *14 March*: they arrive at Dover. After living in lodgings in London and East Sheen they move to 8 Park Shot, Richmond.

1856   *May–August*: holiday in Ilfracombe and Tenby. *12 September*: finishes 'Silly Novels by Lady Novelists'. *23 September*: begins 'Amos Barton'.

1857   'Amos Barton' appears in *Blackwood's Magazine*, to be followed by the other *Scenes of Clerical Life*, 'Mr Gilfil's Love Story' and 'Janet's Repentance'. *4 February*: she adopts the pseudonym 'George Eliot'. In May when she tells him of her union with Lewes, her brother Isaac breaks off all family relations. Barbara Leigh Smith publishes *Women and Work* and founds *The Englishwoman's Journal*, edited by Bessie Parkes; in June she marries Dr Eugène Bodichon. The 1857 Matrimonial Causes Act is passed. *22 October*: Eliot begins *Adam Bede*.

1858   *April–August*: Marian and Lewes visit Germany. *Scenes of Clerical Life* appears in two-volume book form. *January*: Lewes publishes *Physiology of Common Life*.

1859   *1 February*: *Adam Bede* published in three volumes.
          11 February: move to Holly Lodge, Wandsworth.
          March: Marian's sister Chrissey dies. *July: The
          Lifted Veil* appears in *Blackwood's*. *September*: holi-
          day in Dorset, then Lincolnshire, looking at mills
          and rivers. The Society for Promoting the Employ-
          ment of Women is started.

1860   *March—June*: visit to Rome, Naples, Florence and
          Switzerland. Lewes draws her attention to Savona-
          rola as subject for a 'historical romance'. *4 April*:
          The Mill on the Floss published, in three volumes.
          30 September: she begins *Silas Marner*.

1861   *2 April*: *Silas Marner* published. A second visit to
          Florence to gather background for *Romola*, which is
          serialised in the *Cornhill* from July 1862.

1863   *Romola* published in three-volume book form.
          August: Marian and Lewes buy The Priory, North
          Bank, Regent's Park.

1864   *May*: a further visit to Italy. *June*: she begins *The
          Spanish Gypsy*, abandoned February 1859.

1865   *29 March*: begins *Felix Holt, the Radical*. Lewes's
          son Charles marries Gertrude Hill.

1866   *15 June*: *Felix Holt* published in three volumes.
          December: Marian and George leave for Spain,
          returning March 1867, and Marian begins work
          again on *The Spanish Gypsy*. Barbara Bodichon,
          with Emily Davies and Jessie Boucherett, drafts the
          first Women's Suffrage Petition, presented to Par-
          liament by J.S. Mill.

1867   Lewes begins *Problems of Life and Mind* (5 volumes,
          1874—79). Second Reform Act passed; Mill's
          Amendment rejected.

1868   *June*: *The Spanish Gypsy* published. Summer holi-
          day in Germany and Switzerland.

1869   *March—April*: in Italy. *May*: Thornton Lewes
          returns ill from Natal; dies on 19 October. Eliot
          works on her poems and, sporadically, on *Middle-*

march. Girton College founded. J.S. Mill's *On the Subjection of Women* published. Begins *Middlemarch*.

1870   *March–May*: visit to Germany, Prague, Austria. *December*: begins story, 'Miss Brooke'. First Married Women's Property Act passed.

1871   *July*: *Armgart* published. *December*: first book of *Middlemarch* published. It appears in eight books, concluding the following December.

1872   *September*: holiday in Germany; in Homburg they visit the Kursaal gaming rooms.

1873   *June–August*: visits synagogues in Germany.

1874   *June*: *The Legend of Jubal and Other Poems* published. Eliot works on *Daniel Deronda*, falls ill with a kidney-stone, which causes recurrent bouts of pain from now on.

1875   Herbert Lewes dies in Natal.

1876   *1 February–1 September*: *Daniel Deronda* appears in eight books. *December*: Marian and Lewes buy The Heights, Witley, Surrey and spend Christmas with the Cross family at Weybridge.

1877   Height of social acclaim for Eliot and Lewes; for example, they dine with Princess Louise in May. Summer spent at Witley.

1878   Summer at Witley but Lewes very ill with cancer. *30 November*: Lewes dies.

1879   Eliot works on Lewes's *Problems of Life and Mind*. *February*: she begins to see Johnny Cross. Publication of *Impressions of Theophrastus Such*. Founds a G.H. Lewes Studentship at Cambridge.

1880   *9 April*: she agrees to marry Cross. *6 May*: married at St George's, Hanover Square; they leave at once for the continent. *June*: on their honeymoon in Venice, Cross throws himself into the Grand Canal. They return to Witley. *3 December*: they move to 4 Cheyne Walk. On the 19th George Eliot falls ill with a sore throat; fever sets in. *22 December*: she dies, aged 61. *29 December*: she is buried in Highgate Cemetery, next to G.H. Lewes.

GEORGE
ELIOT

INTRODUCTION

Now we think it an immense mistake to maintain that there is no sex in literature. Science has no sex: the mere knowing and reasoning faculties, if they act correctly, must go through the same process, and arrive at the same result. But in art and literature, which imply the action of the entire being, in which every fibre of the nature is engaged, in which every peculiar modification of the individual makes itself felt, woman has something specific to contribute.

('Woman in France', 1854; *Essays*, p. 53)

'you are seeking to escape from the lot God has laid upon you. You wish your true name and your true place in life to be hidden, that you may choose for yourself a new name and a new place, and have no rule but your own will. And I have a command to call you back. My daughter, you must return to your place.'

(*Romola*, 1863; Chap. 40, pp. 428–9)

'you can never imagine what it is to have a man's force of genius in you, and yet to suffer the slavery of being a girl.'

(*Daniel Deronda*, 1876; Chap. 51, p. 694)

All her writing life George Eliot puzzled over the question of what it meant to be a woman artist, and whether men and women had a different kind of imagination – a fundamentally different perspective on life. In this as in so many other areas of her professional and personal life, she was a pioneer. But that passionate declaration about 'a man's force of genius', made by Daniel Deronda's mother, a brilliant singer who gave up her child for her career, is oddly ambivalent when you look at it closely. Eliot can never be drawn easily into the feminist net, whatever powerful currents we may sense beneath the surface of her novels.[1] For despite her lasting friendships with women, her life and her letters suggest that she does seem to have believed that the world of men was where genius flourished, and where the vital discussions and advances took place; that was where she wanted to be.

Nor was she the kind of feminist writer who moved confidently from an analysis of women's oppression to a defiant claim for independence and personal fulfilment, although her novels certainly show the way girls and women are trapped by educational, economic and legal constraints, and are keenly alert to sexual exploitation and what she sees as a male desire for 'mastery' over women. From the 1850s on she knew many of the leading Victorian feminist campaigners, such as Barbara Bodichon (her closest friend), Bessie Parkes, Florence Nightingale, Octavia Hill and Emily Davies. She sympathised with their cause – but always drew back from active involvement. This was partly, one feels, to protect herself – because she could not commit herself to action without encroaching on her life as a writer. Partly, too, because she feared (rightly) that her reputation as a woman living with a married man might damage rather than help the cause. But it was also because she genuinely felt that there was a danger in the emphasis placed by the contemporary women's movement on individual rights; partnership, not personal fulfilment, should be the goal.

Some people would take this further and say that her novels, far from being feminist, are almost repressively conservative. From first publication they have aroused disquiet because the fate of their heroines and the narrow range of opportunities they are offered seem to contrast so strongly with the freedom and achievement of their creator.

Is this true? The novels are rich in a marvellously observed range of portraits of both men and women, including an often neglected group of women who exercise considerable power (for good or ill) in customary or traditional domestic spheres. Mrs Poyser, Dolly Winthrop, Maggie Tulliver's Dodson aunts – all belong to a group Eliot had identified in her essay on the German social historian, von Riehl, when she wrote 'the *wives* and *mothers* here, as elsewhere, are a conservative influence and the habits temporarily laid aside in the outer world are recovered by the fireside' (*Essays*, p. 275). But the women whose lives form the crises of her narratives fall into rather different categories. There are the succession of child-like dreamers – Hetty Sorrel in *Adam Bede*, Tessa in *Romola*, Molly in *Silas Marner* – who are treated as sexual playthings, deceived and often abandoned. There are the strong aspiring heroines – Dinah Morris, Romola, Dorothea Brooke, Mirah – who end by turning their backs on public achievement in favour of domestic duty, content with a filtered, rather than a direct, influence on the world. There are the troubled souls like Maggie, Mrs Transome or Gwendolen Harleth who are ultimately trapped by their own turbulent desires.

But Eliot is describing, rather than prescribing, when she paints these lives so vividly. She is acutely sensitive to the anguish of souls like Dorothea and Maggie who are caught at the wrong moment in history and thus unable to step outside and see their own dilemma clearly. Her novels as a whole often vibrate with anger – no one can read 'Janet's Repentance', *The Mill on the Floss* or *Felix Holt* without receiving a sharp lesson in the way women are excluded from learning and action and are bullied or exploited by men who trade on their physical and economic strength. The reader can sometimes sense a keen desire to avenge the victims, to take the side of the turbulent rebels and the dark heroines who will always lose their happiness to their mild, blonde, goody-goody opposites. Indeed, Eliot's novels do contain a measure of vengeance, enforced either by the fierce goddess Nemesis, or through the intervention of Chance, in the shape of providential death, which pulls strong men like lawyer Dempster, Tom Tulliver and Grandcourt down into its deep unmanageable waters.[2] The underlying drive to avenge wronged womanhood does battle against the overt acceptance that, for women, duty must come before desire – but it never entirely outweighs it.

The message for the lives of women seems to be that although change must come (preferably gradually rather than suddenly), it must not be at the expense of traditional female values. Although it is wrong for women to be excluded from access to common culture and to common stores of power, they should demand them for the sake of partnership with men and for the good of society, not just for their own separate fulfilment. At a more theoretical level it gradually becomes clear that Eliot believes partnership is essential for social harmony because there are integral feminine and masculine attributes which derive from biology, cultural conditioning and individual upbringing which encourage contrasting attitudes to life. Whereas in the past the male approach has been dominant, it is now time to balance and correct it through the female influence. What this often means in fictional practice, and what makes some modern feminists find her novels hard to swallow, is that the traditional roles which seem to oppress women most – the submissive daughter, the self-denying wife, the loving and patient mother – become symbols of woman's social mission. The vital thing is not to launch women into a masculine sphere, but to 'feminise' men, because the feminine strengths have for so long been trampled underfoot and undervalued.

This is also the mission of the woman artist as Eliot saw it. In her own fiction we find it expressed most powerfully not at the level of individual lives – although she does depict a series of men who are made more feminine by their experiences – but at a less explicit level. There is a rich vein of symbolism in the plots and in the language of George Eliot's fiction – those books which seem so bound up in the workings of the everyday world are, when one looks closely, woven through with mystery, with dreams and prophecies and visions. And far from dealing always with 'unfashionable families' they are populated with orphans, children, women and disinherited men seeking a material, but also a spiritual, home. To take just one of the examples which will be examined later, a central image in the early novels is that of a man spiritually renewed by the sacrifice of a woman's life or happiness: Amos Barton, Mr Tryan, Adam Bede, Silas Marner. Philip Wakem in *The Mill on the Floss* describes very clearly the gift of transferred life which has come to him through his love for Maggie and his sharing of her suffering. Through the extension of their feminine sympathies, and through their imagination, a dangerous faculty, but the only one which can apprehend the 'truth of feeling', men and women can grow towards a new, more flexible ethical vision.

The tension in her novels between the angry, desperate striving for learning, autonomy and power and for women's rights, and the ethic of renunciation and suppression, makes one want to reflect a little on George Eliot's own life. The outward pattern is that of the rebel – the girl who defies her father and brother when her principles will not allow her to attend church; the pioneering translator and woman journalist, assistant editor of the prestigious *Westminster Review*, fêted by leading intellectual men of her day; the woman who defied convention by living openly with a married man and yet who ended her life as the darling of the establishment, famous and rich, surrounded by admirers at solemn Sunday afternoon receptions. The inner story however, poignantly conveyed by letters and journals, sets her frustrations, ambitions and 'monstrous ego' against a sense of terrible weakness, despondency and self-distrust. For most of her life, while always aware of her exceptional capabilities, she needed constant reassurance and was haunted by the fear that she would not be able to achieve anything of lasting value.

In her private and professional life the insecurities of the artist were compounded by the insecurities of the woman. She needed reassuring not only about her work but about herself – she had to know that she was loved. This meant that she almost courted dependency and she seems to have longed to excel in traditional roles – good daughter, good wife, good mother. Enormous achievement was accompanied, as it was for many other exceptional Victorian women, by constant physical ailments, devastating headaches, and feelings of lassitude and depression. She had to find a way to link the two worlds to which she wished to belong: that of work, strength and self-assertion and that of domesticity, weakness and submission. Contemporary critics liked to declare that by becoming artists, musicians or writers women lost their essential womanly qualities: Eliot wanted to assert the opposite – that the realm of the imagination was itself essentially feminine and even maternal. It was feeling and not 'masculine reasoning', the ability to identify and to empathise which allowed the artist to create. Furthermore, she suggested with tantalising vagueness, women could use these powers in a distinctive way.

This was one form of resolution. But Eliot had other internal conflicts to resolve. Her progress from devout schoolgirl to radical journalist and novelist ran counter to her family and class background as well as to the normal expectations of a woman's role. By 1856, when she began to write fiction, her father was dead and her union with George Henry Lewes had so outraged her brother Isaac, the most beloved figure in her childhood, that he refused to communicate with her directly and forbade the rest of her family to do so. She was no longer a country girl but an urban intellectual, one of that new floating class dubbed 'The Order of the Quill'. Just as in her worst depressions she yearned to escape from the narrow city streets and a visit to the fields and open sky made her a new person, so in the pages of her English novels she carefully reconstructed that world she had lost, that of her own childhood and of her father's youth.

For while Mary Ann Evans was gradually transforming herself into George Eliot, the Midland society she had left was also undergoing some radical changes. And despite her intellectual allegiance to optimistic notions of progress and development, Eliot regretted those changes. Haunted by the notional innocence of her own childhood she wrote of a world which no longer existed. Although she had been pulled into the new intelligentsia she did not want to turn her back on her past, just as while she revelled in her independence as a professional woman she did not want to abandon the traditional woman's roles. This feeling of being pulled in two directions affects her political vision; a radical hatred of existing abuses of power is balanced by a lingering attachment to the old order. A new order must come, but it must come gently – avoiding any sense of uprooting.[3] This ambivalent stance is very similar to her position on the rights of women. And she resolves the conflict in a curiously similar way by looking for a radical *new* social ethic in *traditional* roles. Indeed she links the two areas in her mind when she tries to show that the old systems of loyalties, especially those practised by the rural artisans, are more organic and also more 'maternal' than the striving, separatist ethic of the emergent industrial society.

These feminist and class contradictions are related to an existential insecurity, which is tied in its turn to the rapid change and economic uncertainties of the mid-nineteenth century. George Eliot had created a life for herself through efforts of will, through her work and through a series of conscious choices which appeared to be the opposite of that to which history had consigned her as the daughter of a provincial surveyor. Her own life therefore contradicted the patterns of gradual development which so profoundly attracted her in the philosophical theories of Comte, the social history of von Riehl, and the natural history studies she undertook with Lewes, confirmed by her later reading of Darwin. She had constructed her own existence – and what was more she had done it all through her skill with words, 'the magic signs that conjure up a world' as she calls them in *Romola*. Her life, like her novels, seemed sometimes to be only a fragile illusion, and every time she finished a book she feared she might never be able to achieve the conjuring trick again.[4]

Eliot's essays, letters and novels all reveal a fascinated delight in language, in its general evolution and in particular words. She is particularly taken with the paradox that language is a living historical system which carries the innuendoes and values of its past development, and yet every act of speech or writing is an act of choice – a course picked out of a myriad possibilities. In *The Mill on the Floss*, stunned by the different implications of the images she could use for Tom Tulliver's education (ploughing and sowing, eating and digesting, writing on a blank slate), she bursts out in amused despair at Aristotle's praise of metaphorical speech as a sign of intelligence, asking that if he were a 'modern' would he not mix his approval 'with a lamentation that intelligence so rarely shows itself in speech without metaphor – that we can so seldom declare what a thing is, except by saying it is something else?'

The effect of this (very 'modern') self-consciousness is to make the whole solid structure of her fictional world seem suddenly impermanent – as if it might fall to the earth like a collapsing card-house, or perhaps a cascade of printer's type. The same tension is there – she loves the independent power of her building, her articulate self, but distrusts and mocks it at the same time. In her fiction, nearly all the most intense and important communication takes place when speech has broken down. Here again feminine symbolism comes to her aid, for she identifies this level of communication (where gestures, looks, touch, food, music and shared experience speak louder than words) with a classic and very double-edged definition of the intuitive understanding of women, the old pre-rational, pre-verbal 'feminine' unconscious as opposed to the rule-bound reasoning of men.

George Eliot's apparently realistic social novels turn on the personal crises of men and women, on marriage, betrayal, child-birth and abandonment and the rediscovery of parents – and in these dramas, characters sometimes defy the literary male and female stereotypes and are sometimes trapped by them. There is little to be learnt by subjecting such rich and varied character-isation to any crude schematic analysis; yet if we look we find that the stories of particular men and women are supported by a background network of references to 'masculine and feminine' qualities and that the meaning of their experience is expressed through a series of provocative ideas and symbols. In a complex and unexpected way the most reactionary positions (from a twentieth-century feminist's point of view) – the good daughter, the loving wife, the self-denying mother – become the sites of a subtle and subversive argument for a radical change in our way of looking at life and organising society.

Fascinated by these paradoxes, I decided to approach George Eliot in the light of their contradictions. My aim is not to seek to assimilate Eliot into a specific tradition of women's writing, or to relate her own belief in sexual difference to a search for a women's language, 'l'écriture feminine', although I have often been stimulated by such thinking.[5] My starting point is more material than theoretical: what I would like to do in a quite free-wheeling manner is simply to trace the double curve of her life and her fiction, seeing where the arcs cross and intersect. I do not believe that literature can be divorced from the conditions of the age in which it is written nor from the gender or background of the writer, especially a writer so very conscious of her own development and aims. So I want to examine the emotional patterns set in her childhood and to see how they relate to conflicts of values in the economic and social life which enveloped her, and I want to follow her self-education and her move into the masculine world of journalism. And because it is so tempting to stress George Eliot's passionate, emotional side at the expense of her wrestling, marshalling, ordering intellect and her moral intensity, I will also look at the places in her essays, letters and novels where she grapples explicitly with issues of women and change, the role of the woman artist or with definitions of 'masculine' and 'feminine'.

One problem of this twofold interest, in her life and in her fiction, is immediate and intriguing: what should I call her? A literary focus seems to demand 'George Eliot' from the beginning, yet this would be absurdly wrong, for it was not 'George Eliot' who travelled the Warwickshire lanes with her father or eloped with G.H. Lewes. As she grew she cloaked herself in names: Mary Ann, Clematis, Apollyon, Marianne, Marian, Polly, George Eliot, M.E. Lewes (perhaps the most significant pseudonym of all) and, at the last, Mrs J.W. Cross.

In the end I have decided to follow her lead, using the principal names she used, Mary Ann and then Marian, and keeping 'George Eliot' for discussion of her writing.

Another result of my dual concern is that this book undergoes a shift of emphasis in the middle, just as Eliot's own life did. In the first chapters, biography dominates and then, with *Scenes of Clerical Life*, the novels take the majority of the space. The chapter ' "George Eliot" and the Woman Question' is a bridge, for many of the feminist concerns of her fiction were fired by the preoccupations of that decade, particularly the arguments about the exclusion of women from culture and from authority, and the tension between the fight for individual rights and the traditional women's role of self-denial and community. Gradually, in the sequence of Eliot's fiction from the *Scenes* to *Daniel Deronda*, the landscape of relations between the sexes, so shifting and various, becomes a metaphor, a means of exploring analogous boundaries: literary, moral, social, political, emotional and spiritual. The charting and crossing of these frontiers is what makes George Eliot, in a supreme sense, a pioneer.

Writing about Eliot is itself a daunting adventure, although the territory has been well mapped by critics and biographers, notably Gordon Haight, Barbara Hardy, Ruby Redinger and, more recently, Gillian Beer. Feminist criticism, in all its variety, is the most stimulating of guides but one may still remain indebted to earlier insights. The afternoon I wrote my last sentence I turned back to Virginia Woolf to check a detail, and found myself re-reading her essay on George Eliot with that shock of recognition which comes when you suddenly understand afresh something which has been taken for granted for a long time. Here is her final judgement:

Save for the supreme courage of their endeavour, the struggle ends, for her heroines, in tragedy, or in a compromise that is even more melancholy. But their story is the incomplete version of the story of George Eliot herself. For her, too, the burden and complexity of womanhood were not enough; she must reach beyond the sanctuary and pluck for herself the strange bright fruits of art and knowledge. Clasping them as few women have ever clasped them, she would not renounce her own inheritance – the difference of view, the difference of standard – nor accept an inappropriate reward. Thus we behold her, a memorable figure, inordinately praised and shrinking from her fame, despondent, reserved, shuddering back into the arms of love as if there alone were satisfaction and, it might be, justification, at the same time reaching out with 'a fastidious yet hungry ambition' for all that life could offer the free and inquiring mind and confronting her feminine aspirations with the real world of men. Triumphant was the issue for her, whatever it may have been for her creations, and as we recollect all that she dared and achieved, how with every obstacle against her – sex and health and convention – she sought more knowledge and more freedom till the body, weighted with its double burden, sank worn out, we must lay upon her grave whatever we have it in our power to bestow of laurel and of rose.[6]

This extravagant, soaring conclusion confidently defines the paradox which is my, more questioning beginning. But for every reader it will feel as if the shores are new and the sand untrodden: we all read and discover George Eliot for ourselves.

CHAPTER ONE

GROWING UP
AT GRIFF

George Eliot returned again and again to the landscape of her youth for the raw material of her novels – incidents, characters, settings. And she returned as well to an inner country of feeling and thought, for the streams of memory which flow most visibly through avowedly autobiographical works like *The Mill on the Floss* never run dry but are merely diverted underground to sustain the rich novels of her later years, *Middlemarch* and *Daniel Deronda*. She revisited the outward scenes most openly in her early work; and although she denied precise identifications her memory was unusually acute, so much so that without a journal and without going back to talk to local people she could recreate events and places with such precision in *Scenes of Clerical Life* that the people of Nuneaton circulated a 'key' to the book – getting almost every one right, except the author.

It is tempting to follow her back, although vital to differentiate between what we know about her early life and what we can conjecture about her relationships and her feelings. The way that the creative imagination uses memory and 'real life' is subtle and indirect, and searching in a childhood for patterns which dictate the shape of adult work can lead us to undervalue later developments and conscious intentions. But Eliot herself, like Wordsworth whom she greatly admired, was extremely interested in the shaping power of childhood. From the first letters which remain to us, written in her late teens, she starts to explain her own development in terms of early experiences and returns to the theme in her poetry, which often analyses, with great sensitivity, the pre-literate stage in her life. What is clear, from her own accounts, is that these years did more than launch her on one of the most extraordinary self-educations of the century. They also laid down emotional directions and needs which remained inner guides to what she demanded from religion, knowledge and social relations and which help to set the formal and moral patterns of her fiction.

The early nineteenth-century Warwickshire countryside with its farms and fields, canals and coach-roads in which George Eliot grew up, and which she wrote about with such clarity, seems like an image of steadfast British solidity. In fact it was already entering an era of fluidity and change, and by the time she came to write *Felix Holt* in 1865, she looked back to it as to a vanished world. The pace of life had accelerated, the railway had pierced provincial seclusion, the traditional political patterns had vanished with the 1832 Reform Act, and the old economic base of farms and market towns was crumbling with the development of the mines and rise of the factory system, which was already throwing local hand-loom weavers out of work when she was a girl.

Eliot's own family's history shows the type of upward movement open to a skilled, hard-working artisan family in Georgian and Regency England. She always remained sensitive to class patterns and the life she chose as an intellectual was one way of escaping the network of rank and respectability which entwined her youth. Her father, Robert Evans, born in 1773, was the fourth son of a Derbyshire carpenter. He took up his father's trade and crossed the county border to work in Ellastone, Staffordshire, where he became friendly with the son of the tenant of nearby Wootton Hall, Francis Parker. He began to work at the Hall, first as a forester and then as a bailiff; in other words taking the same career steps as Eliot's Adam Bede, and Caleb Garth, with whom he shared other attributes – a great physical strength, a keen 'natural' eye for timber and strict notions of honesty. He married his first wife, Harriet, in 1801 and they had two children (Robert, born in 1802, and Fanny, in 1805) before he followed Francis Parker to the estates he inherited from the Newdigates at Arbury, Warwickshire.

In 1809 Harriet died and four years later Robert married Christiana Pearson, the daughter of a prosperous local family, already proud of their 'yeoman' status, who are usually taken to be the models for the Dodson family in *Mill on the Floss*. Like her older sister and brother, Christiana (Chrissey) and Isaac Pearson, born in 1814 and 1816, Mary Ann was to take her name from this side of the family, from two of the three married Pearson sisters who lived nearby. Four months after her birth (on 22 November 1819), the family moved to Griff House, still on the Arbury Estate, at Chilvers Coton on the outskirts of Coventry. This was her home until the age of twenty.

Griff was a large old red-brick house, with a wide, tree-shaded lawn in front and large flower-filled gardens and rough orchards behind, still backed by a jumble of outhouses and stables, with tall fir trees and then the open fields.

'Dear Old Griff,' she wrote on receiving a photograph of it in 1876, 'still smiles at me with a face which is more like than unlike its former self, and I seem to feel the air through the attic above the drawing room, from which when a little girl I often looked towards the distant view of Coton 'College' [the Workhouse] thinking the view rather sublime' (*Letters*, Vol. VI, p. 46). This is Maggie Tulliver's attic, the favourite retreat where she punished her doll, 'fretted out all her ill-humours, and talked aloud to the worm-eaten floors and the worm-eaten shelves and the dark rafters festooned with cobwebs' (*Mill*, Book I, Chap. 4, p. 78).

At first sight it seems that the dominant figures in this landscape were both male: her father and her brother. Mary Ann spent much time with her father driving with him on his trips as consultant to local landowners as well as on his rounds as bailiff. In this way she became one of the 'midland-bred souls' she describes in *Middlemarch* who learn to love every field with its particular shape, 'the things they toddled among, or perhaps learned by heart, standing between their father's knees, while he drove leisurely' (*Middlemarch*, Chap. 12, p. 131). She also learned by heart the world of business conducted by men, the intricate links in the agricultural economy and the class system, and – as she waited in the kitchen, or housekeeper's hall – the separate values of the domestic hierarchy, ruled by women.

Despite their later struggles George Eliot was devoted to her father. When she was a famous writer and was described as a 'farmer's daughter', she said that for her own part she would not mind being labelled a 'tinker's daughter', but felt she must do justice to her father's memory:

Now my Father did not raise himself from being an artizan to be a farmer: he raised himself from being an artizan to be a man whose extensive knowledge in very varied practical departments made his services valued through several counties. He had large knowledge of building, of mines, of plantation, of various branches of valuation and measurement – of all that is essential to the management of large estates.

(*Letters*, Vol. III, pp. 168–9)

But outside practical matters Robert Evans's determination and decisiveness could harden into obstinacy and narrow-mindedness. He deferred to his wife Christiana over many important decisions and, when opposed, fell back on entrenched positions. John Cross, George Eliot's young husband at the end of her life, and her first biographer, suggests that the portrait of the grey-haired father in her last work, *Impressions of Theophrastus Such*, is 'true autobiography', giving us a glimpse of a man whose political and social views were so moulded in his youth by the reaction to the French Revolution that

I was accustomed to hear him utter the word 'government' in a tone that charged it with awe, and made it part of my effective religion, in contrast with the word 'rebel', which seemed to carry the stamp of evil in its syllables, and, lit by the fact that Satan was the first rebel, made an argument dispensing with more detailed enquiry.

(*Impressions*, 'Looking Backward')[1]

When Mary Ann challenged his views on churchgoing in her

twenties, her refusal seemed also a rebellion against this other 'effective religion', ideas of order, control and the rule of the father.

The second influential figure was her brother Isaac. The two children, two years apart, were brought together after the move to Griff. At that point Robert, aged eighteen, left to be the Newdigate agent at Kirk Hallam taking fourteen-year-old Fanny as his housekeeper, and Chrissey, aged five, was sent away to school. Isaac and Mary Ann went to a 'dame school' across the road from their house but, in her memory and in the stories Isaac told Cross, they frequently escaped to play. In 1869, aged fifty-five, when she had not seen Isaac for many years, George Eliot composed a sequence of eleven sonnets called 'Brother and Sister'.[2]

The sonnets she called 'Little descriptive bits on the mutual influence of their small lives', which describe the escape from a protectively fussing mother (who 'stroked down my tippet, set my brother's frill') past the rookery elms through the meadows, waist-high in grass, waving forget-me-nots and tangled wild roses, on into the dark copse where the gypsies have left a cold camp fire. By the brown canal the little girl, her brother's shadow, is left to hold the fishing rod and warned against passing barges. She falls into a daydream and forgets but at the last minute snatches out the line – with a perch on the end. Instead of blame, she receives praise – but the inner guilt remains. The trusting love which gives her the confidence to explore and the security to dream is broken by the shock of being called back, the guilt of irresponsibility. Her love for Isaac, it turns out, was not the union of two buds growing together as she first describes it, but a more complex and troubling emotion which sets both of them free to be themselves.

> Thus rambling we were schooled in deepest lore,
> And learned the meanings that give words a soul,
> The fear, the love, the primal passionate store,
> Whose shaping impulses make manhood whole.
>
> (*Poems*, p. 201)

In comparison with this troubled, nostalgic analysis of a relationship, she hardly returns at all in her later writing to her sister
Chrissey (perhaps the model for neat, passive Lucy in *The Mill
on the Floss*) although she loved her and her growing family
dearly, suffered for their financial plight and grieved at their
estrangement. She is even more reticent about her mother, who
was clearly a strong personality despite being a semi-invalid
since Mary Ann's birth. Little glimpses of her fussing at Isaac
and Mary Ann to keep to the path, of her irritation at the waste
of candles when her daughter developed a passion for books, are
hardly enough on which to build a theory of hostility and rejection. Biographers have identified her with the anxious Mrs
Poyser, fussy Mrs Tulliver or, even worse, with Mrs Hackit in
Amos Barton – a thin, pale, busy woman, with a permanent
eye on the household economy, a strongly independent mind,
blistering tongue and permanent load of knitting; 'in her utmost
enjoyment of spoiling a friend's self-satisfaction she was
never known to spoil a stocking' (*Scenes*, 'Amos Barton', p. 46).
But the comparative silence is strange.[3] Perhaps the lack of
response from her mother made her turn more positively to the
energetic, exploring, managing world of her father and Isaac.
She was to have a succession of close, intense relationships with
women, but she never let herself surrender to their judgement as
she did to that of men.

In 1824 Mary Ann joined Chrissey at Miss Latham's school at
Attleborough. She was dreadfully homesick and terrified at
night, and was treated by the older girls with an indulgent
affection which even then acknowledged her outward gravity
('Little Mamma', they called her) and inner vulnerability. In the
holidays Isaac, like Tom Tulliver, became more impatient with
his shadow, and it is at this age, six or seven, that she seems to
have spent more time with her father and to have buried herself
in books: *The Pilgrim's Progress*, *The Vicar of Wakefield*, *Aesop's
Fables* and less obvious works like Defoe's *History of the Devil*
and *Joe Miller's Jest Book*.

A year later, already recognised as an exceptional student,
Mary Ann moved with Chrissey to Mrs Wallington's school,

Church Lane, Nuneaton. Here she became attached to the gentle evangelical principal governess, Maria Lewis, a close relationship which was to last for fourteen years. An immediate effect was that Mary Ann plunged into the fervent evangelicalism which dominated her adolescence, following her enthusiastic young teacher who was a keen supporter of the stirring preacher John Jones. (Jones's lectures at the parish church in 1828 led to riots in the town and to weeks of violent debate, whose mood was later to be brilliantly evoked in 'Janet's Repentance'.) By thirteen she was so far ahead that her father was advised to send her on to the best school for girls in the neighbourhood, which was run by two sisters, Mary and Rebecca Franklin, daughters of a well-known local minister, Francis Franklin of the Cow Lane Baptist Chapel (the model for Rufus Lyon in *Felix Holt*). Mary, the eldest of ten children, had started the school in the front parlour while Rebecca (like Esther Lyon) went off to finishing school in Paris.

Rebecca's meticulous, carefully weighted prose style and manner of speaking gave added gravity to Mary Ann's already solemn manner – but she gained confidence, for here her intelligence and diligence were regarded as good, not eccentric, qualities. She read widely, in authors from Milton to Scott; she shone at painting, at English composition and at French, apparently translating Maria Edgeworth's novels at the age of thirteen. Her music was also outstanding, and a fellow pupil remembered that she performed well in public but was so nervous that afterwards she 'would rush to her room and throw herself on the floor in an agony of tears'.[4]

During these years, a characteristic that she later described as 'a desire insatiable for the esteem of my fellow creatures' (*Letters*, Vol. I, p. 19) must have been satisfied by the praise she won for her work and for her 'saintly' behaviour – leading prayer meetings, renouncing pleasure with enthusiasm. (It is not surprising that another girl should have found it impossible to imagine her ever having been a baby.) She took the evangelical tenets very much to heart – indeed her Calvinism seems to have been stricter than that of her teachers. She believed that even for the 'elect' few the true life of the spirit could only develop from a profound recognition of the essential sinfulness and unworthiness of the self. Care for the soul must predominate over care for the body and cultivation of the mind, and one should live through good works and renunciation. Her growing spiritual fervour increased her alienation from Isaac, who resisted all her passionate arguments and held to the High Church views of his Birmingham tutor. But it increased her closeness to Maria Lewis, whom she visited in the holidays.

The sequence of existing letters to Maria begins in early 1836. At Christmas Mary Ann left school. Her mother was dying of cancer, her father suddenly became seriously ill. She and Chrissey nursed them both, but although Robert Evans soon recovered he was not his old self – and Christiana, after intense pain, died in the summer. Nowhere does George Eliot write openly of this long illness and grim death, which must have put a terrible strain upon an imaginative sixteen-year-old. She seems to have chosen to identify with her father's grief rather than show her own, throwing herself into the task of cheering him, buying furniture, reading aloud. In May 1837 when Chrissey married a doctor, Edward Clarke, Mary Ann took over control of the house, refusing her father's offer to employ a housekeeper, perhaps not only out of duty but out of a feeling that this was one of the few ways she could attain autonomy and status.

Her active if limited life brought her into contact with the gentry (she continued to study in Arbury Hall library), with the prosperous middle classes (through church bazaars and meetings) and with the poor, through clothing clubs for the families of out-of-work ribbon-workers. She ran the large house and dairy methodically, although often groaning at the endless succession of tasks, and she was also caught up in the social round appropriate to a well-off young woman, paying and receiving calls most afternoons. Maria Lewis and her old schoolfriend Martha Jackson (Patty) came to stay, and she in turn visited them and others like Rebecca Franklin in Coventry. Her close family also made demands on her time – she often visited Chrissey, and she read aloud to her father each evening.

Yet in the interstices of this packed routine she continued her own reading. She read while dressing, walking, making jam: she literally devoured books, especially evangelical biographies and essays. Praising Isaac Taylor's controversial study *Ancient Christianity and the Doctrines of the Oxford Tracts*, she told Maria, 'I have gulped it, pardon my coarseness, in a most reptile like fashion; I must *chew* it thoroughly to facilitate its assimilation with my mental frame.' She also had teachers from Coventry to tutor her in music, German and later Italian, and her letters show her serious interest in contemporary debates on theology and religious history. Desperate to find some way of using all this knowledge she spent six months of 1839 labouring like a young female Casaubon on a chart of ecclesiastical history, only to lay it aside when another more complex chart was published. Gradually, however, by the end of that year her reading altered – the Romantic poets and the High Church Oxford Movement writers crept into favour and by 1840 these were alternating with an extraordinary amount of scientific literature. She herself provides the most arresting image of her eclectic learning and her frustrating, fragmentary life in a letter to Maria complaining that her mind

never of the most highly organised genus is more than usually chaotic, or rather it is like a stratus of conglomerated fragments that shows here a jaw and rib of some ponderous quadruped, there a delicate alto-relievo of some fernlike plant, tiny shells and mysterious nondescripts, encrusted and united with some unvaried and uninteresting but useful stone. My mind presents just such an assemblage of disjointed speci-mens of history, ancient and modern, scraps of poetry picked up from Shakespeare, Cowper, Wordsworth and Milton, newspaper topics, morsels of Addison and Bacon, Latin verbs, geometry, entomology and chemistry, reviews and metaphysics, all arrested and petrified and smothered by the fast thickening every day accession of actual events, relative anxieties and household cares and vexations.

(*Letters*, Vol. I, p. 29)

This self-education is an astounding achievement, the more so because, although we know she was attracted to her Italian teacher Brezzi, there was virtually no one with whom she could discuss her growing knowledge. Her women friends were vital to her and in 1840 they adopted fashionable 'flower names' – Veronica for Maria (Fidelity in Friendship), Ivy for Patty (Constancy) and Clematis for Mary Ann (Mental Beauty). But letters to Maria and Patty – both of whom expressed awe and backed away when she suggested that they choose improving topics to correspond on – were simply not enough. It must have been hard, dispiriting work, especially as at this period she could see no possibility of ever *using* the intellectual achievements which she felt were her only attributes, compensating in part for her physical plainness.

She was terribly lonely, complaining of numbing languor and headaches, symptoms of the tension of her pent-up existence in a 'walled-in world'. She longed for escape: 'Oh how lusciously joyous to have the wind of heaven blow on one after being *stived* in a human atmosphere', and could only check her 'Byronic invective' by reminding herself

of Corinne's or rather Oswald's reproof, La vie est un *combat*, pas un *hymne*. We should aim to be like plants in the chamber of sickness, dispensing purifying air even in a region that turns all pale its verdure and cramps its instinctive propensity to expand . . .

(*Letters*, Vol. I, pp. 70–3)

The reference to Corinne, Madame de Stael's inspiring heroine, the poet, writer and actress who could thrill all Rome with her improvisations, is significant and poignant in contrast to this young girl's 'walled-in' existence.[5]

She never forgot this early despair, telling Cross at the end of her life 'the only thing I should care never to dwell on would be the absolute despair I suffered from of ever being able to achieve anything. No one could have felt greater despair.'[6]

Her reading of theology, of books like Carlyle's *Chartism* and *Sartor Resartus*, and of certain novels, was beginning to shake her intellectual acceptance of religious doctrine. And, at the same time, her knowledge of her own powers made her rebel against the self-abasement of evangelicalism. 'I make the most

humiliating and appalling confessions with little or no corresponding feeling' (*Letters*, Vol. I, p. 19) she told her aunt, and her
letters are permeated by protests at her own egoism and ambition.

Anecdotes about these years demonstrate her mingled feelings
of fear, longing and suppression, and there is a suggestion that
she needed her religion to banish anything which might be too
emotionally overwhelming. For example, her first visit to
London in 1838 with Isaac turned into a battleground; she
strictly evangelical, refusing to go to the theatre, deprecating
sightseeing, shopping only for a copy of Josephus's *History of the
Jews*; he, with strong traditional Anglican views, and a comfort-
able sense of the importance of pleasure, buying – in the same
shop – a couple of hunting sketches. The same note of protest-
ing too much sounds in her stricture against church music,
countered by the emotional outburst which caused a commotion
when she had a fit of hysterics during the Birmingham festival –
again at an emotionally upsetting time, when Isaac's engagement
had been announced and they were visiting his fiancée, Sarah
Rawlins. Similar hysterics are recorded at a party – brought
on, so she said, because of her feelings about the frivolity of
dancing. The hysterical note is most noticeable of all in the
denunciation of imaginative literature in a famous letter of 1839
to Maria Lewis. In it she condemns the power of fiction to
embody fantasy (like the strength of music to embody unspecified longings) as straightforwardly pernicious. In her view, apart
from a canon of classics including *Don Quixote*, *Hudibras*,
Robinson Crusoe, Scott, Byron and Southey's romances (how
do they escape?) and the great (but morally problematic)
Shakespeare, most other fiction and poetry is dangerous to
youth. And she makes the astonishing declaration:

I am I confess not an impartial member of a jury in this case for I owe
the culprits a grudge for injuries inflicted on myself. I shall carry to my
grave the mental diseases with which they have contaminated me.
When I was quite a little child I could not be satisfied with the things
around me; I was constantly living in a world of my own creation, and

was quite contented to have no companions that I might be left to my own musings and imagine scenes in which I was chief actress. Conceive what a character novels would give to these Utopias. I was early supplied with them by those who kindly sought to gratify my appetite for reading and of course I made use of the materials they supplied for building my castles in the air.

(Letters, Vol. I, p. 22)

Eighteen months later we have a further glimpse of how painful she found her unconquerable impulse towards fantasy, in another letter to Maria:

My imagination is an enemy that must be cast down ere I can enjoy peace or exhibit uniformity of character. I know not which of its caprices I have most to dread – that which incites it to spread sackcloth 'above, below, around', or that which makes it 'cheat my eye with blear illusion, and beget strange dreams,' of excellence and beauty in beings and things of only 'working day price'.

(Letters, Vol. I, pp. 65–6)

Interestingly, this last letter begins with a joking reference – from which she disassociates herself – to female irrationality, 'women's privilege to give no reason for her actions'. Mary Ann's youthful evangelicalism was deeply marked by the destructive self-restraint which, as George Eliot, she was to criticise so bitterly in some nonconformist sects in her novels. But her religion offered her radical visions – of justified rebellion against any faith, and of the rightness of conscience, of the individual. It also provided a model for expressing the spiritual power of women. Women teachers like Maria and the Franklins were matched by women preachers like her own aunt Elizabeth, and by stories of the many female visionaries of earlier sects, like Joanna Southcott. Evangelical teaching often linked two ideas, which one can trace in Eliot's fiction – that women were the more sensitive, emotional sex and that their 'natural' maternal instincts were inseparably linked to an ethic of self-renunciation. The next stage in evangelical argument was to link this maternal self-denial to God's sacrificial love for erring humanity, and thus to forge symbolic bonds between the suffering of women and the suffering of Jesus, and between the redemptive power of Christ and the redemptive moral power of women's love. Such suggestive ideas were outlined in books like Louis Aimé-Martin's *Education des mères de famille et de la Civilisation de genre humain par les femmes* (1834), which Mary Ann read with great enthusiasm in October 1840, although rather sternly explaining to Patty that the author was 'not an orthodox Christian'.

But at this point, since she also resisted her maternal destiny, and shuddered at the thought of perpetual domesticity, books such as Aimé-Martin's or Sarah Lewis's *Women's Mission* perhaps increased her discomfort.[7] By the time she was twenty her intellectual horizon was widening to embrace social and political issues like franchise reform, the repeal of the Corn Laws, the operation of the poor law and spreading agricultural unrest, and her broader view simply made her own situation seem more intolerable. She could see no place for herself in her sister's domestic world, where she might become 'a stunted growth'. She felt marriage, the sphere of women's maternal mission, was not for her and she spurned every spark of attraction she felt for men (an unknown friend, her Italian teacher Brezzi). Yet everything she achieved outwardly, although exciting, and even 'beguiling' like her study of languages, seemed hollow unless given life by feeling. Unable to generalise her experience, she could not see it in terms of the conflict many contemporary women felt between their abilities and ambitions, and the submission and surrender that was expected of them. Her isolation was not something she could share, but a personal cross. She felt no one would ever love her: she was both victim and culprit – and could only anticipate further punishment:

And to tell you the truth I begin to feel involuntarily isolated, and, without being humble, to have such a consciousness that I am a negation of all that finds love and esteem as makes me anticipate for myself – no matter what; I shall have countless undeserved enemies if my life be prolonged, wherever my lot may be cast, and I need rigid discipline, which I have never yet had.

(*Letters*, Vol. I, p. 51)

This feeling of loneliness and separation is a dominant strand in her childhood and youth, summed up in the description Cross gives of the five-year-old schoolgirl shivering outside the circle of larger girls blocking the narrow fireplace, trembling at night with indescribable terrors. Even before this she seems to have felt different from other girls and somehow disapproved of, a situation she tried to escape by immersing herself in a series of roles – as she recognised quite early, 'we are all *Dramatis Personae* in our own life'. These roles included tomboy sister, dutiful daughter, model pupil, 'saintly' young woman. Each performance extended her vision by sympathy, yet left her incomplete. Even her love for Isaac denied some aspect of her personality:

> His sorrow was my sorrow; and his joy
> Sent little leaps and laughs through all my frame;
> My doll seemed lifeless and no girlish toy
> Had any reason when my brother came.
>
> (*Poems*, p. 206)

Ironically, while these roles brought her esteem – she caught the fish, won the prizes – they actually cut her off from affection, setting her even more apart: 'her school fellows loved her as much as they could venture to love one they felt to be so immeasurably superior to themselves'. Towards the end of her life she told a friend, Edith Simcox, that when she was young the women and girls around her thought her 'uncanny'. They sensed the unconventional power beneath the public face.

The other strand is that of the secret self: the passionate, rebellious, dreaming nature of her heroine of *Mill on the Floss*, Maggie Tulliver, and the dangers it entails. Maggie suffers because she falls, finally, under the spell of her fantasy. But for her creator, as a child, the world of the imagination, whether sensual daydream or fantasy given form by fiction, was a world where one could be solitary without fear, alone without loneliness. In the 'Brother and Sister' sonnets of 1869 she slips into a metaphor which associates the world of the imagination with a female power common in the nineteenth century – from

Coleridge's 'damsel with a dulcimer' to Tennyson's Lady of Shalott. Yet these romantic images have a threatening air – such power is far from normal, and can be self-destructive as well as creative. The damsel may inspire, but the Lady of Shalott is a victim. What Eliot seems to have feared when she wrote 'my imagination is an enemy' is the transforming, subverting power which presents the mundane world in a new perspective and can disable the victim of the trance from dealing with the 'real' (male) world of action and responsibility. Here, she is left to watch the fishing line:

> Proud of the task, I watched with all my might
> For one whole minute, till my eyes grew wide,
> Till sky and earth took on a strange new light
> And seemed a dream-world floating on some tide –
>
> A fair pavilioned boat for me alone
> Bearing me onward through the vast unknown.

But the brother sees a barge coming and shocks her back into fearful awareness:

> Nearer and angrier came my brother's cry,
> And all my soul was quivering fear. . .
>
> *(Poems,* pp. 203–4)

By 1840, as the letters on the imagination show, her inner mental and emotional life was at odds with her restricting daily life. There are aspects of her novels which smack of the same forced restraint as the letters of her late adolescence – a certain flat-footed heaviness, a refusal to let her characters spring away from the path of duty without dire results; a fearful dread of escapism, an insistence that the cool clear gaze is the only means of reaching truth. Many readers long, I know, for a touch of chaos, madness, irresponsibility.

What holds the reins so tight? Fear perhaps, a vertiginous sense that, unless conscience controls mind, all mental effort may trickle away in ventures like Casaubon's 'Key to All Mythologies'; unless reason controls desire, the tide of emotion may swirl unchecked like the tide which carries away Maggie and Stephen Guest; unless moral principles check self-interest, integrity may weaken and be lost – as it is by Tito, or by Lydgate. George Eliot's fictional world seems so weighty and ballasted by details of landscape, behaviour, intricate social codes and practices but, like the stable Warwickshire community she grew up in, and like the carefully packed routine of her early life, it is a structure built on sand. What gives her fiction its eternal appeal is the balance of forces experienced by her heroes and heroines within the books, and by the author herself, who knows that the solidity of her meticulous realist novels, like the social systems they demonstrate, is mere illusion, created by the sorcery of words.

CHAPTER TWO

FROM COVENTRY TO GENEVA

In 1841 Isaac married and took over Griff. Mary Ann was whisked with her father away from her rural childhood world to Bird Grove, Foleshill, on the outskirts of the growing city of Coventry. Ten years later, aged thirty, she left for London, her base for the rest of her life. Although at the end of the decade she was still intense, passionate and emotionally dependent, she had grown from an awkward girl into a woman, with a justified confidence in her powers, a firm base for her evolving personal philosophy and a public reputation as the translator of Strauss's *Das Leben Jesu*, one of the most influential books of the century. The transition was far from easy, but although there were periods of intense depression one rarely hears in her letters the despair of those adolescent appeals to Maria Lewis. The dominant tone is one of struggle. Here she is, for example, writing a quick note to her closest friend Sara Hennell during the hard months of nursing her father through his final illness in 1848:

more anon – this from my doleful prison of stupidity and barrenness with a yawning trap-door ready to let me down into utter fatuity. But I can even yet feel the omnipotence of a glorious chord. Poor pebble as I am left entangled among the slimy weeds I can yet hear from afar the rushing of the blessed torrent and rejoice that it is there to bathe and brighten other pebbles less unworthy of the polishing.

(*Letters*, Vol. I, p. 274)

The self-deprecating tone is typical, but the alliterative lilt of the conceit gives it a tongue-in-cheek air, and her favourite imagery of music and flowing water conveys a real sense of energy, as if at last she had access to a life-giving current of ideas which fed her imagination, and caught her up in the tide of change which was rushing through Europe in that revolutionary year.

Trying to sketch her inner development in these ten years is like hurtling on a journey through the varied landscape of new ideas and movements for reform. Renan called George Sand 'the Aeolian harp of our time' and the phrase also applies to Mary Ann, at least at this stage, for she responded to, and later drew on in her art, every intellectual wind that blew. Her crisis of faith in 1842 may have led her to grasp new approaches more eagerly, for she was in that state which Froude was to catch so evocatively, in his book on Carlyle:

All around us the intellectual lightships had been broken from their moorings, and it was then a new and trying experience. The present generation which has grown up in an open spiritual ocean, which has got used to it and has learned to swim for itself, will never know what it was like to find the lights all drifting, the compasses all awry, and nothing left to steer by but the stars.[1]

In this heady but anxious freedom she responded with sensitivity to a series of mentors, movements and prophets: to Combe's phrenology and mesmerism; to Lyell's geology, with its evolutionary implications; to Carlyle's passionate denunciation of industrialism and theories of enlightened leadership; to Emerson's transcendentalism with its hope in human perfectability; to Sand's liberating fictions of sexual and social passion, to Frederika Bremer's sterner feminism.

But she did not merely respond – she analysed, argued and wrestled with each theory and each author, enjoying the way they forced her to clarify her own opinions and feelings. She felt this 'electrical thrill' even when she disagreed (as she did with Rousseau) and looking back on 1855 she probably included herself, despite the gender, when she wrote of Carlyle, 'Many of the men who have the least agreement with his opinions are those to whom the reading of *Sartor Resartus* was an epoch in the history of their minds.' [2]

Whereas the first two decades of her life tell a tale of solitude, an inner landscape of longing, faith, doubt and imagination, the third was to look outwards, carrying her by stages from a quiet backwater into the mainstream of British intellectual life.

The initial impetus came from the new circles which opened up to her in Coventry. The Evangelical community welcomed her at once: her old teacher Miss Franklin introduced her to her neighbours the Pearses (Abijah Pears was later Mayor of Coventry), Rev. and Mrs Sibree, their daughter Mary who was soon to be a devoted pupil, and their son John, then a theological student. Mrs Pears in turn introduced her to her brother Charles Bray and his wife Cara, both vital catalysts in her life.

The Brays and the Hennells – Cara's family – were associated with ribbon manufacture in Coventry, but Cara's father had moved to Hackney as a merchant, and after his early death she and her six sisters and two brothers had been brought up in the Unitarian faith. Charles Bray, after a severe Evangelical period resembling Mary Ann's, gradually moved through arguments with Unitarians and others to a personal theory of 'philosophical necessity'. During the 1830s, while he managed his father's booming business, he became an apostle of phrenology. This new 'science' confirmed his view that the ways of man must be subject to unalterable laws, analogous to those of the material world. A similar feeling resides in the 'Nemesis' of Eliot's novels and some of her portraits of characters reflect another belief of phrenology: that separate mental faculties had specific positions in the brain, so that qualities like intellect, tolerance or anger could be estimated by taking precise measurements of the skull.[3] Bray expounded his determinism in *The Philosophy of Necessity; or the Laws of Consequences as Applicable to Mental, Moral and Social Science*, published in 1841.

His wife Cara, subjected to Charles's free-thinking opinions on their honeymoon in 1835, appealed to her brother (also called

Charles) to investigate his alarming claims and provide reassurance about the supernatural basis of her belief. But Charles Hennell, an intuitive and original scholar, was slowly drawn from his Unitarian standpoint to a complete rejection of the revealed element in Christianity and, after much argument, his sisters were also persuaded. Mary Ann had already bought his book *An Inquiry into the Origins of Christianity* (1838) and was now prompted to re-read it.

Bray's exuberant nature led to action as well as theory. His wide interests were typical of the radical streak associated with dissenting manufacturing families: non-sectarian education, labour cooperatives and unions, repeal of the Corn Laws and extension of the franchise. An oft-quoted passage from his autobiography describes how 'everyone who came to Coventry with a queer mission, or a crotchet, or was supposed to be a "little cracked" was sent up to Rosehill' (Bray's house) where they joined the easy conversations on the bearskin under the acacia tree.[4] When she crossed the threshold, Mary Ann told Mary Sibree, she felt as if she shut the real world outside, and Mathilde Blind describes the Rosehill set as belonging more to a novel than to a Warwickshire country town, as they 'used to spend their lives in philosophical speculations, philanthropy and pleasant social hospitality, joining to the ease and *laisser aller* of continental manners, a thoroughly English geniality and trustworthiness'.[5] The Evans family never shared Mary Ann's enthusiasm, fearing as much for her marriage prospects as for her changing ideas since 'Mr Bray, being a leader of mobs, can only introduce her to Chartists and Radicals' (*Letters*, Vol. I, p. 157).

Among the cracked individuals Mary Ann met at Rosehill were James Simpson, pioneer of elementary education; John Connolly, who worked for reform of insane asylums; the mesmerist Lafontaine; the socialist Robert Owen and the philosopher Emerson. But at the beginning it was the small domestic circle, rather than the wider network, which was vital. Responding to Charles Bray's warmth and Cara's sensitivity she realised that she could talk about anything and everything that interested her, and as she talked so her thoughts crystallised and she was brought up sharply against the nature of her own doubt. Within a fortnight of entering this atmosphere she was writing, warningly, to Maria Lewis:

My whole soul has been engrossed in the most interesting of all enquiries for the last few days and to what results my thoughts may lead I know not – possibly to one that will startle you, but my only desire is to know the truth, my only fear to cling to error.

(Letters, Vol. I, p. 120)

Her adherence to the Bible as the source of 'truth' (key word of these years) had been undermined by her wide reading, her observation of local religious life, and her new scientific studies. Since the publication of Lyell's *Principles of Geology* (1830–3), geology had seemed to offer new 'truths' about how the laws of erosion, movement and subsidence guided the gradual evolution of the earth. A letter of Charles Hennell to Cara in 1834 shows how he had caught that first excitement: 'When Aunt comes to town we will talk in the first place on Geology, after that, Geology, and lastly a little more Geology'.[6] Mary Ann followed the debate with enormous interest: in 1841 she was deep in John Pye Smith's *Relations between the Holy Scripture and Some Parts of Geological Science* (1839) and one finds geological metaphors buried in much of her writing on personal and historical development.

But after her first exciting meeting with the Brays she seems to have plunged back into theology, not only studying Hennell's *Inquiry* but allegedly re-reading the Bible before she began. Hennell's patient, reverent approach and instinctive scholarship reached to the depths of her own concern: Cross's *Life* includes her own later resumé of the book in which she emphasises the discussion of the historical and cultural context. She was especially interested in the analysis of the character of Jesus (Hennell's approach is rather like that of a Romantic literary critic), and of the way Jesus believed that he had a national mission which had supernatural sanction. In the context of the 1840s, which were to end in a burst of nationalist revolution,

Hennell's work may have assumed even greater relevance. But his essential message was twofold: first, that the miraculous element in Christianity must be discarded; second, that this need not involve rejecting its central teachings about love, ethics and responsibility. Christianity will not disintegrate, for instead of appearing as ancient history, it 'will rest its claims on evidence clearer, simpler and always at hand, – the thoughts and feelings of the human mind itself'. The reliance on 'thoughts and feelings' was to prove central to George Eliot's philosophy and fiction, but in 1841 the destructive element in Hennell's conclusion made the greater impact. After a troubled family Christmas she decided that she could no longer accompany her father to church. His terse diary entry forces its way into all accounts of her life.

Went to Trinity Church in the forenoon. Miss Lewis went with me. Mary Ann did not go. I stopd the sacrement and Miss Lewis stopd also.

(*Letters*, Vol. I, p. 124)

Robert Evans's extreme anger had multiple components: hurt pride, embarrassment, rejection and bewilderment. It clearly applied not so much to his daughter's beliefs as to her refusal to behave like the eligible, marriageable daughter of a now prosperous middle-class townsman. The argument raged for the next two months as he declared his intention of leaving Foleshill, and Mary Ann faced the prospect of life as a governess – even going to Maria in Leamington to look for work. Her evangelical friends – the Pearses, Sibrees and Franklins – tried unsuccessfully to win her back, bringing in as reinforcements a local clergyman and the tutor at John Sibree's theological college. All confessed themselves beaten by her superior knowledge of theological controversy and by her passion. The vehemence which left her shaking after an argument with the Rev. Sibree can be felt in her long, reasoned and imploring letter to her father; for she now regarded Christian doctrine to be as 'pernicious' as she had felt imaginative literature to be three years before.

Such being my very strong convictions, it cannot be a question with any mind of strong integrity, whatever judgement may be passed on their truth, that I could not without vile hyprocrisy and a miserable truckling to the world for the sake of my supposed interests, profess to join in worship which I wholly disapprove. This and *this alone* I will not do even for your sake – anything else however painful I would cheerfully brave to give you a moment's joy.

(*Letters*, Vol. I, pp. 128–9)

Eventually, after a month spent at Griff with Isaac (whose initial intense irritation had given way to resigned intercession on her behalf), Mary Ann returned to Foleshill, and to a compromise, conforming in public but retaining her private opinions. Eighteen months later in October 1843, she reflected on her actions in another significant letter, this time to Sara Hennell:

The first impulse of a young and ingenuous mind is to withhold the slightest sanction from all that contains even a mixture of supposed error . . . But a year or two of reflection and the experience of our own miserable weakness which will ill afford to part even with the crutches of superstition must, I think, effect a change. Speculative truth begins to appear but a shadow of individual minds, agreement between intellects seems unattainable, and we turn to the *truth of feeling* as the only universal bond of union.

(*Letters*, Vol. I, pp. 161–3)

Her letter tumbles on through a wealth of images describing the mental positions which like seaweed and 'incrustation have grown into the living body' and cannot be wrenched away without destroying the life of the whole organism. Change, she insists, must be gradual, organic, natural and not imposed: 'I think the best and the only way of fulfilling our mission is to sow good seed in good i.e. prepared ground, and not to root up tares where we must inevitably gather all the wheat with them.'

In this letter one can recognise the approach to life which lies behind the moral teaching of the fiction, not least in the realisation that the lesson of an event comes home only slowly, after careful analysis and reflection – it is the consequences of the consequences which matter. Here is the quality of tolerance (which does not necessarily imply agreement), which allows her to write so sensitively about individuals holding intellectual and sectarian positions far removed from her own; here too is the conviction – born of experience and not intellectual persuasion – that change must grow from within, and cannot be arrogantly imposed. 'We begin to find that with individuals, as with nations, the only safe revolution is one arising out of the wants which their *own progress* has generated.' And finally, here is the humility which acknowledges that reason is not all and that those who may be confused or in error may be 'richer in the fruits of faith'.

Her friendship with Sara Hennell, the sister of Cara and Charles Hennell, had begun in the spring of 1842 and during these years their correspondence was often the place where she worked out her ideas and feelings. Sara was a governess and a German scholar, as interested in theology as Mary Ann herself. The letters show how Mary Ann grew in confidence until Sara, initially the leader in the relationship, became the suppliant. The terms of endearment grew in strength from 'my dearest friend', to 'Lieber Gemahl', and 'Beloved Spouse'. By 1847 Mary Ann – or, as she now called herself Pollian (a pun on Apollyon, the Angel of Destruction) – signed her letters 'Husband', and two years later confessed that she gave Sara a 'sad excuse for flirtation' but pleaded, 'I come back to you and all a husband's privileges and command you to love me . . . I sometimes talk to you in my soul as lovingly as Solomon's Song' (*Letters*, Vol. I, p. 279). Even allowing for the emotional excesses common in Victorian female friendship, there is a sexual ambivalence here which was to pervade many of Eliot's friendships, although it describes emotional dependence rather than physical desire. But it was not just Sara, it was the whole circle that she loved: she became increasingly caught up in the life of Rosehill, even accompanying the Brays on holiday, and at the same time continued her wide reading, and began working on a translation of Spinoza – probably the *Tractatus Theologico-Politicus.*

In 1843 Charles Hennell married Rufa Brabant, the daughter of a Dr Brabant of Devizes, who had been involved in arranging for Hennell's *Inquiry* to be translated into German, and who had obtained an introduction to the book from George Friedrich Strauss. This marriage had great consequences for Mary Ann. The first was her infatuation with the doctor himself, which has led to much speculation. After the wedding, at which she was bridesmaid, she accepted his invitation to Devizes, and was soon sending back to the Brays rapturous accounts of her status as 'Deutera', his second daughter, of long walks and ecstatic scholarly sessions: 'I am in a little heaven here, Dr Brabant being its archangel'. Although she felt she was only plucking the apple of knowledge, she was, however, soon expelled from this little paradise when Dr Brabant's blind wife, aroused by her sister's suspicions, delivered an ultimatum.

The importance of the episode – which left a lasting smart – lies in the way it illustrates George Eliot's unconscious habit of seizing with excitement on new teachers, friends and advisers and later, pupils and admirers, a habit which was endlessly misinterpreted. Or perhaps not misinterpreted, for in her fiction she frequently talks of how 'ideas can have the force of sensations' and she expressed this excitement physically, by touching, gazing, almost leaning on the people she argued with. In 1845 there were rumours of an engagement to an unidentified young painter or picture restorer: she told Sara she would enter this under the heading, 'Precipitancy, ill effects of', and this precipitancy was to cause her frequent heartache – most notably with John Chapman and Herbert Spencer in the following decade. Chapman's diary (following Rufa's account) credits the intimacy between Mary Ann and Dr Brabant to 'the simplicity of her heart and her ignorance of (or incapability of practising) the required conventionalisms'.[8]

One result of the encounter with Dr Brabant may have been to give the mature George Eliot a model for Casaubon in *Middlemarch*, the dry scholar, who sits like a spider in the middle of an endless web of words, bewildered by – yet fully ready to exploit – the enthusiasm of a starry-eyed young woman. From the Hennell–Brabant marriage also came Mary Ann's first substantial published work, for in January 1844 Sara, on Rufa's behalf, asked if she would take over the translation of Strauss's *Das Leben Jesu*, which Rufa had begun before her marriage. This was her major task for the next two years, involving the translation of 1,500 pages of densely argued theological argument, which she undertook so conscientiously that she even learnt Hebrew so that she could follow Strauss's comments on the original material. It became 'soul-stupefying' work, on which she concentrated every morning for four intense hours, *still* leaving plenty of time for her to help Cara in her infants' school, assist in Bray's newly founded industrial school, attend lectures at the Mechanics' Institute on chemistry and astronomy, hear O'Connell speak on Home Rule for Ireland, and support Charles Bray in his anti-Corn Law campaigns in Coventry. She then relaxed with novels – her letters are dotted with casual references to Disraeli and George Sand.

But sometimes the Brays whisked her away from her work, on holidays to Scotland, to the Lake District and trips to the theatre. In her friends' letters one catches glimpses of her as she must have appeared to strangers at this time, for example dazzling a dinner party in Liverpool on their return from Scotland by her knowledge. Through connections of the Brays her acquaintances were now stretching to include a nationwide network of radical, especially Unitarian, reformers such as the Rathbones and Martineaus.

During these years the Brays may also have widened Mary Ann's horizons by showing her an alternative morality to that of her own strict family, for Charles Bray, who was known locally as a 'village Casanova', had a child by another woman. The Brays adopted her briefly in 1844–5, and then later adopted his second illegitimate daughter by the same woman, Elinor (Nelly), whom the childless Cara loved dearly until her death from consumption at the age of nineteen.[9] And although always close to Charles, Cara herself formed a romantic attachment to a close friend, Edward Wood. We have no information about how much Mary Ann or her family knew of this, or what they felt, but gossip, from which she could never escape, even after her death, implied that Mary Ann herself was infected by Bray's ideas of sexual freedom. As recounted gleefully by her daughter this was the view of Bessie Parkes, who first met Mary Ann at Rosehill:

I am bound to say that I know my mother has always held the secret view that she had a passionate affair before she ever came to London, with that very attractive man, I think a Doctor Something with whom and with whose wife she was intimate as a girl.[10]

But over all the varied life of Rosehill, the translation of Strauss cast its shadow. Strauss came at the end of a line of German theological critics who had, like Hennell, demolished the supernatural element in Christianity through a combination of logic, textual criticism and historical analysis. He found both the 'natural' and 'supernatural' approaches to the gospels unsatisfactory, and suggested that problem sequences – the virgin birth, transfiguration, resurrection and many miracles – could be best explained as 'myths'. *Das Leben Jesu*, which cost him his job and his reputation in Germany, looked minutely at every single gospel narrative.

In a rather similar way to her crisis of faith in 1842, Mary Ann learned less from the theory itself than from her own reaction to it. As she progressed through the three volumes, her work rate slowed down and her involvement turned slowly to revulsion and, according to Cara, by February 1846 'she said she was Strauss-sick – it made her ill dissecting the beautiful story of the crucifixion'. Only fixing her eyes on the model of Thorwaldsen's statue of Christ in her study helped her get through.

A reaction set in. She was reluctant to reduce the person of Christ, whom she regarded as an unparalleled charismatic teacher, to a mere pawn of cultural consciousness. Strauss seemed to drain Christianity of any application to life, and she realised, in rejecting his negative position, that she *did* value the

symbolic importance of the Christian teaching, indeed of all
religions based on notions of self-sacrifice, of spiritual community, of supporting love.

Finally the translation was finished, the proofs read, the
'many awkward blunders' all corrected, and the book published
on 15 June 1846. For her labours Mary Ann received £20; no
mention of her name appeared on the title page. At once she
plunged into reading Shakespeare, poetry, new novels, learning
Greek. But the oppression of Strauss was almost immediately
replaced by another labour of duty, familiar to generations of
women – the task of looking after her ageing and ill parent.
Despite their differences, she loved and was dependent on her
father. In her forthright letter of 1842 she had written, 'I fear
nothing but voluntarily leaving you.' But now the shape of her
days was dictated by his demands, as she implies in a letter to
Sara: 'I am sinning against my daddy by yielding to the strong
impulse I felt to write to you, for he looks at me as if he wanted
me to read to him'. And read to him she did, particularly the
works of Scott, almost every evening until his death four years
later. Sometimes she felt impatience and despair – 'my soul's as
barren as the desert' – but beneath this barrenness were hidden
springs, nurtured by her close relationships and fed by her
engaged response to everything she read, studied and discussed.

For what was also happening during her Strauss years was a
reaffirmation of the importance of the imagination. This must be
linked, I think, to her conviction of the truth of feeling. At the
same time as she rejected her adolescent evangelicalism, so she
re-embraced the creative world that evangelicalism had crushed
– particularly fiction and music which moved her so deeply. By
1843, she was arguing with Mary Sibree for 'works of the
imagination', maintaining that 'they can perform an office for
the mind which nothing else can'. She may have turned towards
writing fiction herself at this time, for in October 1846 Sara
wrote to her mother, 'M.A. looks very brilliant just now – we
fancy she must be writing her novel' and the articles which she
wrote in December 1846–February 1847 for the *Coventry
Herald and Observer* (bought by Charles Bray as a vehicle for his

ideas) begin with the creation of a character 'Macarthy', described through the eyes of his devoted friend. Macarthy (who
has echoes of Carlyle's 'Sartor') has allegedly never fulfilled his
youthful brilliance, hampered by his morbid sensitivity to the
discrepancies between the ideal and the real, and his friend
proposes to publish merely some scraps and reflections from his
notebooks in these articles: 'Poetry and Prose from the Note-
book of an Eccentric'.

Beneath their laboured frivolity these articles show Mary Ann
grappling with ideas about the imagination and the feelings as a
guide to understanding and behaviour. Macarthy is a Romantic
figure, and it is not surprising that the first of his articles begins
with a tribute to Rousseau, and to the notion that the 'proper
result of intellectual cultivation is to restore the mind to that
state of wonder and interest with which it looks on everything
in childhood' (*Essays*, p. 19). Did she feel now that her appre-
hension of reality had been more 'truthful' in her day-dreaming
state than after its 'perversion' through education and religion?

One can trace in her later novels the latent influence of many
works she read and admired, from the slow, detailed moral
analysis of Richardson's *Sir Charles Grandison*, whose 'fat little
volumes' she took on holiday to the Isle of Wight, to the
passionate analysis of industrial alienation in Carlyle's *Past and
Present*, published in 1843, and the women poets, novelists and
essayists she enjoyed. Her reading showed her sensitivity to the
diversity of contemporary culture which she remembered in
detail and reflected upon just as she remembered the Nuneaton
riots of 1832, or the 'traditions' of her Pearson aunts.

But in that period of release and excitement there were some
figures she turned to with a special sense of exuberant gratitude.
These included Emerson, Carlyle, Rousseau and – perhaps of
the greatest interest to readers of the novels – George Sand.
Sand made a huge impact on British readers in the 1840s; she
was read, reviewed, endlessly discussed in 'middle-class drawing
rooms', and had devoted admirers and vehement detractors.
Her lifestyle unnerved many: she had an arrangement with her
husband whereby she spent half the year with him and their son

on their estates in Berry, and half in Paris, where she made a living as a professional writer; she dressed in men's clothes, had a succession of lovers including Chopin, and was an active socialist during the 1840s. Her novels of the 1830s and '40s such as *Indiana*, *Jacques*, *Lelia* and *Mauprat* – 'novels of personal revolt and passion, turbulent self-expression and feminism'[11] – were followed in the 1840s by works like *Spiridion* and *Consuelo*, full of both a mystical doctrine of democratic reform, and an assertive feminism, summed up for many in the dark-haired Consuelo herself, opera singer, outsider, doomed to lose her lover to a blonde respectable wife, but imposing her individuality on the future through their daughter.

Rosehill was, of course, swept up in the debate over Sand as they were in every major movement of the decade – but this time it was Mary Ann, or the future George Eliot, who was the most radical. As she told Sara, it was not Sand's iconoclasm or ideology which attracted her but her ability, in six pages, to:

delineate human passion and its results – (and I must say in spite of your judgement) some of the moral instincts and their tendencies – with such truthfulness such nicety of discrimination such tragic power and withal such loving gentle humour that one might live a century with nothing but one's own dull faculties and not know so much as those six pages will suggest.

(*Letters*, Vol. I, pp. 277–8)

Much of the turbulence, the idealism, the restlessness and the suppressed, tingling, physical passion in heroines from Maggie to Dorothea and Gwendolen Harleth (as well as many details of incident and description) grew from her response to Sand's liberating depiction of women. Perhaps she bore her example in mind in her own life as well, when she defied convention to live with George Henry Lewes – and took his first name, which was incidentally also the first name of her favourite writer's pseudonym – for her own pen name.

Eliot's radicalism never approached Sand's active involvement in revolutionary politics. Her belief in slow, educative change was already well established. But, as her letters to her young friend John Sibree show, she did respond to the turmoil of 1848. She could find no time to pity 'Louis Philippe and his moustachioed sons . . . when the earth has its millions of unfed souls and bodies', and she was excited by the French spirit – 'the *mind* of the people is highly electrified – they are full of ideas on social subjects – they really desire social *reform*' – which she saw as so different from the comparable movement in England with its 'larger proportion of selfish radicalism and unsatisfied, brute sensuality (in the agricultural and mining districts especially) than of perception or desire for justice' (*Letters*, Vol. I, p. 252). She also confided to John her need to discuss all these issues: 'It is necessary to me, not simply to *be*, but to *utter*, and I require utterance of my friends . . . It is like a diffusion or expansion of one's own life to be assured that its vibrations are repeated in another, and words are the media of those vibrations.'

The history of George Eliot in the 1840s is very largely an account of her sensitivity to all the vibrations of the period. At the end of the decade, when she had returned to her task of translating Spinoza, and was reading Thomas à Kempis's *De Imitatione Christi* with its 'cool air as of cloisters', she reviewed J.A. Froude's *Nemesis of Faith*, an account of his loss of faith and the family crisis this caused which must have reminded her, despite the very different setting, of her own experience.

Her review in the *Coventry Herald* called forth an interested response from Froude, who unearthed her identity, and tracked her down to Rosehill. But 1849 was darkened by her father's dying and her anxiety emerged again in devastating headaches, sickness and a feeling of spiritual paralysis: 'I am living unspeakable moments and can write no more' (*Letters*, Vol. I, p. 282). Robert Evans died on 30 May 1849. On the evening of his death she wrote:

where shall I be without my Father? It will seem as if a part of my moral nature were gone. I had a horrid vision of myself last night becoming earthly sensual and devilish for want of that purifying restraining influence.

(*Letters*, Vol. I, p. 284)

She did collapse after his death, but not at first, and not into devilish sensuality. The Brays took her away, through Paris and down the Rhône to Milan and Como, crossing back via Chamonix to Geneva. Her inner fear took the form of absolute terror of losing her balance, of falling not from moral, but from real precipices. Her early biographer, Mathilde Blind, heard from the Brays that she was emphatically *not* a mountaineer and 'her frequent fits of weeping were a source of pain to her anxious fellow travellers'.[12]

From the crisis she emerged a new person, and signed herself with a new name – Marian, occasionally Marianne. This was the name she wrote from Geneva, where she stayed on while the Brays returned home. For the first time she was alone among strangers. She stayed first at the Pension Plongeon, entertaining Rosehill with brisk pictures of the other residents and then, as winter approached, she moved further into the town to stay in the apartment of the d'Albert Durades. François d'Albert Durade was a fine painter, a gentle, hunchbacked man who has, from early days, been taken as an element in the portrait of Philip Wakem in *The Mill on the Floss*. The kindly understanding of Madame Durade and the invigorating conversation of their circle helped to heal her spirit. Although the period at Geneva seems among the quietest in her life, it was there that she took stock of her needs, and realised her life must lie away from Warwickshire and her family. And when she visited Isaac at Griff on her return, as she wrote ruefully to Sara, she discovered that they, in turn, had little time for her:

Oh the dismal weather and the dismal country and the dismal people. It was some envious demon that drove me across the Jura to come and see people who don't want me. However I am determined to sell everything I possess except a portmanteau and carpet-bag and the necessary contents and be a stranger and a foreigner on the earth for ever more.

(*Letters*, Vol. I, p. 335)

Her great exile was about to begin.

CHAPTER THREE

THE WESTMINSTER REVIEW

It was in 1851 that Marian eventually packed that portmanteau and set off, 'a foreigner on the earth', to make her literary fortune in London. For a young single woman the step was daring and unconventional, although she was not alone; women such as Harriet Martineau and Eliza Lynn were among those to take similar steps.

In October 1850 John Chapman, the London publisher, had visited Rosehill, bringing with him the philosopher R.W. Mackay. Mackay's new book, *The Progress of the Intellect, as Exemplified in the Religious Development of the Greeks and Hebrews*, related to many of Strauss's ideas, so he asked Marian to review it for *The Westminster Review*. So impressed was Chapman that the following year when he himself bought this leading radical journal (founded in 1824 by Bentham, with the help of John Stuart Mill) he asked Marian to become his assistant editor. Thus began five years packed with hard work, vast amounts of reading, the continuing intellectual excitement of absorbing and responding to advances in contemporary thought, deep emotional involvements with men – John Chapman, Herbert Spencer and George Henry Lewes – and stimulating new friendships with women – Bessie Parkes, Barbara Leigh Smith, Clementia Taylor.

The energy and exhaustion of this period are, as always, vividly present in Marian's letters, especially those to the Brays and to Sara Hennell. But curiously, because the turmoil of her sexual and emotional feelings was not something she could write about easily to these friends, it is in her public writing, the anonymous reviews and essays, that one gets the strongest sense of her working out issues which she felt to be vitally important. Just as in her conversations with Bray, in her reading of Hennell, in her translation of Strauss, she first absorbed and then questioned and re-stated propositions to satisfy herself, so, once embroiled in London liberal circles, whether as an editor seeking contributors to *The Westminster Review* or as a reviewer and journalist, she pursued every avenue and wrestled with the implications of each line of thought: Lamarck's evolutionary theory, Spencer's views on development and degeneration, Lewes's and Harriet Martineau's approaches to Comte's positivist philosophy, Faraday's lectures on geometry, Mary Wollstonecraft's feminism. Initial strong reactions to people and to ideas are often qualified by later reflection. From a century later, as through a telescope, we seem to see her in the company of many of her contemporaries circling and returning to certain ideas, seeking constantly and urgently for explanations of her own desires, of the natural world, of the workings of her society and for keys which will unlock the mysteries, clues which will thread a maze of unresolved complexities and inconsistencies.

The same combination of emotional, intellectual and sensual excitement was present in her personal relationships. Impetuous, searching, ambitious of literary and intellectual eminence, she reached out for what people could give her; one of the things she was searching for, as she admitted herself, being quite simply someone to love. En route, because she gave herself so generously and because she demanded so much, she was bound to suffer. Interestingly, the three men with whom she fell in love in rapid succession – John Chapman, Herbert Spencer and George Henry Lewes – came, like herself, from that newly emerging class of intellectuals, journalists and writers whose achievement and ambitions cut them off from a sense of solidarity with their past (Eliza Lynn and William Hale White are two other examples in their immediate circle), and so the society of like thinkers they created around them became their principal support, often a precarious one.

Marian's initiation into this world was painful in the extreme.[1] In November she had taken her Mackay article to London and stayed with the Chapmans, who lived, and took lodgers, above their bookshop at 142 Strand. Eliza Lynn unkindly remembered her arrival on the scene, an ungainly young provincial who 'held her hands and arms kangaroo fashion, was badly dressed; had an unwashed, unbrushed, unkempt look altogether, and . . . assumed a tone of superiority over me which I was not then aware was warranted by her undoubted leadership. From first to last she put up my mental bristles.'[2] But she got on better with others she met. She liked the busy, argumentative, lively atmosphere so much that she returned the following January, determined to try her luck as a freelance writer. At once she found herself at odds with Chapman's mistress – the children's governess Elizabeth Tilley – and his wife Susanna. The two women, who existed in an uneasy truce, resented her obvious attraction to Chapman, and her close dealings with him, which included advising him on editing the morally 'delicate' passages in Eliza Lynn's new novel *Realities*, giving personal piano recitals to him in her room, and lengthy German lessons, also in private. She failed to get the literary work she wanted and much of her concentration seems to have been diverted into the domestic passions and dramas, stirred no doubt by Chapman himself, despite the ingenuous disclaimers in his diary: 'I am sure I have no other feelings on the subject than to obtain peace at any cost'. Although there is no evidence that they were lovers the rumours flew. After a final storm in March 1851, she was put on the train back to Coventry, in tears at his parting assertion that, although he felt great affection for her, he loved Elizabeth and Susanna too, both in different ways.

She was smarting deeply, and it took all Chapman's diplomatic skills to woo her back to 142 Strand again, when he really needed her the following summer, to help him edit *The Westminster Review*. He concluded negotiations in May, and took over formally in October. Although he wanted to control the review himself, he knew he had not the intellectual breadth or rigour to take on the detailed editing. Marian would do the job perfectly – and anonymously – and he needed her help immediately to write a new prospectus. This editorial labour was unpaid work, and remained so, although she was paid for individual articles, and she existed chiefly on the small inheritance from her father.

Over several visits he smoothed out problems with her and with those at number 142, but one of his diary entries reveals how intensely she still felt. After a trip to Kenilworth Castle Chapman burst into effusions about 'the beauties of nature which men and women jointly present'. He continues: 'I dwelt also on the incomprehensible mystery and witchery of beauty. My words jarred upon her and put an end to her enjoyment. Was it from a consciousness of her own want of beauty? She wept bitterly.'[3] In this one may read, perhaps, Chapman's own insecurity. Aware of her mental predominance he needed to reassure himself of his physical power over her, and to put her at a disadvantage by pushing her back into his idea of conventional female competition at which she could not win.

Calming herself (as her heroine Maggie Tulliver was to do) by reading Thomas à Kempis, Marian worked on the prospectus, visited Devon with Cara and went to the Great Exhibition where Charles Bray was exhibiting. She finally moved to the Strand in September. There she began work at once on planning the January issue of *The Westminster Review*, the first under the new editors.[4]

Over the next two years her letters show her dealing with contributors both tactfully and firmly. As assistant editor, involved with everything from planning and commissioning to production problems, Marian was associated with five issues from 1851 to April 1854. She worked with an impressive team of writers; W.J. Fox, F.W. Newman, Froude, James and Harriet Martineau (brother and sister, at daggers drawn), W.R. Greg, J.S. Mill, Herbert Spencer and G.H. Lewes. For each issue they had to find five or six main articles under sections dedicated to social reform, politics, history, religion, philosophy, science and literature, while there was also a lengthy review section with shorter articles, covering a large number of books published in America and Europe as well as in Britain.

By mid 1852 she was a real professional, proud of her achievement and not above keeping a knowing, jealous eye on the opposition like the new *British Quarterly*: 'Its list of subjects is excellent . . . They have one subject of which I am jealous "Pre-Raphaelism in Painting and Literature." We have no good writer on such subjects on our staff. Ought we not, too, to try and enlist David Masson, who is one of the British Quarterly set. He wrote that article in the *Leader* on the Patagonian Missionaries, which I thought very beautiful' (*Letters*, Vol. II, p. 48). The tone would be recognised in any publisher's office today. By then, too she had got used not only to balancing conflicting philosophies but also to balancing the review's unstable finances. Any money it made was drained by Chapman's other publishing ventures, and they survived on loans from benefactors like Joseph Parkes, Samuel Courtauld and later, Harriet Martineau. There is a weary irony in her self-deprecating comment, 'I feel that I am a wretched help-mate to you, almost out of the world and incog. so far as I am in it. When you can afford to pay an Editor, if that time will ever come, you must get one.'

Certainly there was no financial reward in the job, but there was some satisfaction and she was delighted when Lewes – whom she did not then know well – wrote in the *Leader* that the new editors had restored the review to the status it had enjoyed under J.S. Mill's editorship years before. And she was not entirely incognito. Her editorship and her life at 142 Strand brought her into contact not only with reformers and theorists but with the political exiles who had arrived in the wake of the 1848–9 European revolutions and for whom she seems to have had a special liking – such as Pierre Leroux, Louis Blanc, Mazzini. Many of this circle were now familiar figures: George Combes, Robert Owen and his brother, Richard Mackay, the Martineaus, W.E. Forster, W.R. Greg ('a short man, with hooked nose and an imperfect denunciation from defective teeth – when you see him from across the room, you are unpleasantly impressed and can't believe that he wrote his own books'). Foreign visitors included Horace Greeley, editor of the New York *Tribune*, and Frederika Bremer, the Swedish feminist novelist whose books had been translated into English in the 1840s by Mary Howitt. Sharp, even cruel little vignettes like that of Greg fill her letters, in which phrenological judgements ('the anterior lobe very fine and a moral region to correspond'), mingle with acutely observed details. And vignettes of herself at this age also survive. The young William Hale White, Chapman's proofreader, was later to write novels as 'Mark Rutherford' whose unconventional heroines reflect his admiration for the vibrant, sympathetic personality. After her death he wrote, 'I can see her now, with her hair over her shoulders, the easy chair half sideways to the fire, her feet over the arms and a proof in her hands, in that dark room at the back of No 142'.[5]

Bessie Parkes remembered her at one of the distinguished dinner parties given by Joseph Parkes, wearing her black velvet 'then seldom adopted by unmarried ladies'. Descending the great staircase 'She would talk and laugh softly, and look up into my father's face respectfully, while the light of the great hall lamp shone on the waving masses of her hair, and the black velvet fell in folds at her feet.'[6] This picture of her alone, triumphant in a world of men, was popular for many years, and there is truth in it but, as the next chapter will show, she was also extending her friendships with women.

Her most important new friendship was with Herbert Spencer. She knew him slightly through the Brays and had abstracted his book *Social Statics or The Condition Essential to Human Happiness Specified* for Chapman's 'analytical catalogue'. One of the arguments of the book is the fundamental equality of men and women, but it puts forward an ideal of autonomy which, while attractive, is opposed at a profound level to the belief in the give and take of social responsibility which is at the heart of George Eliot's novels. The difference is typical of their natures and their relationship. When they met in London they at once realised they had much in common (as well as a commitment to theories of development). They were the same age, both from the Midlands, both from rather anti-intellectual backgrounds (Spencer had trained as an engineer before becoming a journalist) and both were now working as assistant editors on liberal journals. Spencer worked for the *Economist* and lived above its offices on the other side of the Strand. Using his free reviewer's tickets to indulge another common bond, a love of the theatre and music, from early 1852 they were constantly together.

She could not argue fervently with someone she admired without becoming emotionally involved. But Spencer, nervous, perhaps physically timid, could not take the pressure of her feelings. From Broadstairs, where she fled from the dusty London summer, she wrote to him, cloaking her longing in playfulness, thanking him for the 'few lumps of ice which I carried with me from that tremendous glacier of yours', and suggesting he visit her, to enjoy the 'delicious, voluptuous laziness' of the sea side. He did visit her, and her next letter abandons suggestive imagery for the plain language of 'hopeless wretchedness', sharp self-knowledge and head-tossing pride:

I want to know if you can assure me that you will not forsake me, that you will always be with me as much as you can and share your thoughts and feelings with me. If you become attached to some one else, then I must die, but until then I could gather courage to work and make life valuable, if only I had you near me . . . Those who have known me best have always said, that if ever I loved any one thoroughly my whole life must turn upon that feeling, and I find they said truly. You curse the destiny which has made the feeling concentrate itself on you – but if you will only have patience with me you shall not curse it long. You will find that I can be satisfied with very little, if I am delivered from the dread of losing it.

I suppose no woman ever before wrote such a letter as this – but I am not ashamed of it, for I am conscious that in the light of reason and true refinement I am worthy of your respect and tenderness, whatever gross men or vulgar-minded women might think of me.

(*Letters*, Vol. VIII, pp. 56–7)

In her eventual, wholly satisfying love for Lewes she was to challenge these 'gross men and vulgar-minded women' head-on, but now she withdrew into work and (as she had done in adolescence) turned any resentment she felt against herself, in her next letter chastising her strong feelings as egotism and hugging renunciation, as she had clasped her volume of Thomas à Kempis while smarting under Chapman's attentions:

The fact is, all sorrows sink into insignificance before the one great sorrow – my own miserable imperfections, and any outward hap is welcome if it will only serve to rouse my energies and make me less unworthy of my better self.

(*Letters*, Vol. VIII, p. 61)

The language is almost a reversion to her feverish evangelicalism and so is the imagery in which she describes the despair of the 'walled-in' world of Bird Grove repeating itself amid the bustle of London: 'ever since I have come back I have felt something like the madness which imagines that the four walls are contracting and going to crush one'.

But she pressed on, and over the next winter a new name crept into her letters which give a vivid glimpse of her packed life:

I will just tell you how it was last Saturday and that will give you an idea of my days. My task was to read an article of Greg's in the North British on Taxation, a heap of newspaper articles and all that J.S. Mill says on the same subject. When I had got some way into this *magnum mare*, in comes Mr Chapman with a thick German volume. 'Will you read enough of this to give me your opinion of it?' Then of course I must have a walk after lunch, and when I had sat down again thinking that I had two clear hours before dinner – rap at the door – Mr Lewes – who of course sits talking till the second bell rings. After dinner another visitor – and so behold me at 11p.m. still very far at sea on the subject of taxation but too tired to keep my eyes open.

(*Letters*, Vol. II, pp. 68–9)

Marian was introduced to George Henry Lewes in Jeff's bookshop in the Burlington Arcade, on Monday 6 October 1851. Her first impressions (as so often with her) were far from good – his habitual flippancy made her dismiss him as an exhibitionist, and he seemed too ostentatiously assertive and versatile. When they met he was 34, a potent irritant in the London literary establishment. With Thornton Hunt he had founded a new radical journal, the *Leader*, in 1850; as Slingsby Lawrance he adapted French plays for the London stage; he had written (fairly bad) romantic novels; had published an excellent popular *Biographical History of Philosophy* and was now working on a life of Goethe.

Lewes's charm, like his intelligence, was inescapable. Small, thin, so ugly that Jane Welsh Carlyle called him 'Ape', his mobile face, unpredictable wit and curiosity almost always won people over. Absolutely at his ease in city life – as Marian never was – his background was far wider than hers or Spencer's and had the free, cosmopolitan excitement of Europe. Born into a theatrical family, educated in Jersey, France and London, he had dabbled in medicine and taught for a year in Germany, while his knowledge of European literature, his bold championship of women writers, his interest in Goethe, Spinoza and Comte all made him a stimulating, intellectual companion.

But during 1851 and '52, Lewes's vivacity was largely superficial. His personal life was a desert. In 1841 he had married the young and beautiful Agnes Jervis, and, with their close friends the Thornton Hunts, they had determined to follow a Shelleyan free-thinking approach to marriage. The ideal proved difficult in practice, and despite Lewes's own reputation as a philanderer his principles were tested when Agnes became deeply involved with Thornton Hunt – who was also still living with his own wife. When Agnes gave birth to Hunt's son in 1850 Lewes gave him his own name, Edmond Alfred Lewes. Since he had condoned the liaison out of his affection for them both and his loyalty to the open principles on which they had agreed to conduct their marriage, his acceptance of the child ruled out the possibility of divorce – he was tied to a dead marriage. In 1851 Thornton's wife Katharine and Agnes were both pregnant again – Agnes's baby, Rose, was born in the month that Marian and George met.

Herbert Spencer had become a close friend of Lewes during this 'dreary wasted' period and through Spencer he met Marian. The office of the *Leader* in Wellington Street was very near 142 Strand, and Lewes called in, at first with Spencer, and then alone. In April of 1853 Marian was telling Cara of trips to the opera and of how 'kind and attentive' Mr Lewes was: 'like a few other people in the world, he is much better than he seems – a man of heart and conscience wearing a mask of flippancy' (*Letters*, Vol. II, p. 98). During the summer Lewes seems to have confided in her thoroughly – Agnes was pregnant again by Hunt, and her daughter Ethel was born in October. In that same October Marian left 142 Strand and rented rooms at 21 Cambridge Street off Edgware Road, where she could have greater privacy for a blossoming private life.

They kept their relationship very quiet, although in letters to the Brays, and in her professional dealings with Chapman, Marian may have defended Lewes rather too obviously. In fact, in the winter and spring of 1853 they became increasingly close – when Lewes fell ill she did his work for the *Leader* as well as her own. Because Lewes was still technically a married man, their relationship had an air of the clandestine, of defiance, even before they became lovers. It may well be that the intensity of their supportive and enduring relationship came partly from their very freedom from legal bonds. For this freedom strengthened the sense of voluntary commitment to each other, not only in 1854 but in all the later years when, as George Eliot, she dedicated each manuscript in turn to her 'beloved husband'. All of the novels emphasise how much more vital are the laws of conscience and of human community than the Law of State or Church.

During that first winter together Marian gave up the unpaid drudgery of her work on *The Westminster* to concentrate on her own writing, a translation of the German philosopher Ludwig Feuerbach's *Essence of Christianity* (1841). This translation, it has often been suggested, may have provided Marian with the conceptual authority – if she needed it – which justified her decision to live openly with Lewes as his wife. *The Essence of*

Christianity contains one of the most remarkably radical nineteenth-century interpretations of Christ, locating the sense of divinity which Christians experience in the general awe and yearning for human perfection, of which Christ's life has become a symbol. Feuerbach also takes as the symbol of the human desire for unity the ideal of love, whose most perfect earthly expression is in sexual harmony within the 'free bond of love'. Any marriage which is not free in this sense is really an empty formality (like that of Lewes and Agnes). In the light of this argument the step Marian wanted to take, which would be condemned by the world as immoral, was in fact exactly the opposite:

That alone is a religious marriage, which is a true marriage, which corresponds to the essence of marriage – of love. And so it is with all moral relations. Then only are they moral, – then only are they enjoyed in a moral spirit, when they are regarded as sacred in themselves.[7]

Shortly after the translation was published, with her name firmly on the title page as if in affirmation of what she had told Sara Hennell ('with the ideas of Feuerbach I everywhere agree'), she and Lewes took the irreversible step. On 19 July she sent a note to Sara and the Brays:

Dear Friends – all three
I have only time to say goodbye and God bless you. Poste Restante, Weimar for the next six weeks, and afterwards Berlin.
Ever your loving and grateful
Marian

(*Letters*, Vol. II, p. 166)

At 11 o'clock on 20 July she took a London cab to St Katharine's wharf, boarded the Steamer *Ravensbourne* and paced the decks:

I had 20 minutes of terrible fear that something should have delayed G. But before long I saw his welcome face looking for me over the porter's shoulder and all was well.[8]

Her journal describes sailing, the beauty of sea and sky, the night spent on the deck, the dawn rising as they sailed up the Scheldt, and Europe, and a new life, opened before them.

They were to spend eight months abroad, three in Weimar where they came under the spell of Liszt ('For the first time in my life I beheld real inspiration', she said of his piano playing) and five in Berlin. Everywhere they were accepted without hesitation; one gets a strong sense of that easy-going freemasonry of European artists and intellectuals which had accepted the liaisons of Goethe, of Liszt, of George Sand – enjoying the dramas rather than relishing the scandals. Berlin was not dramatic and they missed the English sense of humour, but life was full – they read Shakespeare together, Lewes worked on his biography of Goethe and on articles for the *Leader*, and Marian on 'Woman in France', the first of her major articles for *The Westminster*. They were certainly ruffled by the breath of gossip and disapproval from England (Carlyle labelled the back of a self-vindicating letter from Lewes 'G.H.L. and strong-minded woman') but they did not feel the full blast until they landed in Dover on their return in March 1855.

From Germany Marian had written to Chapman, to Bray and then to Sara. But she was concerned more to defend Lewes against the charge of abandoning his family than herself against a charge of immorality. In September 1855, responding to overtures from Cara, whose initial response had been cool and hurt, she expressed her clear-eyed conviction that what she had done had been not only right but admirable:

light and easily broken ties are what I neither desire theoretically nor could live for practically. Women who are satisfied with such ties do *not* act as I have done – they obtain what they desire and are still invited to dinner.

(*Letters*, Vol. II, pp. 214–5)

She was convinced of the morality of her decision, making allowances for accusations of immorality by reminding herself 'how subtle and complex are the influences that mould opinion'. (Again and again in her novels, this complex movement behind the public definition of morality was to be exposed and displayed.) The feeling that theirs was a 'true' marriage (and the more immediate difficulty of appeasing landladies who might not see things in that light) led Marian to ask her friends to call her Mrs Lewes. It was unity, not autonomy, that she valued, and the bold gesture of the joint name was significant. Although retaining her single name might have seemed to her more feminist friends like Bessie to have emphasised her freedom of choice, her challenge to society was, in fact, a more radical one for she was asking them to redefine a 'true marriage' as something different from legal forms.

The Leweses began life together in a series of lodgings: two weeks in Bayswater, then a few months in East Sheen, before moving to 8 Park Shot, Richmond, in October 1855 where they stayed until February 1859. Life was quite hard, for in addition to providing for themselves and for Lewes's boys, Marian wanted to send money back to Chrissey, whose husband had died the previous winter, leaving her with six children. John Chapman, proving a loyal and helpful friend, provided the basis of Marian's income, commissioning her to write the Belles Lettres section for *The Westminster Review* and occasionally the travel, history and biography section of the paper as well as some major articles. But Lewes encouraged her to look elsewhere as well, and she also wrote for *Fraser's Magazine* (her recollections of Weimar), for the *Saturday Review* and, on numerous occasions, for the *Leader*. In addition to her paid writing she worked on her translation of Spinoza's *Ethics*, a major project which was to help her crystallise her views of personal responsibility, but which was destined never to be published. She still found time to start studying the classics – a new stage of her never-ending self education – beginning with the Odyssey and the Iliad, while with Lewes she read (and re-read) the modern authors who most appealed to them – Ruskin, Browning, Stowe, Charlotte Brontë, George Sand and Jane Austen.

To all this the couple added a keen amateur interest in science and biology, which they pursued on holidays like that at Worthing in September 1855 and at Ilfracombe and Tenby in 1856.[9] 'You would laugh', she told Charles Bray, 'to see our room decked with yellow pie-dishes, a *footpan*, glass jars and phials, all full of zoophytes or molluscs or annelids – and still more to see the eager interest with which we rush out to our 'preserves' in the morning to see if there has been any mortality among them in the night' (*Letters*, Vol. II, pp. 252–3). Lewes's observations and her atmospheric descriptions are mingled in his *Sea-Side Studies* (1858) and in her marvellous journal in which she mixes Exeter cathedral, Ilfracombe rock-pools, the back street shops of collectors of marine animals (nature study was all the vogue in the 1850s) and Tenby cockle women 'treading the earth with unconscious majesty'. It is full of excitement, the pitfalls of amateurism, the luscious rolling of new Latin names, '*Eolis pellucida . . . Doris Billomellata*, and an *Aplysia*', but also with a conscious delight in the act of writing and an awareness of *how* she wants to write, filling in broad backgrounds with precise particulars, like a Pre-Raphaelite painting.

I have talked of the Ilfracombe lanes without describing them, for to describe them one ought to know the names of all the lovely wild flowers that cluster on their banks. Almost every yard of these banks is a 'Hunt' picture – a delicious crowding of mosses and delicate trefoil, and wild strawberries, and ferns great and small . . . I never before longed so much to know the names of things as during this visit to Ilfracombe. The desire is part of the tendency that is now constantly growing in me to escape from all vagueness and inaccuracy into the daylight of distinct, vivid ideas.

(Letters, Vol. II, pp. 250–1)

It was this holiday with its passion for naming things, she later wrote, which brought her to the brink of 'a new era in my life, for it was then I began to write fiction'. And, appropriately, the spur came when she was half asleep as she put a name to an unwritten story and to a man. '"The Sad Fortunes of the Reverend Amos Barton". I was soon wide awake again and told G. He said "Oh what a capital title!" and from that time I had settled in my mind that this should be my first story' ('How I Came to Write Fiction', *Letters*, Vol. II, pp. 406–10).

The Ilfracombe Journal, however, combines this delight in

naming particulars with a desire to place the particulars against a general background; it is the crowded banks as well as the individual plant which she admires, the whole rock-pool as well as the individual sea anemone. And going further, the journal makes the connections between all the different worlds she is currently observing – that of man, of landscape and of marine life. Not only do the themes weave in and out, so that she is as it were constantly crossing margins, 'the sea stretching beyond the massive hills towards the horizon looked all the finer because we had been turning our backs on it and contemplating another sort of beauty', but often the worlds clash in a comic way as in her efforts to put the sea anemones into glass wells when 'they floated topsy-turvy in the water and looked utterly uncomfortable; and I was constantly called upon to turn up my sleeve and plunge in my arm up to the elbow to set things right' (*Letters*, Vol. II, p. 243). She fuses her experience and understanding of the different realms at a deeper imaginative level when she describes Lantern Hill

a picturesque mass of green and grey surmounted by an old bit of building that looks as if it were the habitation of some mollusc that had secreted its shell from the material of the rock . . . In hilly districts, where houses and clusters of houses look so tiny against the huge limbs of Mother Earth one cannot help thinking of man as a parasitic animal – an epizoon making his abode on the skin of the planetary organism . . . we begin to think of the strong family likeness between ourselves and all other building, burrowing, house-appropriating and shell-secreting animals.

(*Letters*, Vol. II, pp. 241–2)

'Look at man in the light of a shell fish', she concludes, and he will certainly come off worst in terms of the beauty and design of his architecture.

The passage is fanciful but it is absolutely typical of her desire to keep the sense of diversity and individuality without losing a feeling of inter-relatedness of phenomena, and a second desire to combine keen observation with moral sentiment – we end by looking at both shellfish and men in a quite different way. As she says at another point in this journal, noting the effect of sunset and clouds on some ugly little houses, 'what is it that light cannot transfigure into beauty?' This, it seems to me, is very close to her theory of fiction – the observation must still be accurate, but the sense of connections and the arrangement will throw a transfiguring light over the whole scene suggesting new interpretations of a familiar world.

If one looks back over the impressive series of reviews and major essays Marian had written since she returned from Germany one can see this habit of mind developing to the point where the analogies through which she argues almost obtain a life of their own, threatening to overwhelm the argument. Her fondness for exploring lines of thought through imagery drawn from different fields – biology, art, music, history, the human body, reflects her openness and her feeling that different sets of experiences may share an underlying pattern which is not clearly visible at first glance. This gives a richness and subtlety to her writing so that arguments which interpret her novels in terms of one single theory such as Comtean positivism, Darwinian theory, phrenology, Ruskinian 'realism' or Victorian feminism are at once illuminating *and* inadequate. The vivid images, to be replaced in fiction by complex characters and minutely observed communities, are symptoms of her growing distrust of abstract argument and generalisations, whether based on religious doctrine or theoretical philosophy. She saw that such arguments could become enclosed in their own circles of logic and language and lose all touch with the human experience they were supposed to describe. This falsification draws her fiercest condemnation: 'pernicious'. Her own problem was to reconcile the theoretical explanations of natural and human development which satisfied her intellectually – a deterministic model which saw all activity as the consequence of 'necessary laws' – with the feeling that when one actually looked at how people behaved, at first glance they were motivated by combinations of habit, emotion, self-interest and confused principles which seemed to defy these logical laws. There *was* an underlying pattern, but the web which bound individuals together was a much finer structure, woven of emotional and moral ties which were hard to articulate and which could be comprehended through sympathy or empathy ('the truth of feeling') in a way which would be lost if they were reduced to argument. This is why the artist is so important, and particularly the novelist, who can not only demonstrate through example but has at her, or his command, a concrete, living language full of nuances and half-lights, resonant with past experience in a way that the language of the scientist or economist can never be.

In her journalism Marian returned frequently to her concept of artists' responsibility to their material and to their audience. She admired Goethe, for example, because he was content to draw out, rather than force upon his material, the pattern of action and consequence to demonstrate the saving grace of a 'noble impulse' among 'mixed and erring and self deluding' human beings. 'He quietly follows the stream of fact and life; and waits patiently for the moral processes of nature as we all do for her material processes. The large tolerance of Goethe, which is markedly exhibited in *Wilhelm Meister*, is precisely that to which we point as the element of moral superiority.'[10] Tolerance, the quality which she believed she had acquired over the past few years in her personal and professional life, was to be the prime requisite for the artist, and with it went an ability to judge not by conventional rules and taboos but by a sensitivity of the intention, motive and judgements of individuals – the human heart.

The insistence on sympathy with individuals does not necessarily imply that to understand is to forgive – judgement counts as much as intention, and her novels are littered with the victims of weak, well-intentioned men like Arthur Donnithorne or Fred Vincy. It is by action, not motive, that characters are ultimately judged: in their relationships, not as isolated beings. And they can only judge a correct course of action by weighing personal inclination, responsibility to others and loyalty to particular principles (a belief in the importance of scientific research, for example) in a fine balance. Those who seek to replace this allegiance to humanity by allegiance to dogma or abstraction receive a passionate denunciation, like the dazzling condemnation of the tenets of the evangelical preacher Dr Cumming:

A man is not to be just from a feeling of justice; he is not to help his fellow-men out of good-will to his fellow-men; he is not to be a tender husband and father out of affection: all these natural muscles and fibres are to be torn away and replaced by a patent steel-spring – anxiety for the 'Glory of God'.

(*Essays*, p. 187)

The notion of God can, however, be a force for good if it embodies 'pure elements of human feeling':

In this light the idea of God and the sense of His presence intensify all noble feeling, and encourage all noble effort, on the same principle that human sympathy is found a source of strength: the brave man feels braver when he knows that another stout heart is beating time with his; the devoted woman who is wearing out her years in patient effort to alleviate suffering or save vice from the last stages of degradation, finds aid in the pressure of a friendly hand which tells her that there is one who understands her deeds, and in her place would do the like.[11]

But in order to judge, we must have a model which allows us to compare the behaviour of an individual with those of their fellows, and so in the novels each individual is introduced or 'placed' as an example of a particular social or spiritual type, just as the anemones in the rock-pools, beautiful in themselves, could yet be studied in a book as a species or sub-species. And, yet again, accuracy and delicacy of delineation are essential if we want to identify the type correctly.

Throughout her time as a journalist and, it has been convincingly argued, as a novelist as well,[12] many of her underlying analogies were always provided by contemporary discoveries in the natural sciences and structured by the implications of evolutionary theory. In one of her best essays on the German social historian Riehl, 'The Natural History of German Life',[13] she develops this position with marvellous clarity and absorbing detail.

This essay is the theoretical equivalent of the impressionist

Ilfracombe Journal, and was written at the same time. Like the Journal, only explicitly, it sums up many of her central ideas.

Describing his 'socio-political-conservatism', she defines her own belief that social, like natural, development reveals 'the gradual operation of necessary laws', that social forms represent the current aspirations of their members, and that individuals are not merely influenced by the society they inherit but can influence them in turn. Above all, she points to Riehl's view of society as one in which we use inherited forms without reflection, just as we all use a language rich in buried meaning and 'hoary archaisms familiar with forgotten years' or just as

The nature of European men has its roots intertwined with the past, and can only be developed by allowing those roots to remain undisturbed while the process of development is going on, until that perfect ripeness of the seed which carries with it a life independent of the root.

(*Essays*, p. 288)

This represents quite a change from her sympathy with the 1848 revolutions and the current of change sweeping over Europe, and there must have been times when she felt a conflict between her theory and the demands of the humanitarian justice she had approved in Dr Cumming – for example over such issues as slavery, which called out for immediate imposition of change – but in her novels she was rarely to deviate from this gradualist political stance.

In the essay, Marian chooses to concentrate on Riehl's picture of the peasantry and begins with a passage on language, a subject she returned to constantly. Here she is fighting not the dogmatic rhetoric of evangelical preachers, but the sloganising abstractions of political scientists – 'the people', 'the masses', 'the proletariat', 'the peasants': empty labels which often hide a complete lack of concrete knowledge. But she condemns as equally false the iconography of pastoral art or the idyllic rustic convention of opera and the stage which 'represents the still lingering mistake, that an unintelligible dialect is a guarantee for ingenuousness, and that slouching shoulders indicate an upright disposition . . . To make men moral, something more is requisite

than to turn them out to grass' (*Essays*, p. 270). If labourers or
Dickensian roadsweepers are really virtuous under appalling
conditions of servitude and ignorance then there is little argument for reform. (She was to use similar arguments about
idealised pictures of women.) Realism and precision is what she
demands, and she calls for someone who will write not about the
'working classes' but about different sections of the working
class, or about the 'small shopkeepers artisans and peasantry, –
the degree in which they are influenced by local conditions, their
maxims and habits, the points of view from which they regard
their religious teachers, and the degree in which they are influenced by religious doctrines, the interaction of the various
classes on each other, and what are the tendencies in their
position towards disintegration or towards development . . .'
(*Essays*, pp. 272–3). This could be a prescription for her own
early fiction.

Riehl's four-volume work on German society, the result of
years of travelling and observation, fills the criteria she lays
down – it is a 'natural history of . . . social classes'. In tracing
his analysis of the part played by tradition in the life of German
peasants, and their confused response to new economic pres-
sures of the market, to new administrative changes and to new
political doctrines such as Communism, she draws a picture of a
stubborn, custom-bound, litigious class which could stand in
many ways as a prototype for the Dodsons and Pearsons in *The
Mill on the Floss*. And indeed it is in this essay that she begins to
look back on her own society with the eye for significant detail
which distinguishes her later fiction. In *How I Came to Write
Fiction*, a note written in 1857, she tells us that she had once
written an introductory chapter describing 'a Staffordshire
village and the life of the neighbouring farm houses' and perhaps
this lies behind the evocative paragraph in which, ostensibly to
bring home to British readers the nature of Riehl's peasantry,
she compares it to the life of a tenant farmer in England fifty
years ago. It is a passage which takes us to the threshold of
her fiction, but which also conveys the deep regrets and doubts,
the acceptance of casualties and losses which accompanied her

fidelity to the idea that development inevitably implies 'progress'. She is turning the clock back to the early 1800s, the time of *Adam Bede* and of her own father's youth:

when the master helped to milk his own cows, and the daughters got up at one o'clock in the morning to brew, when the family dined in the kitchen with the servants, and sat with them round the kitchen fire in the evening. In those days, the quarried parlour was innocent of a carpet, and its only specimens of art were a framed sampler and the best tea-board; the daughters even of substantial farmers had often no greater accomplishment in writing and spelling than they could procure at a dame-school; and, instead of carrying on sentimental correspondence, they were spinning their future table-linen, and looking after every saving in butter and eggs that might enable them to add to the little stock of plate and china which they were laying in against their marriage. In our own day . . . we can hardly enter the least imposing farm-house without finding a bad piano in the 'drawing-room', and some old annuals, disposed with a symmetrical imitation of negligence, on the table; though the daughters may still drop their '*h*'s, their vowels are studiously narrow; and it is only in very primitive regions that they will consent to sit in a covered vehicle without springs, which was once thought an advance in luxury on the pillion.

(*Essays*, pp. 273–4)

There is little doubt which period she prefers.

CHAPTER FOUR

'GEORGE ELIOT' AND THE WOMAN QUESTION IN THE 1850S

In 1855 when Charles Bray identified her as the author of the devastating article in *The Westminster Review*, 'Evangelical Teaching: Dr Cumming', Marian begged him to keep her identity secret: 'The article appears to have produced a strong impression, and that impression would be a little counteracted if the author were known to be a woman . . .' (*Letters*, Vol. II, p. 218). She feared discovery on general and on particular grounds. First, to know that the Cumming piece was written by a woman might be to re-read it as an emotional outburst rather than a reasoned analysis, given the current view of women as intuitive rather than intellectual. And secondly, any acceptance of the moral argument in the article would almost certainly be forfeited if the author of this brilliant attack on the hypocrisy and false thinking of fashionable evangelicalism was known not only as a woman, but as that particular 'strong-minded woman' ostracised from polite society because she was living with a married man who had 'run away' from his wife and children.

As a journalist, Marian therefore cherished her anonymity and the general assumption that reviewers in leading periodicals would all be men. Yet at the same time in many of her pieces, directly or indirectly, she was sorting out precisely what it meant to be a woman in the mid-nineteenth century, and particularly what the implications were for a woman like herself, an intellectual, a professional writer, a potential novelist. With her usual thoroughness she explored the question from every angle, trying to use her knowledge of philosophy, physiology, history and literature to come to her own conclusions about the nature of women in society and as artists. Her most sustained writing on the issue comes in her articles written in 1855 and '56, such as that on the seventeenth-century Madame de Sablé and her influential literary salon, entitled 'Woman in France'; the comparison of the books of two influential feminists, Margaret Fuller's *Woman in the Nineteenth Century* and Mary Wollstonecraft's *A Vindication of the Rights of Woman*, and the scathing criticism of contemporary fiction writers, 'Silly Novels by Lady Novelists'. This last piece was finished only ten days before she began writing her first story 'Amos Barton' – under a male pseudonym.[1]

But these three articles only hint at her deep preoccupation with the subject, which recurs frequently in her letters from 1850 onwards, and in her reviews, particularly of women novelists. Thus, writing from Berlin about possible topics for articles to John Chapman in January 1855, she notes, 'I still think the "Ideals of Womanhood" a good subject and one I should like to treat', but proposes that first she will write on

'Woman in Germany' – not simply the modern German woman, who is not a very fertile subject (metaphorically speaking) but woman as she presents herself to us in all phases of development through which the German race has run.

(*Letters*, Vol. VIII, pp. 133–5)

Her interest in problems of gender was stimulated by what she read, by her friendships and by her own ambitions. She had followed the growing debate about women's position in her years among the Rosehill circle, where Sara Hennell, in particular, was developing strong feminist sympathies, and she knew of works like Mrs Hugo Reid's *A Plea for Women* (1843), with its perceptive exposure of the ideology of 'separate spheres'. *The Westminster Review*, which the Brays and Marian read, had carried occasional provocative articles, such as Harriet Martineau's *Criticism of Women* (1838–9) and Mylne's *Woman and Her Social Position* (1841). Gradually other periodicals joined the debate. By 1850 'The Woman Question' in all its dimensions was pushed to the fore in reviews, articles, pamphlets and tracts, and in books like *Thoughts on Self-Culture: Addressed to Women* (1850) by Emily Shirreff and her sister Maria Grey.[2] In London she was drawn increasingly into liberal middle-class circles which were fervently debating the issues and were moving from the plight of single women and the condition of governesses and seamstresses, to the legal rights of married women, the divorce and custody laws, the right of all women to work and possess their earnings and the oppression of the double sexual standard.

The Chapman soirées brought her new friends like Clementia Taylor, wife of a member of the Courtauld silk factory family, a friend of Mazzini and a lifelong feminist. Partly through Sara Hennell's connections as a former governess to the Bonham Carter family she met Hilary Bonham Carter, a talented painter, her cousin Florence Nightingale, just returned from studying nursing in Germany, and Mrs Samuel Smith, their aunt, a stalwart women's rights campaigner and loyal supporter of Florence's fight against her family. Another older member of this group was the extraordinary Mary Clarke Mohl, who passed her life between England and Paris, where her salon was a meeting place for revolutionaries and romantic writers from the 1820s onwards. Later the Leweses stayed with her in Paris when they visited France. Then through Barbara Leigh Smith, to whom she was introduced by Bessie Parkes in 1852, she met Anna Jameson, one of the most successful professional women writers, whose works on art history and iconography were extremely influential and who developed her own altruistic feminist theory in her *Communion of Labour* (1856). (Jameson's horror at Marian's 'running-off' with a married man when she herself had been separated for years because of an unhappy marriage is just one instance of the contradictions within Victorian feminist attitudes.) At the Chapmans' she also met celebrities like Anna Swanswick, the translator of *Faust*, who was on the council of Queen's and Bedford College, and the elderly American Sara Pugh, whom she described to the Brays as a great abolitionist, 'one of the Women's Convention that came to England in 1840 and was not allowed to join the *Men's* Convention. But I suppost we shall soon be able to say "*Nous avons changé tout cela*", in spite of Mr Bray and all retrogradists.' Marian must have enjoyed a rare opportunity to tease Charles Bray for holding reactionary views. When we see her in this context the possibilities she gives to the heroines of her novels seem more limited than ever. Florence Nightingale, for example, attacked the portrayal of Dorothea in *Middlemarch* as a frustrated St Theresa, pointing out that Eliot could see women around her (like Octavia Hill) who were managing to make their philanthropic ideals 'very real indeed'.[3]

Although in her joking letter to Bray she had sided with the rebels against male dominance, elsewhere Marian often stood back from her women friends, ranging herself with the men, registering shock in a tone of heavy playfulness as if disturbed by assertive feminism. She is cruel, until she knows her better, about Frederika Bremer's appearance: 'she is old – extremely ugly and deformed – Her eyes are sore – her teeth horrid'. Unimpressed by Mary Clarke Mohl's colourful life she sneers that 'her *make-up* was certainly extraordinary, but I suppose she is a superior woman'; at Anna Swanswick's she passes 'a stupid evening – 12 women and 2½ men' while she is clearly taken aback by Clementia Taylor's niece who 'smoked her cigarette with a charming nonchalance'. One of the traits she is most suspicious of – a principal target in 'Silly Novels' – is feminine learning, perhaps defensive of her own. She groans, for example, at the thought of meeting a prodigy like Caroline Cornwallis, scholar, friend of Sismondi, who was to write powerful articles for *The Westminster Review* on the legal position of women in 1856 and '57, and who in 1853 was receiving a prize for an essay on juvenile delinquency: 'A lady who reads

Egyptian Hieroglyphs and for all I know the arrow-headed cuneiform characters to boot.'[4] But while she patronised these clever women she had even less time for the mass from which they sprang, witness this aside in another letter to Charles Bray after she had read John Wharton's *Summary of the Laws relating to Women*: "Enfranchisement of Women" only makes creeping progress; and that is best, for woman does not yet deserve a much better lot than man gives her' (*Letters*, Vol. II, p. 86).

The irony is characteristic of her detachment even at this most 'feminist' stage in her career. Her single wholehearted commitment was to Barbara Leigh Smith.[5] Barbara (whose radical father Benjamin Leigh Smith had never married her mother, a young servant, and who provided for his daughter on her majority equally with her brothers) was an inspirational figure – intelligent, well informed and fiercely determined, a talented landscape painter who fought her own battles for recognition as a woman artist with male critics like Ruskin who admired, but patronised, her work. She immediately endeared herself to Marian and her warmth, vitality and spontaneous verve always kept them close. (She is often considered the model for the tall, red-haired heroine of Eliot's *Romola* with her 'expression of proud tenacity and latent impetuousness'.) A famous instance of their friendship which illustrates Barbara's nature well is her response to *Adam Bede*. She knew from the reviews even before she read the novel that Marian was the author, and wrote at once from Algiers (where she had married a French doctor, Eugène Bodichon): 'I can't tell you how I triumphed in the triumph you have made . . .' She wrote again later:

Now the more I get of the book, the more certain I am, not because it is like what you have written before, but because it is like what I see in you. It is an opinion which fire cannot melt out of me, I would die in it at the stake . . . That YOU, that *you* whom they spit at should do it! I am so enchanted with the good and bad of me! Both angel and devil triumph!

(*Letters*, Vol. III, p. 56)

Marian responded to this warm feminist outburst with an

equally warm, but very different emphasis, asking Barbara to keep the secret, and giving the tribute which she had been offered as an unconventional outcast woman to her 'dear husband' Lewes – 'he is the prime blessing that has made all the rest possible to me'.

When Barbara visited Marian and Lewes, on holiday at Tenby in the summer of 1856, she herself had become involved with the charismatic irresponsible John Chapman, who was fascinated by her red-haired beauty and independence (and probably by her independent income). In 1855 he had quoted the example of Marian and George in an attempt to persuade Barbara to live with him openly, a course she rejected, influenced by the obdurate disapproval of her father, and the arguments of her brother. Barbara was then on the brink of beginning her campaigns for legal reform and for the extension of educational and professional opportunities for women. She was to become a key figure in the founding of *The Englishwoman's Journal* in 1857 and in the activities of the 'Langham Place group' who campaigned tirelessly for educational and professional opportunities and legal rights. She herself wrote *A Brief Summary of the Most Important Laws Concerning Women* (1854) and *Women and Work* (1857).

Marian's attitude to the organised feminism in which her friends were so active was ambivalent. She shared their resentment at blatant inequities, at legal disabilities and at the denial of educational opportunities. She resented the silencing of women, their exclusion from particular topics and from access to knowledge, and she disliked the cant surrounding double sexual standards. She also admired the courage of the feminist leaders. But she resisted any idealisation of women – arguing that *realism* about women's dependency, like Mrs Stowe's realistic pictures of slavery – made a better argument for change. And she resisted a thoroughgoing acceptance of equality for she did not believe that men and women had the same capacities, differentiated only by conditioning. Instead she clung fast to the notion of sexual difference, the idea that women had a specific culture, a language, a section of experience from which men would always be excluded. Unfortunately the notion of 'special qualities' associated with biology, maternity and domesticity has more often been a force for conservatism than change, and this conservatism sometimes overwhelms the subtleties of argument in George Eliot's own novels.

But Marian believed wider opportunities would both enhance women's capacities *and* maintain their 'precious speciality', the capacity for sympathy. She quotes with approval Mary Wollstonecraft's words, 'I contend that the heart would expand as the understanding gained strength, if women were not depressed from their cradles.' All she asks is that change should be moderate and gradual:

On one side we hear that woman's position can never be improved until women themselves are better; and, on the other, that women can never become better until their position is improved – until the laws are made more just, and a wider field opened to feminine activity. But we constantly hear the same difficulty stated about the human race in general. There is a perpetual action and reaction between individuals and institutions; we must try and mend both by little and little – the only way in which human things can be mended.

(*Essays*, p. 205)

The articles written in 1855 and '56 are exploratory rather than final statements. But they do give us clues as to her views on gender difference which she saw as deriving both from 'nature' and 'nurture'. They also reveal her, in line with moderate feminists of her day, justifying equal access to education and to employment opportunities, not on the grounds of basic justice so that women could fulfil themselves, but for the good of society as a whole.

In 'Woman in France' written in 1855, Marian attempted to define the 'special nature' of woman as universal, and as deriving from a physical base, notably 'comparative physical weakness' and childbearing:

Under every imaginable social condition, she will necessarily have a class of sensations and emotions – the maternal ones – which must remain unknown to man.

(Essays, p. 53)

But she then had to explain why women's achievements and behaviour varied so much in different eras and different cultures. Victorian science tended to explain psychological and cultural differences (whether between men and women or between races) through their biology, increasingly so after the publication of Darwin's *The Origin of Species* in 1865 and Spencer's *Principles of Biology* in 1867. Evolution suggested, comfortingly to many, that if the male and female roles were not ordained by God, they were laid down by something almost as deterministic. Thus even in the pre-Darwinian 1850s we find the scientifically oriented Marian turning first of all to physiology (and phrenology), opposing the 'small brain and vivacious temperament' of Frenchwomen to the larger brain and slower temperament of the Germans and English (and, critics have suggested, of herself). Her bewildering conclusion is that the poor Saxon woman is doomed, for

The woman of large capacity can seldom rise beyond the absorption of ideas; her physical conditions refuse to support the energy required for spontaneous activity; the voltaic-pile is not strong enough to produce crystallizations; phantasms of great ideas float through her mind, but she has not the spell which will arrest them, and give them fixity. This, more than unfavourable external circumstances, is, we think, the reason why woman has not yet contributed any new form to art, any discovery in science, any deep-searching inquiry in philosophy.

(Essays, p. 56)

In 'Woman in France' she turns swiftly to different arguments: to the pattern of sexual relationships, and the general cultural milieu. With an astounding leap she moves from arguing that it is not the size of her brain which has allowed the mind of the Frenchwoman to 'pass like an electric current through the language', but the laxity of the marriage tie. After a pious disclaimer – 'Heaven forbid that we should enter a defence of

French morals!' – she points to the good influence of free, mature, unforced unions (like that between herself and Lewes), which brought men and women into 'intelligent sympathy'; 'gallantry and intrigue are sorry enough things in themselves, but they certainly serve better to arouse the dominant faculties of women than embroidery and domestic drudgery'. But her desired goal is partnership, not free expression for women: so at the end of the article she stresses the relationships, rather than the singularity of the truly cultured Madame de Sablé:

In this combination consisted her pre-eminent charm: she was not a genius, not a heroine, but a woman whom men could more than love – whom they could make their friend, confidante and counsellor; the sharer, not of their joys and sorrows only, but of their ideas and aims.

(*Essays*, p. 80)

This anticipates with uncanny clarity the final achievement of Dorothea Brooke.

The 1856 review of the writing of Margaret Fuller and Mary Wollstonecraft is equally revealing of attitudes which pervade George Eliot's novels. First, she applauds their moderate, rational tone: Fuller's *Woman in the Nineteenth Century* is praised because

There is no exaggeration of woman's moral excellence or intellectual capabilities; no injudicious insistence on her fitness for this or that function hitherto engrossed by men; but a calm plea for the removal of unjust laws and artificial restrictions, so that the possibilities of her nature may have room for full development.

(*Essays*, p. 200)

Similarly, she recommends Wollstonecraft's *Rights of Woman* because it is 'eminently serious, severely moral'. Almost as important, she discerns in both authors

Under the brave bearing of a strong and truthful nature, the beauty of lovely woman's heart which teaches them not to undervalue the smallest office of domestic care or kindliness.

(*Essays*, p. 201)

The point which immediately strikes her is the insistence on the dangerous power that ill-educated women – the Rosamund Vincys of the day – exert over their husbands, and through them over the local community and the wide workings of society. In 'Silly Novels by Lady Novelists' she picks up the same theme when she attacks the effect of a superficial half-measure of education which will *not* make women 'rational' but merely bombastic, pompous and affected. A truly cultured woman, she concludes, 'does not give you information, which is the raw material of culture – she gives you sympathy, which is its subtlest essence'.

In the Fuller–Wollstonecraft piece she goes on from education to discuss in a way less usual among contemporary feminists the confining power of a whole set of ideas and expectations of 'woman-hood'. She quotes with approval Margaret Fuller's plea for the non-conformists, the women who have masculine tastes, the men who have feminine ones, the little girls who like woodcarving: 'where they are forbidden, because "such things are not proper for girls" they grow sullen and mischievous'. (Here is Maggie Tulli-ver, barred from Tom's world.) And she agrees with the point that as there will always be plenty of natural mothers 'to make the nest soft and warm' there should be 'no need to clip the wings of any bird that wants to soar and sing or finds in itself the strength of pinion for a migratory flight unusual to its kind' (*Essays*, p. 204). This anticipates her own, rather more pessimistic, introduction to Dorothea: 'Here and there a cygnet is reared uneasily among the ducklings in the brown pond, and never finds the living stream in fellowship with its own oary-footed kind' (*Middlemarch*, p. 26).

The most disabling ideology, she avers, must be that of 'the lady' since it enshrines the idea of uselessness, and she even suggests that men bolster this sanctification of drawing-room idleness (which superficially is much to their disadvantage) because it ensures their continued power and removes any threat of competition:

Anything is more endurable than to change our established formulae about women, or to run the risk of looking up to our wives instead of down on them . . . let them be idols, useless absorbents of precious things, provided we are not obliged to admit them to be strictly fellow-beings, to be treated, one and all, with justice and sober reverence.

(*Essays*, p. 205)

This is strong stuff, very like the argument that women may still be actual slaves at the same time that they are revered as saints, which had been put forward in an article which she (and probably Barbara Leigh Smith as well) had helped John Chapman to write, entitled 'Women's Position in Barbarism and among the Ancients', in *The Westminster Review* in 1855.

Eliot's essays are a delight to read, not only for her trenchant arguments but also because her fascination with detail brings individuals to life – for example Madame de Sablé's fear of death, her passionate female friendships, her greedy delight in fine food. But these discussions of de Sablé, Fuller and Wollstonecraft also reveal another, less likeable, characteristic – a persistent intellectual elitism. She constantly separates the extraordinary woman from the mass, a pattern she continues in the aspiring heroines of her fiction.

A George Eliot heroine, whether historical or fictional, must, it seems, be above all a woman of passion, with a hunger for ideals and a great capacity for love. In his selection of Eliot's essays, Thomas Pinney points out how she identified with Margaret Fuller, who had died in 1850, when she read Emerson's *Memoirs* in 1852:

How inexpressibly touching that passage from her journal – 'I shall always reign through the intellect, but the life! the life! O my God! shall that never be sweet?' I am thankful, as if for myself, that it was sweet at last.

(*Letters*, Vol. II, p. 15)

Much later she wrote of Mary Wollstonecraft in the same vein, brooding on the way she soaked her dress in the rain before leaping into the Thames:

it occurred to her as she was walking in this damp shroud, that she might live to be glad that she had not put an end to herself – and so it turned out. She lived to know some real joys, and death came in time to hinder the joys from being spoiled.

(*Letters*, Vol. V, p. 160)

While she responds to the intellectual rebellion of these intellectual women, Marian's definition of 'sweetness' in 'real' joy clearly invokes physical love and family life. She desperately wants them to win these 'feminine delights'. It reminds one of the way she reacted to the longing in *Villette* 'almost preternatural in its power' (*Letters*, Vol. II, p. 87) and to Charlotte Brontë herself: 'Lewes was describing Currer Bell to me yesterday as a little, plain, provincial, sickly-looking old maid. Yet what passion, what fire in her! Quite as much as in George Sand, only the clothing is less voluptuous' (Letters, Vol. II, p. 91).

In 'Silly Novels by Lady Novelists' Marian turns back from the unconventional, defiant individuals to the norm, the women who were writing according to accepted standards for 'women's fiction'. Extremely funny, the attack is withering in its scorn. She cannot even excuse their 'twaddle' on the grounds that they write out of necessity, the only career open to them:

It is clear that they write in elegant boudoirs, with violet-coloured ink and a ruby pen; that they must be entirely indifferent to publishers' accounts, and inexperienced in every form of poverty except poverty of brains.

(*Essays*, p. 304)

Here again, Marian was contributing to a contemporary debate. The journals of the 1850s devoted more space to the question of the contribution of 'the woman novelist' than those of any other decade and Mrs Oliphant could justifiably say, in the ringing tones of one who might be opening the Great Exhibition, that this was pre-eminently the age of the female novelist.

In fact the proportion of professional women writers in London had not increased since 1800, but their impact and success was more marked: they edited journals, they produced annuals, they wrote everything from penny dreadfuls to three-decker novels. In 1850 G.H. Lewes (before he met

Marian) had made fun of the alarm among male literary hacks, pretending to join them in wishing these busy women would return to making dumplings and embroidering braces, a 'graceful and useful devotion of female energies' and leave the market to the men. His mock concern extended to a vision of husbands with stockings undarned, with no one left to pet, flatter or flirt with them. Female authors, who put work before home, carried the threat of revolution.

Lewes wrote with tongue in cheek, and his piece is partly a tribute to the women authors he enjoyed:

How many of us can write novels like Currer Bell, Mrs Gaskell, Geraldine Jewsbury, Mrs Marsh, Mrs Crowe and fifty others, with their shrewd and delicate observation of life? How many of us can place our prose beside the glowing rhetoric and daring utterance of social wrong in the learned romances and powerful articles of Eliza Lynn, or the cutting sarcasm and vigorous prose of Miss Rigby? What chance have we against Miss Martineau, so potent in so many directions?[6]

But while he appreciated good women writers, he still located the source of female creative energy in biological difference, and astonishingly declared that the weaknesses of Brontë's *Shirley* were due to her not having children: 'the grand function of woman, it must always be recollected, is, and ever must be Maternity'. In his article of 1852 on 'The Lady Novelists', he wrote that female literature is bound to be different not only because of different domestic experiences but because of speciality: 'the masculine mind is characterised by the predominance of the intellect, and the feminine by the predominance of the emotions'. Therefore 'love is the staple of fiction, for it forms the story of a woman's life'. Men will be better at structure, plot and character; women at illustrative detail and at conveying passion and sentiment.[7]

Lewes developed his ideas in reviews of some of the great women's novels of the decade for *The Westminster Review*, such as Mrs Gaskell's *Ruth* and Brontë's *Villette*. He described the latter as the work of a strong, struggling soul: 'we hear the cry of pain from one who has loved passionately, and who has sorrowed sorely'.[8] But meanwhile other critics were applying different criteria, which often effectively segregated women's novels from serious – i.e. male – literature. Domestic novelists like Catherine Gore, Anne Marsh, Charlotte Yonge, whose childish heroines overcame all obstacles to be rewarded with happy marriages, received copious praise for the truly 'feminine' tone of their work, but were criticised for their restricted outlook. On the other hand, women writers of power and originality were being condemned as 'coarse'. Lewes was unusual in acknowledging that women like Charlotte Brontë not only could but should write about sexual desire and he praised George Sand for 'the forlorn splendour of a life of passionate experience'. Rarely did a 'powerful' woman's novel win universal acclaim, although an exception was Harriet Beecher Stowe's *Uncle Tom's Cabin*, whose strength derived, it was felt, from its very feminine emotional base – the overflowing feelings of a 'wife and mother' crying out against the outrage of a cruel system (but it must be remembered that southern anti-abolitionist critics had described her as a 'termagant virago'). It seemed there was no escape from this double trap.

'Silly Novels' therefore attacks not only the novels, but the critics who praised such rubbish:

By a peculiar thermometric adjustment, when a woman's talent is at zero, journalistic approbation is at the boiling pitch; when she attains mediocrity, it is already at no more than summer heat; and if ever she reaches excellence, critical enthusiasm drops to the freezing point. Harriet Martineau, Currer Bell and Mrs Gaskell have been treated as cavalierly as if they had been men.

(*Essays*, p. 322)

Although the last sentence seems to ask for women to be treated more gently than men, the main drift of the piece is that it is the duty of anyone who cares about women's literature to criticise all the novels by the same high standards. The last thing women needed to prove was their intuitive sensitivity: they must show that they could be accurate, diligent and self-critical with 'an appreciation of the sacredness of the writer's art'. Their work must be cleared of the 'rotten and trashy books so that the essential women's tradition can be exposed. For there is a distinctive women's writing, 'a precious speciality', lying quite apart from masculine aptitude and experience'. Women, as well as men, can shape the amorphous novel form into something beautiful if only they pour in the right elements – genuine observation, humour and passion. This, Eliot felt when she reviewed *Aurora Leigh* in 1857, was just what Elizabeth Barrett Browning had managed to do, adding the 'peculiar powers' of her sex to 'masculine' tradition.

But Eliot's main target in the devastating 'Silly Novels' is the falseness of female literature – the novels contain false pictures of sexual relationships, false and improbable characters, false and ridiculous pictures of female learning. The total effect, she argues, is to make women, their achievements and their aspirations look negligible and even ludicrous. She points out how the novels concentrate on an enclosed world of wish-fulfilment, entirely centred on a woman character:

The men play a very subordinate part by her side. You are consoled now and then by a hint that they have affairs, which keeps you in mind that the working-day business of the world is somehow being carried on, but ostensibly the final cause of their existence is that they may accompany the heroine on her 'starring' expedition through life.

(*Essays*, p. 302)

As if in reaction Eliot's first fiction places story-book heroines firmly in the world of work, marrying them to dull curates or drunken lawyers and not to prime ministers or aristocratic evangelical curates. The fairy-tale ending is seen as a pernicious dream, and a series of misguided women – Hetty, Rosamund Vincy, Gwendolen – are doomed because they absorb the fantasy offered by this romantic literature and believe, or convince themselves, that love, wealth, fame and fortune will come simply because they desire it. But Eliot also reacted against the opposite fairy-tale ending, as Gillian Beer has shown.[9] In her reviews of novels such as Geraldine Jewsbury's

Constance Herbert or Frederika Bremer's *Hertha*, she resisted the alternative feminist fantasy, that of fulfilment through altruism gained by an independent woman who has renounced romantic love and its pitfalls. Beer suggests that in *Romola* Eliot herself succumbs to the lure of such an ending, but in the struggles of Maggie and Dorothea she surely shows the pain, and loss, which might be involved in such a choice.

The 'feminist' George Eliot was partly formed by the pre-occupations of the 1850s. The nature of womanhood; the fear of change; the exclusion of women from the realm of the intellect and from effective power; the alliance in oppression of women, workers and slaves which gives them a shared rhetoric of freedom and resistance; the conflict between the new drive for autonomy and the older ethic of self-sacrifice; the difficulty of achieving independence without losing the possibility of sexual passion and family life – all these provide structures for the inner drama of her fiction. Thus *Scenes of Clerical Life* explore (and demonstrate) the attraction of the notion of fruitful sacrifice, but they also show the suppressed anger of women trapped in unequal relations with men. *Adam Bede* investigates differences between 'feminine fantasy' and female vision and sympathy. *The Mill on the Floss* battles with problems of exclusion and rejection, duty and desire, and *Silas Marner* pits the claims of the maternal ethic of community and care against the legal rights of property-owning 'fathers'.

As the years passed, the feminist arguments of Eliot's work were made subtle and complex by her own experience and unresolved dilemmas. *Romola* and *Felix Holt* contain contrasting studies of enabling maternal sympathy and disabling possessiveness, which can be translated from personal into political terms. But these two novels also assert the right of a woman to be an active participant in her own story, a right which (with all its pains and uncertainties) is the subject of the heroine's struggle in *Middlemarch* and *Daniel Deronda*. George Eliot's novels are the work of a writer who felt that a woman artist had special gifts and special responsibilities. Ironic then, that in 1856, at the start of her bold career, 'the strong-minded woman' could only speak out if she was wearing the mask of a man.

CHAPTER FIVE

SCENES OF CLERICAL LIFE: FRUITFUL SACRIFICE

After their return from Tenby at the end of July 1856 the Leweses settled down to work on their journalism. In late August George went to Switzerland to settle his three boys, Charles, Thornton and Herbert, into a new school – a liberal, progressive boarding-school at Hofwyl, near Lucerne. Marian remained in Richmond, working chiefly on 'Silly Novels by Lady Novelists', increasingly irritated by what she read, and increasingly determined to prove for herself that 'women can produce novels not only fine, but among the very finest; – novels too that have a precious speciality, lying quite apart from masculine aptitudes and experience' (*Essays*, p. 325). On 12 September she finished her article: two weeks later she began her first story.

The three *Scenes of Clerical Life* – 'Amos Barton', 'Mr Gilfil's Love Story' and 'Janet's Repentance' – were conscious experiments. Marian wanted to see if she could write fiction – a hidden longing for many years, as she explains in her journal note, 'How I Came to Write Fiction' (*Letters*, Vol. II, pp. 406–10). The scene at Cross Farm and even Milly's death in 'Amos Barton' were, in part, technical exercises to see if she could master dialogue and pathos. She wanted to put to the test her theories about realism and the social novel, and to propose an alternative to the false view of women's lives and the phoney presentation of social and religious movements she had castigated in 'Silly Novels'. Finally, she wanted to prove that a woman novelist could combine her special quality, flexible sympathy and tolerance, with the skills she most admired in her favourite male novelists such as Scott, Richardson and Thackeray: humour, observation and passion.

Ironically, she could only be free to make this experiment by posing as a man. She took a male pseudonym, like many of her contemporaries, to avoid being caught in a net of critical prescriptions and sanctions – no one laid down rules about 'men's novels'.

The disguise, though, went further than mere protection and gave a peculiar double focus to her early fiction, for although the *Scenes* appeared anonymously in *Blackwood's Magazine* in 1857 she went beyond the simple assumed masculinity of her reviews. She carefully gave her male narrator a personal history: a local childhood, classical education, cosmopolitan experience. It was knowingly and deliberately done and no one, not even her sympathetic publisher, John Blackwood, penetrated the disguise. (Only Dickens made a lucky guess at her sex.) The hints she dropped were quickly picked up:

There was clearly no suspicion that I was a woman . . . when G. read the first part of 'Amos' to a party at Helps's, they were all sure I was a clergyman – a Cambridge man. Agnes thought I was the father of a family – was sure I was a man who had seen a great deal of society etc, etc.

(*Letters*, Vol. II, p. 408)

She was delighted at the success of her impersonation, a fictional trick in itself and one which questions her realism in an intriguing way. She drew many portraits from life, and based incidents like the persecution of the evangelical Mr Tryan in 'Janet's Repentance' on actual incidents remembered from her childhood. But the authorial comment, – for example in the eulogies on 'gentle womanhood' – comes not from the 'real' memory of Marian Evans but from a man, granted the status,

education and social confidence she had been denied. The mask
also sets her free, in one swoop, to rewrite her own history. She
now had power over that complex, demanding Midland society
which had so constrained her – she could control actions, pin
down motives, re-design fates. The narrator too responds as she
wills; as a novelist, one feels that she comes close to Mr Gilfil's
definition of God, enjoying intoxicating power and insight:

Our thoughts are often worse than we are, just as they are often better
than we are. And God sees us as we are altogether, not in separate
feelings or actions, as our fellow-men see us. We are always doing each
other injustice, and thinking better or worse of each other than we
deserve, because we only hear and see separate words and actions. We
don't see each other's whole nature. But God sees that you could not
have committed that crime.

('Mr Gilfil's Love Story', Chap. 19, *Scenes*, p. 235)

It was several weeks before this omniscient narrator received a
name, 'as a tub to throw to the whale in the case of curious
inquiries' (*Letters*, Vol. II, p. 292) – 'George Eliot', a clever
name, deceptively simple. She said she chose George as a tribute
to Lewes, and Eliot because it was 'a good, mouth filling, easily
pronounced word'; but it also had resonances of a hidden female
tradition – George reminding us of her beloved George Sand,
and Eliot perhaps a nod to Jane Austen, since it was about the
delayed blossoming of Anne Elliott in *Persuasion* that she was
reading aloud that spring. For in these stories she operates
through subterfuge: as a free-thinker in clerical guise she used
the well-known struggles of nineteenth-century sects to embody
her belief in a radical, non-theological 'religion of humanity'; as
a women disguised as a man she used well-known fictional
images of the virtuous wife, the scheming adventuress, the
romantic orphan to embody her belief in the power of feminine
sympathy to change relations between the sexes, and to alter
society's restricted moral views. In her fiction, love and marriage
– the traditional preserve of women writers – become the
fulcrum of self-knowledge and potential change.

★

Literary duplicity pervades *Scenes of Clerical Life*. At first the point of the stories seems to be the way they are rooted in historical reality and in their claim to embody common experience. They all open in the 'working-day' world dominated by men and by social institutions: the Church; the landed aristocracy; the law and the market place. Change is measured in this male public world by 'the New Police, the Tithe Commutation Act, the penny-post'. Women know their place and run their own affairs, ostensibly as subservient helpmates.

In this acutely observed historical world the women seem to take on the conservative role she noted in the essay on Riehl, when she wrote that the wives and mothers, here as elsewhere, are a conservative influence, and 'the habits temporarily laid aside in the outer world are recovered by the fireside'. As the story progresses the narrator asks us to extend our sympathy to the prototype of the 'ordinary man', Amos Barton, the blundering, tactless but well-intentioned curate:

and perhaps I am doing a bold thing to bespeak your sympathy on behalf of a man who was so very far from remarkable, – a man whose virtues were not heroic, and who had no undetected crime within his breast; who had not the slightest mystery hanging about him, but was palpably and unmistakably commonplace; who was not even in love, but had had that complaint favourably many years ago.

('Amos Barton', Chap. 5, *Scenes*, p. 80)

The interesting thing, in addition to her determination to paint the 'ordinary' with the fidelity of Dutch art, is that Amos is seen not as one individual but as representative of 'eighty out of a hundred' British men 'of complexions more or less muddy'. And she defines their existence in negative terms – they do not conform to any literary stereotypes at all. Now if we re-read the passage above applying it to the central women characters it immediately seems false. Amos's wife Milly *does* have heroic virtues, while her rival the Countess *does* have a hidden past if not a crime, and *is* shrouded in mystery. Milly, if not 'in love', rules her whole life by its guiding light. In fact, to show patterns of conflict and resolution which transcend the mundane 'male' existence, George Eliot turns back to the stereotyped literary forms she pretends to eschew – the novel in which domestic virtue is opposed to 'wicked and fascinating women'; the Gothic tale of love and revenge; the nonconformist spiritual autobiography of confession. And by and large she uses her heroines to bridge the gulf between the literary and the real worlds.

The story-book quality of the central women characters is openly acknowledged. Milly is introduced as a 'large, fair, gentle Madonna' and left with the same image: 'they laid her in the grave – the sweet mother with her baby in her arms'. The reader is forced to realise with astonishment that such a figure can descend from 'the serene dignity of *being* to the assiduous unrest of *doing*', that she can be married not to a 'fellow of fine proportions and aristocratic mien' but to blundering Amos Barton who sniffs and 'gets more kicks than halfpence'. The testing of the ideal image against the real world illustrates more fully her 'sublime capacity for loving'.

The Countess Czerlaski, who jeopardises Amos's reputation and Milly's health, is the stylised opposite of Milly:

Look at the two women on the sofa together! The large, fair, mild-eyed Milly is timid even in friendship: it is not easy to her to speak of the affection of which her heart is full. The lithe, dark, thin-lipped Countess is racking her small brain for caressing words and charming exaggerations.

('Amos Barton', Chap. 3, *Scenes*, p. 69)

But in this story the opposition of silent good and articulate hypocrisy gains a new significance, for the cliché of the devious adventuress, the heartless Becky Sharp, is tempered by giving her a 'real' history, with which we can sympathise.

Caterina, the heroine of 'Mr Gilfil's Love Story', is less successful, because she is conceived almost entirely in cultural terms and remains stereotypical despite George Eliot's insistence in her letter to Blackwood that she wanted to present 'mixed human beings in such a way as to call forth tolerant judgement, pity, and sympathy' (*Letters*, Vol. II, pp. 298–9). An Italian orphan, collected like an *objet d'art* on a rich British couple's grand tour, Caterina is a singer, the first of a series of portraits Eliot was to draw of the woman artist as musician. Cheverel Manor is full of stiff ancestral British portraits and Caterina lives in a world of formal poses which embody class ideals: Sir Christopher and Lady Cheverel are Reynolds characters, their heir Captain Wybrow has a cameo profile, and gives himself to Caterina only in the form of a miniature portrait. To this artificial plastic world of art and architecture (Cheverel Manor has been remodelled on Italian lines), Caterina brings the mobility and emotion of the theatre; the passion of Gothic melodrama is contrasted with aristocratic rigidity.[1]

In 'Janet's Repentance' we move from these obvious, though useful, clashes of genres to something which was to be characteristic of almost all George Eliot's later fiction, a thorough blending of her literary inheritance with 'realistic' qualifications. Janet Dempster is the first of those large, statuesque heroines, on whom their simple dresses hang so beautifully that they resemble Greek statues;[2] who are spontaneously noble and unselfish yet whom circumstances or flaws in temperament render incapable of carrying out their good intentions. She is rescued at her weakest point by the sympathy of the evangelical clergyman Mr Tryan, who is also persecuted (like herself) by her bullying husband Dempster. And both she and Tryan describe their dark night of the soul in terms which would have been recognisable to George Eliot's readers, familiar with non-conformist traditions – the spiritual autobiographies which worshippers who wished to be accepted as 'full members' of a particular church often had to write or read to the full congregation. By pitting literary forms against a realistic medium George Eliot can give extra weight to her heroines' stories, for the readers' expectations are already guided by the conventions to which those heroines belong: often romantic conventions.

In 'Mr Gilfil's Love Story', Caterina, like Milly, dies in childbirth. Her thwarted love for the aristocratic heir, Captain Wybrow, which makes her want to kill him (he dies in the nick of time from a 'diseased heart') is seen as destructive to her, but fruitful for Mr Gilfil, her faithful admirer. For Gilfil gains, from her night-long confession of inner guilt, the quality of sympathy which makes him such an admirable pastor:

Mr Gilfil felt as if in the long hours of that night the bond that united his love for ever and alone to Caterina had acquired fresh strength and sanctity. It is so with the human relations that rest on the deep emotional sympathy of affection; every new day and night of joy or sorrow is a new ground, a new consecration, for the love that is nourished by memories as well as hopes – the love to which perpetual repetition is not a weariness but a want, and to which a separated joy is the beginning of pain.

('Mr Gilfil's Love Story', Chap. 19, *Scenes*, p. 236)

'Hallowed', 'consecrated' and 'sacred' love arises from men's response to suffering women: a theme which George Eliot was to elaborate in different ways in *Adam Bede*, *Silas Marner* and *Felix Holt* and which echoes in the background of her later novels. But in 'Janet's Repentance' the idea of sacred love is joined to that of Eros, to a powerful undercurrent of sensual abandonment. We know that despite their present misery Dempster and Janet were happy once, 'when they sat on the grass together, and he laid scarlet poppies on her black hair, and called her his gypsy queen'. She has a wild, elemental energy which endows her with reserves of power – a power which terrifies her dying husband and inspires her dying friend, Mr Tryan. The relationship between Janet and Tryan has a suppressed eroticism, which reminds one of Feuerbach's symbolic use of sexual union as an emblem of spiritual harmony.

In this story it seems as if it is the men who die and the women who survive. But not so: Tryan himself has reached grace, it turns out, through his remorse over the suffering of Lucy, a woman he seduced, and who eventually became a prostitute, drinking poison and dying on a London doorstep. This melodramatic account parallels Janet's fate, driven to drink by her husband. In her own worst moment, she stands as the absolute embodiment of female vulnerability, an image which haunts Eliot's fiction. (The description of her total loss of confidence could, for example, apply equally to Gwendolen, when she is tormented by Grandcourt in Eliot's last novel, *Daniel Deronda*.)

In this close presence of the dreadful man – of this huge crushing force, armed with savage will – poor Janet's desperate defiance all forsook her, and her terrors came back. Trembling, she got up and stood helpless in her night-dress before her husband.

('Janet's Repentance', Chap. 14, *Scenes*, p. 342)

When she is thrown out on the street, even death seems preferable to the blank future of a woman alone, but she works through her suffering to understanding. Janet survives, unlike Milly and Caterina (and unlike the Nuneaton woman who was her model). But her energy is spent: both 'anguish and joy' have died with the men who inspired them:

Janet felt a deep stillness within. She thirsted for no pleasure; she craved no worldly good . . . Life to her could never more have any eagerness; it was a solemn service of gratitude and patient effort.

('Janet's Repentance', Chap. 28, *Scenes*, pp. 411–2)

The women in *Scenes of Clerical Life* are holy sacrifices through whom men's lives are given spiritual meaning. They take the brunt of structural as well as personal alienation and distorted values. Milly works herself to death because Amos is poor, not because he is bad. Caterina suffers because no one takes her seriously – she is regarded as property by her adoptive father, and as a minor diversion by Anthony, who sees her devotion as the natural due of a handsome young man: 'to find oneself adored . . . is an agreeable sensation, comparable to smoking the finest Latakia'. Janet is beaten by Dempster because he expects the world to serve him; he is still 'the first born darling of a fair little mother'. For a man like Dempster every lost account, every extra glass of brandy has its place in a personal economy as strict as that of the market-place, adding to 'the little superadded symbols that were perpetually raising the sum of home misery'. His sadism and his use of a wife as scapegoat for his own failure are seen as common traits:

an unloving, tyrannous, brutal man needs no motive to prompt his cruelty; he needs only the perpetual presence of a woman he can call his own. A whole park full of tame or timid-eyed animals to torment at his will would not serve him so well to glut his lust of torture; they could not *feel* as one woman does; they could not throw out the keen retort which whets the edge of hatred.

('Janet's Repentance', Chap. 13, *Scenes*, p. 335)

The sketches carry a pessimistic analysis of the relative power of men and women to a logical conclusion. Gentle women are used blindly by selfish men, who in turn reflect the blindness of the unreformed social institutions to which they belong. Milly Barton and Janet Dempster are victims of a dependency and isolation which society, in the person of the narrator, persists in reading as noble:

A loving woman's world lies within the four walls of her own home; and it is only through her husband that she is in any electric communication with the world beyond.

('Amos Barton', Chap. 7, *Scenes*, pp. 99–100)

There is, however, a compensatory picture of a strong 'women's culture', even a women's economy, quite separate to men's while overlapping with it: the dairy money guarded jealously by Mrs Hackit and Mrs Patten; the talk of 'women's matters' common to Milly and the Countess; the evangelical women with their lending library, and clubs to provide clothes for the poor, which contrasts with the male society of pubs and meetings. Widows and single women *do* have control of their property: Dempster's will makes Janet into a figure of independence although she then chooses to put her money at the disposal of others. And while among this community of women there is as much silliness and backbiting as there is in the world of men, there is also considerable support, most noticeably in 'Janet's Repentance' where Mr Tryan's rescue of Janet from despair is supported by a mass of 'secondary helpers', the love of her mother, and her women friends.

There is anger too in these stories, and a sense of latent power which emerges in crucial incidents: when the maid Nanny bursts out at the Countess, or Janet refuses to pick up Dempster's clothes (clothing and nakedness are central images in the story). One is made aware of the heroine's withheld strength – the tall, statuesque figures of Milly and Janet, the artistry of Caterina. And in the last two women we are offered a vision of a darker side, a hint of women who are not angels or songbirds but tigresses, witches, murderesses.[2] In his delirium Janet appears to Dempster as a Medusa dragging him into a black fathomless sea – foreshadowing the interlocked fate of Maggie and Tom and the drowning of Grandcourt.

Defiance does lurk beneath the surface, but it is firmly suppressed. The overt approval of the male narrator and, one feels, of the female author, is given to 'quiet submissive sorrow, patience and gratitude'. It is a hard message for modern readers (particularly women) to swallow, that we should cherish our dependency and work through it to alter consciousness, rather than strive for autonomy. And perhaps the hardest moment of all is Milly's deathbed bequest of this mission to her daughter Patty, emphasising the continuity of a tradition of self-sacrifice. At the end of 'Amos Barton' we see Patty at thirty, after the other children have attained independence, re-visiting her mother's grave: 'Patty alone remains by her father's side and makes the evening sunshine of his life.'

Nowhere in Eliot's later fiction is this put in such an extreme form – indeed, the sacrificial stance is criticised as much as it is admired in Romola, who is also the sunshine of her father's life, and in Dorothea, ready to sacrifice herself for Casaubon. But there is no doubt that Eliot viewed these self-sacrifices as heroic – just as the pelican pierces its breast to feed the young, so women give themselves to succour those close to them. And as in each case these loved ones are clergymen (Amos Barton, Mr Gilfil, Mr Tryan), so their influence may spread throughout the community. Thus personal love is linked to the development of sympathy, a new religion of humanity. We see how this chain can work in the way Mr Tryan learns from his experience, and is then able to offer the necessary sympathy to Janet:

Blessed influence of one true loving human soul on another! Not calculable by algebra, not deducible by logic, but mysterious, effectual, mighty as the hidden process by which the tiny seed is quickened and bursts forth into tall stem and broad leaf, and glowing tasseled flower. Ideas are often poor ghosts; our sun-filled eyes cannot discern them; they pass athwart us in thin vapour, and cannot make themselves felt. But sometimes they are made flesh; they breathe upon us with warm breath, they touch us with soft responsive hands, they look at us with sad sincere eyes, and speak to us in appealing tones; they are clothed in a living human soul, with all its conflicts, its faith and its love. Then their presence is a power, then they shake us like a passion, and we are drawn after them with gentle compulsion, as flame is drawn to flame.

('Janet's Repentance', Chap. 19, *Scenes*, p. 364)

In this passage Eliot is describing, in her own way, the 'Word made flesh' and the role of love in its incarnation. The imagery is organic, sensual, celebrating the physical world and rejecting the realm of abstractions. To her, arguments are inadequate without embodiment and without conflict – and this is one of the reasons she turns from essays to fiction. A final point, related to this theme of embodiment, and to the contrast between masculine and feminine forms of expression, can be made about all three of the *Scenes* which brings us back again to the duplicity of the bluff, sincere figure of the narrator, Eliot's masculine mask. For all three sketches are, in part, about fiction itself, about the gulf between words, acts and feelings.

In 'Amos Barton', the most declaredly 'realistic' piece, we soon find that the people of Shepperton themselves cannot stand realism. They spend their time making up stories. The gossip at Cross Farm, in which both men and women join; the whisperings of the Misses Farquhar; the jealous suppositions of Mrs Phipps, the baker's wife, and Mrs Lander, the attorney's wife; the speculation of the clerical meeting and the servants' gossip all turn the lives of Amos, Milly and the Countess into something as sensational as any 'silly novel': 'There's fine stories i' the village about her', is a typical opening. Repeatedly Eliot stresses how disappointed they would be if they knew the plain truth, as if we could not bear very much reality. The adults, until sobered by the shock of Milly's death, prefer to live in a fantasy world. They are not much better than the children, Fred and Sophy, at their mother's funeral, who,

though they had seen mamma in her coffin, seemed to themselves to be looking at some strange show. They had not learned to decipher that terrible handwriting of human destiny, illness and death.

('Amos Barton', Chap. 9, *Scenes*, p. 110)

And like Dicky, who wants to play at funerals when he gets home, most adults merely repeat the experiences of life without understanding them. Amos has to force himself, by re-reading Milly's tombstone, to recapture the immediacy of his grief.

The difficulty of correctly reading a story which is being played out in front of our eyes is also a theme of 'Mr Gilfil's Love Story'. Here the Gothic genre is particularly appropriate, for as the story gradually uncovers a series of secrets we realise how blind we are. The revelations of Mr Gilfil's past life, of Caterina's love, of Anthony's perfidy, make us feel with Sir Christopher when he learns of Caterina's hidden passion: 'Poor dear little one! God help me! I thought I saw everything and was stone blind all the while.'

In 'Janet's Repentance' the issue of 'the story' is treated in a more complex and subtle manner. Dempster, the lawyer, is introduced as a monster of words, displaying unparalleled eloquence, particularly in abuse – his skill with language wins him comparisons with the Devil. Words are to be distrusted, but they do have their place: when Janet and Mr Tryan pour out their confessions, forcing themselves to read a pattern in their own personal histories, they learn from them as the Paddiford miners are supposed to do from the exemplary autobiographical confessions in the Evangelical lending library, or as Janet learns from reading *The Life of Henry Martyn*. The impulse to confession is important in this story, for confessing creates human bonds between relative strangers and also allows men and women to impose a form on their lives. It is therefore a means of asserting identity and solidarity in the face of annihilating fear and guilt. In describing Janet's longing for Tryan's reassurance Eliot uses the image of the rope thrown to someone trembling on an edge above yawning depths, an image which recurs throughout her fiction to the end of her writing life, most notably in *Romola* and *Daniel Deronda*:

If she felt herself failing, she would confess it to him at once; if her feet began to slip, there was that stay for her to cling to. O she could never be drawn back into that cold damp vault of sin and despair again.

('Janet's Repentance', Chap. 24, *Scenes*, p. 385)

But in this final story, which is very much about the emotions and the body, Eliot is concerned to point out the inadequacy as well as the power of words. She does this in two ways. First she points to a realm of experience which defies rationalisation:

There are unseen elements which often frustrate our wisest calculations – which raise up the sufferer from the edge of the grave, contradicting the prophecies of the clear-sighted physician, and fulfilling the blind clinging hopes of affection; such unseen elements Mr Tryan called the Divine Will, and filled up the margin of ignorance which surrounds all our knowledge with the feelings of trust and resignation.

('Janet's Repentance', Chap. 22, *Scenes*, p. 374)

Secondly, she shows that even at the most crucial moments, language may fail. We have to move into silence and uncertainty in a world where the gesture replaces the word. In his last moments Dempster struggles to speak:

But the moment of speech was for ever gone – the moment for asking pardon of her, if he wanted to ask it. Could he read the full forgiveness that was written in her eyes? She never knew; for, as she was bending to kiss him, the thick veil of death fell between them, and her lips touched a corpse.

('Janet's Repentance', Chap. 24, *Scenes*, p. 388)

Later in the story Janet will again kiss a dying man, Mr Tryan – and then too it is a silent embrace, not of forgiveness, but a 'sacred kiss of promise'.

Despite the narrator's assumption of god-like power his

boast to show all sides of human personality is actually a hoax. In *Scenes of Clerical Life* George Eliot shows knowledge or 'truth' to be veiled by prejudice, gossip, self-deception, death and the mists of history, and she also insists that there are areas of human contact so mysterious or so deep as to defy expression in language. The only way to lift these veils is by feeling the 'power of sympathy'. Sympathy finds expression in touch and symbolic action more readily than in abstractions or fine phrases. In Mrs Hackit's care for Milly's children, in Mr Jerome's practical kindness to Mr Tryan, in Mrs Pettifer's acceptance of the outcast Janet into her bed, feeling goes beyond words:

Janet turned her dark eyes on her old friend and stretched out her arms. She was too much oppressed to say anything; her suffering lay like a heavy weight on her power of speech; but she wanted to kiss the good kind woman. Mrs Pettifer, setting down the cup, bent towards the sad beautiful face, and Janet kissed her with earnest sacramental kisses – such kisses as seal a new and closer bond between the helper and the helped.

('Janet's Repentance', Chap. 15, *Scenes*, p. 347)

Here are foreshadowed Dinah, helping Hetty in prison; Dorothea, clasping Rosamund's hand; Daniel Deronda, pulling Gwendolen from her soul-stupefying despair. It is such wordless living sympathy which Eliot identifies with feminine 'affectionateness'. But it is central to the message of her fiction that men, as well as women, can draw from this bottomless well.

CHAPTER SIX

ADAM BEDE: THE MYSTERY BENEATH THE REAL

By 1857 life at Richmond had settled into a steady pattern of working, walks in the park, reading aloud, enjoying music together. Although the Leweses had few visitors they were not completely cut off: for George's work took him to London and sometimes Marian went with him. Her old friends like Rufa Hennell and Bessie Parkes were reluctant to lose sight of her and set aside the raised eyebrows of society – a fact she appreciated, although she did object to the feminist Bessie introducing her to Emily Faithful as 'Miss Evans'. But on the whole their life was solitary, wholly bound up in their work and in each other, its mood summed up by Marian's description in her journal of Christmas Day 1857:

George and I spent this lovely day together – lovely as a clear spring day. We could see Hampstead from the park so distinctly that it seemed to have suddenly come nearer to us. We ate our turkey together in a happy 'solitude à deux'.[1]

She felt, she confided again to her journal on New Year's Day, that her happiness had deepened, 'the blessedness of a perfect love and union grows daily . . . Few women, I fear, have had such reasons as I have to think the long sad years of youth were worth living for the sake of middle age'.

But even in this calm atmosphere her writing was proving agonisingly slow work, for she was attempting something quite new. She began *Adam Bede* in October 1857 immediately 'Janet's Repentance' was in proof: even at the planning stage she knew that her story would break the bounds of the *Scenes* format, as she told John Blackwood:

I have a subject in mind which will not come under the limitations of the title 'Clerical Life', and I am inclined to take a larger canvas for it and write a novel.

(*Letters*, Vol. II, p. 381)

Five weeks later she wrote to him: 'My new story haunts me a good deal, and I shall set about it without delay. It will be a country story – full of the breath of cows and the scent of hay' (*Letters*, Vol. II, p. 387). But the writing proved slow work. She finished only three chapters between October and Christmas 1857 and, despite the critical success of *Scenes*, she was reluctant to show her new manuscript to Blackwood who hoped to have it for a serial. But by March she was ready to part with the first few chapters and almost at once author and publisher agreed that the boldness of the story and the sexual nature of the tragedy – which was 'very different from anything the magazine has carried before' – might make publication in book form a better plan.

She wrote almost all the rest of the novel in Germany where she and Lewes spent the months of April to September. George visited his boys at their school at Hofwyl, Switzerland, but most of the time he was working on his book *The Physiology of Common Life*.[2] The interest his work aroused in Marian can be sensed in the language of *Adam Bede* where society and even the workings of the mind are often described in terms of the human body – of veins, muscles and connecting tissue, language which contributes to the scorching pain and the notion of healing and new growth of the later chapters.

In Munich, where there was a brilliant and scholarly court including historians, writers, scientists and painters, the Leweses were immediately made welcome. Apart from the joyous relief of appearing openly as a couple, Munich and Dresden offered one supreme pleasure – their quantity of fine art. Marian visited the galleries daily, particularly the collection of Dutch painters. French critics, followed by Ruskin, had coined the term 'réalisme' to explain the quality of Rembrandt's painting.[3] Marian had already allied her short stories with such Dutch realism and in *Adam Bede* she develops her theme with passion, acknowledging the place of idealism and formal beauty in art, but continuing:

> But let us love that other beauty too, which lies in no secret of proportion, but in the secret of deep human sympathy. Paint us an angel, if you can, with a floating violet robe, and a face paled by the celestial light; paint us yet oftener a Madonna, turning her mild face upward and opening her arms to welcome the divine glory; but do not impose on us any aesthetic rules which shall banish from the region of Art those old women scraping carrots with their work-worn hands, those heavy clowns taking holiday in a dingy pot-house, those rounded backs and stupid weather-beaten faces that have bent over the spade and done the rough work of the world – those homes with their tin pans, their brown pitchers, their rough curs, and their clusters of onions.

> (*Adam Bede*, Chap. 17, p. 224)

An aesthetic judgement quickly turns into a moral principle and a rule of literary practice, as her narrator insists that it is more needful to have 'a fibre of sympathy' with the tradesman in the street than with heroes 'I shall never know except by hearsay'. This chapter, written in Munich like an excited letter home and hardly revised, is a manifesto for a literalism in art and a commitment to describing the mundanities of life which is not carried through in the novel as a whole, despite its vivid farmhouse scenes. But it is important to notice that Eliot does not wish to banish the Madonna altogether, she merely demands that she be balanced by the old women scraping carrots. This is true of *Adam Bede* and all her own work, where conventions and idealised portraits are alternately enriched and undercut by pictures of the 'rough work of the world'.

In the peaceful interlude in Dresden, of work, walks and evenings alone reading aloud, *Adam Bede* progressed rapidly. It was completed by November, after their return to England, having taken almost exactly a year. Six months later Marian wrote on the fly-leaf of her manuscript (which she dedicated to Lewes) that while large parts of it had been written twice with small revisions,

other parts [were written] only once, and among these the description of Dinah and a good deal of her sermon, the love scene between her and Seth, 'Hetty's World', most of the scene in the Two Bedchambers, the talk between Arthur and Adam, various parts in the second volume which I can recall less easily, and in the third of Hetty's Journeys, her confession, and the cottage scenes.[4]

In other words, the dramatic, romantic sections of the book rather than the comic pastoral set her imagination racing. Yet it was the evocation of English rural life which first caught readers' attention and which continues to do so. It is difficult not to respond to that extraordinarily realised world – the kitchen of Hall Farm with its polished oak and gleaming pewter; the cool dairy with the guelder roses trailing through the windows; the bow-legged labourer who puts on his Sunday dress to come and stand in admiration in front of the newly thatched ricks. The speech rhythms and idioms of country speech, varying according to occupation, background, religion and region, are captured with uncanny precision and the great set scenes, like Arthur Donnithorne's coming-of-age or the Harvest supper – read like lyrical celebrations of the solidarity of the rural community.

It is a world which seems to be constructed from memory, yet, of course, it lies before the author's lifetime. The action of the novel is set in 1799, and the detail draws on her careful research into everything from Methodist practices of divination to the dates when particular flowers bloomed or books were published. And, as in all her novels, every detail counts, like the mention of Wordsworth's *Lyrical Ballads*, a work which also had the avowed aim of transforming the ordinary by the light of the imagination.

But the germ of the book came, she said, from some events in the early life of her father and from a story told her by her aunt Elizabeth Evans: a combination of origins which sets the masculine world of work, quantity, judgement against the 'feminine' realm of the spirit, caring and tenderness. The portrait of Adam is both a tribute to and a criticism of her father; Hayslope is based on Ellastone, the village on the Staffordshire-Derbyshire border where he worked as a young man and where he was married; Snowfield (Dinah's workplace) resembles Wirksworth, a former mining town on the high Derbyshire moors, where the workers of the Arkwright Mills lived. Here the eight-year-old Mary Ann had visited her aunt and uncle Elizabeth and Samuel Evans. Elizabeth, who became a close friend of the young girl, had been a lace-mender who was converted to Methodism in 1797 and travelled as a lay-preacher before she married Samuel, a carpenter. In 1802 she and other Methodist women stayed all night in the cell of Mary Voce, a nineteen-year-old woman convicted of poisoning her child. They brought about such a transformation that, according to local papers, broadsheets and ballads, Mary went to the scaffold 'with a triumphant and heavenly smile on her countenance'.[5]

The return to the legends and memories of her family past had added poignancy because while working on the *Scenes* her terrible anxiety about her sister Chrissey's illness had led Marian to tell Isaac of her union with Lewes, an admission which led him to break off all communication with her and to insist that his sisters did likewise. The links with the world which she was bringing to life in her fiction were being cruelly severed.

★

Adam Bede was at first conceived as another 'Scene of Clerical Life', and, like those earlier sketches, it explores the way religious feeling is expressed through active sympathy rather than doctrine. In a book where symmetry guides our understanding, this theme is largely carried by the two contrasting preachers – the Anglican clergyman, Mr Irwine, and the young Methodist, Dinah Morris.

Both Irwine and Dinah preach to congregations, the man in the old lichened church with the arms of the Donnithornes on its walls, emblem of a patriarchal authority of church and state, the woman to a spontaneous gathering on the village green. He concentrates on ethics, she on sin and salvation; but they share an inner quality which is not conveyed through their words but through their talent for comradeship and compassion. At the end of the novel tragedy overwhelms the village of Hayslope as Hetty Sorrel, by then the bride-to-be of the carpenter, Adam Bede, is discovered to have been seduced by the young squire, Arthur Donnithorne, and to have left her baby to die. In this crisis Mr Irwine steps forward to help her and her stricken family, standing by the tenant farmer Martin Poyser 'like a neighbour', while Dinah brings comfort and healing of soul to Hetty herself in her prison cell. Both are distinguished by their sense that religion makes them part of a community and does not set them apart or above. Their ability to love the ordinary people links them to the narrator and to the author's driving motive in writing the novel:

the way in which I have come to the conclusion that human nature is loveable – the way I have learnt something of its deep pathos, its sublime mysteries – has been by living a great deal among people more or less commonplace and vulgar.

(*Adam Bede*, Chap. 17, p. 229)

Through this knot of suffering, unravelled by the sympathy of these two very different pastoral figures and by the compassionate gestures of others (such as his old teacher Bartle Massey), Adam himself learns that 'human nature is loveable' and is able to take his full place in the community.

The *Scenes* had developed a counterpoint structure which was to be a permanent feature of George Eliot's fiction, where plots based on literary conventions are played out against a background of realistic description, each mode of writing commenting on the other's validity – poetry against prose, reason against imagination, science against art – oppositions which demonstrate the inadequacy of a single kind of vision. The opening of

Adam Bede encapsulates these contrasts, its promise of exotic magic rushing us not to far-flung shores but into a mundane scene precisely labelled with names, places and dates:

With a single drop of ink for a mirror, the Egyptian sorcerer undertakes to reveal to any chance comer far-reaching visions of the past. This is what I undertake to do for you, reader. With this drop of ink at the end of my pen I will show you the roomy workshop of Mr Jonathan Burge, carpenter and builder in the village of Hayslope, as it appeared on the eighteenth of June in the year of our Lord 1799.

(*Adam Bede*, Chap. 1, p. 49)

With his magic words the sorcerer creates an illusion of reality which seems concrete, solid, thoroughly material. It appeals to all the senses – we smell, feel, see and hear the scent of pinewood and elder-bushes, the warmth of the sun and the roughness of the dog's coat, the dust glinting in the light, the strong baritone voice of the unidentified singer. Yet the 'ideal' enters almost at once, in this case as the disembodied hymn which will echo through the book, asserting the virtues of industry and of honesty:

> Awake my soul and with the sun
> Thy daily stage of duty run
> Shake off dull sloth . . .

and

> Let all thy converse be sincere
> Thy conscience as the noonday clear.

Adam will be a good workman, a clear-eyed realist, while his brother Seth – poetry to Adam's prose – will prove a poorer carpenter but a man of finer inner vision. From the start it is suggested that Adam's heroic manly philosophy, while cherished and respected, is somehow lacking. He can measure the world, sum up at a glance the value of timber in a wood, plan and draw and create improvements which will last a century, but these skills will not help him understand the mysteries of humanity. Realism has its weaknesses.

There is a flaw in Adam's mode of judgement, and in the dictates of the 'sensible' characters like Mrs Poyser and old Mrs Irwine. Not everything can be assessed by its appearance, nor every man by his work. The truth may lie beyond the reach of commonsense. Adam's own heart, for example, is clearly not guided by his head when he prefers Hetty above his master's daughter, Mary Burge. As Seth points out to their grumbling mother, 'There's nobody but God can control the heart of man.' A fascinating exchange follows, in which Seth tries to get Lisbet to 'take no thought for the morrow', explaining that this means that human destiny follows the will of God. But she doubts his reading:

'I donna see how thee't to know as "take no thought for the morrow" means all that. An' when the Bible's such a big book, an' thee canst read all thro 't, an' ha' the pick o' the texes, I canna think why thee dostna pick better words as donna mean so much more nor they say. Adam doesna pick a that 'n; I can understan' the tex as he's allays a-sayin', "Gods helps them as helps theirsens."'

'Nay, mother,' said Seth, 'that's no text o' the Bible. It comes out of a book as Adam picked up at the stall at Treddles'on. It was wrote by a knowing man, but over-worldly, I doubt. However, that saying's partly true; for the Bible tells us we must be workers together with God.'

'Well, how 'm I to know? It sounds like a tex.'

(*Adam Bede*, Chap. 4, p. 90)

Lisbet's bewilderment alerts us to the unreliability of any authority which depends on subjective interpretation, whether it be the Bible or the worldly wisdom of Benjamin Franklin discovered in the market-place.

An insistence on the arcane runs right through *Adam Bede*. The most down-to-earth characters seek explanations which defy reason, from Martin Poyser who fears to work on Sunday lest his oxen be 'sweltered', to the observers in the courtroom who swear that Hetty 'looked as though some demon had cast a blighting glance upon her'. Religion becomes a matter of divination, traditional knowledge is cast in obscure proverbs, love is 'frankly a mystery'. By the end of the novel the narrator mistrusts even language itself, acknowledging that even the most moving words are merely a set of arbitrary sounds which gain their power because they are 'the signs of something unspeakably great and beautiful'. All outward signs are cloaks of an inner, possibly different, meaning. Nature itself is incurably capricious. Old Mrs Irwine playfully, but with a terrible hidden irony, remembers her certainty, when looking at her baby godson, that Arthur had inherited the character-istics of his mother's and not his father's family when her son stops her:

'But you might have been a little too hasty there, mother,' said Mr Irwine, smiling 'Don't you remember how it was with Juno's last pups? One of them was the very image of its mother but it had two or three of its father's tricks notwithstanding. Nature is clever enough to cheat even you, mother.'

'Nonsense, child! Nature never makes a ferret in the shape of a mastiff. You'll never persuade me that I can't tell what men are by their outsides.'

(*Adam Bede*, Chap. 3, p. 108)

In fact, all appearances are deceptive. Even the country life which seems to provide such a solid backdrop to the action is by no means as settled as it seems. The farming community is flung out across hills and dales and the novel is punctuated by journeys, by figures disappearing into and emerging from a vast landscape. Again and again Eliot places her characters as anxious watchers and listeners, waiting by a door or a stile for the appearance of a loved figure as 'a speck in the distance'. The mellow farmhouses are like islands in swirling currents of motion which swell into the hectic journeys of Adam and Hetty and Arthur. The rich farmland itself is not trustworthy, but is dependent on men to make it work; a good farmer like Martin Poyser and a bad one like Luke Britton can create different countrysides. The rhythms and rituals of the farm – sowing, hay-making and harvest, so lovingly and humorously described that they seem like an inevitable progress – are suddenly thrown into doubt when we learn that the Poysers' tenancy is dependent on the whim of the landlord: after Mrs Poyser 'has her say' the whole family may be out by Lady Day.

Hidden contradictions can also exist within personalities: individuals can be taken by surprise when they realise how their minds are operating. Thus it is his work, the expression of his down-to-earth nature, which releases Adam's unexpected powers of imagination. The practical man becomes a seer, like the Egyptian sorcerer:

While his muscles were working lustily, his mind seemed as passive as a spectator at a diorama: scenes of the sad past, and probably sad future, floating before him, and giving place one to the other in swift succession.

(*Adam Bede*, Chap. 4, p. 91)

Adam sees himself leaving home with his 'mensuration book' in his pocket but without a measured plan; 'he would go and seek his fortune, setting up his stick at the crossways and bending his steps the way it fell.' In a moment he will hear the magic rap of the willow wand, portent of death which he does not understand, while unknown to him his father tumbles to his death in the nearby brook. As he muses, he draws out texts for himself and interprets them with proverbs, using his dreamy intuition to reveal – too late – the truth which has escaped his arguing reason:

' "They that are strong ought to bear the infirmities of those that are weak, and not to please themselves." There's a text wants no candle to show 't; it shines by its own light. It's plain enough you get into the wrong road i' this life if you run after this and that only for the sake o' making things easy and pleasant to yourself.'

(*Adam Bede*, Chap. 4, p. 93)

Finally, when he discovers Thias's body and makes his first great step towards losing his disabling hardness of soul, he does this not through reason but through the experience Eliot promised her own readers, 'far-reaching visions of the past':

Adam's mind rushed back over the past in a flood of relenting and pity.

When death, the great Reconciler, has come, it is never our tenderness that we repent of, but our severity.

(*Adam Bede*, Chap. 4, p. 97)

The reader is taught to look for secret signs, to weigh the hidden more carefully than the openly expressed: for example, to judge Bartle Massey less by his harsh words than by his anxiety for his dog, and Mrs Poyser less by her fierce tongue than by her adoration of little Totty.

The way people can deceive themselves, even about their own feelings, is illustrated by the justly famous scene where Arthur arrives at the rectory with the intention of confessing his feelings about Hetty to his friend Mr Irwine, but cannot bring himself to do so. His first feeling, that the conversation was too general, is replaced by the new excuse that it is too personal:

Was there a motive at work under this strange reluctance of Arthur's which had a sort of backstairs influence, not admitted to himself? Our mental business is carried on much in the same way as the business of the State: a great deal of hard work is done by agents who are not acknowledged. In a piece of machinery, too, I believe there is often a small unnoticeable wheel which has a great deal to do with the motion of the large obvious ones. Possibly, there was some such unrecognised agent secretly busy in Arthur's mind at this moment – possibly it was the fear lest he might hereafter find the fact of having made a confession to the Rector a serious annoyance, in case he should *not* be able quite to carry out his good resolutions? I dare not assert that it was not so. The human soul is a very complex thing.

(*Adam Bede*, Chap. 16, p. 218)

The narrator, denying the knowledge of the omniscient author, is content to sow a doubt.

Arthur, Hetty and Adam are all shown to be blind to the workings of their own nature, and to be swayed by irrational motives when they claim to be thinking clearly about their actions. But the blindness of the lovers is still more complete than that of Adam, for he is always guided by a sense of res-ponsibility towards others, while Arthur and Hetty look inwards and blot out the claims of the outside world. Their vision is totally self-reflecting and when they gaze into their looking-glasses they literally see only their own desires. In Chapter 15 Hetty in her coloured stays and black shawl transforms herself into a grand lady who will 'dress for dinner in a brocaded silk, with feathers in her hair', while Arthur enjoys 'seeing his well-looking British person reflected in the old-fashioned mirrors, and stared at, from a dingy olive-green piece of tapestry, by Pharaoh's daughter and her maidens, who ought to have been minding the infant Moses' (Chap. 12, p. 169).

The playful image anticipates Hetty's distraction from her duties. What these two are guilty of is 'magical thinking', the dangerous refusal of realism which allows them to believe they can control the future merely by wishing. George Eliot conveys with terrifying power the way that dreams unchecked can dissolve the sure outlines of the familiar world:

But for the last few weeks a new influence had come over Hetty – vague, atmospheric, shaping itself into no self-confessed hopes or prospects, but producing a pleasant narcotic effect, making her tread the ground and go about her work in a sort of dream, unconscious of weight or effort, and showing her all things through a soft, liquid veil, as if she were living not in this solid world of brick and stone, but in a beatified world, such as the sun lights up for us in the waters.

(*Adam Bede*, Chap. 9, p. 144)

The imagery takes one forward to the young girl in the 'Brother and Sister' sonnets, dreaming by the side of the gleaming canal, about to be rudely awoken by the crash of the oncoming barge, shamed by her brother's shout. Hetty's summer dream, shimmering on the waters, will lead to a fearful awakening beside a barren winter pool.

Hetty indeed retreats so far within her dream that by the end the powerful feeling that she can control destiny merely by wishing takes over completely. She not only denies killing her child but refuses to admit, against all the outward evidence, that she ever gave birth to a baby. The depiction of a woman cut off behind a wall of shock and suffering resembles the crisis scene of

'Janet's Repentance' and has an uncanny resemblance to modern psychological accounts of victims of sexual assault or violence. But with a difference, for Eliot seems to see Hetty's isolation as self-induced and treats her as significantly responsible for her own disaster. She is encouraged to express not anger, but forgiveness, even at the point when it appears that her seduction may lead to her death. It is the man, Adam, stung partly by his own humiliation, who fights Arthur in the wood and who is allowed to voice rage at the sexual double standards involved:

'It's *his* doing,' he said; 'if there's been any crime, it's at his door, not hers. *He* taught her to deceive – *he* deceived me first. Let 'em put *him* on his trial – let him stand in court beside her, and I'll tell 'em how he got hold of her heart and 'ticed her t' evil, and then lied to me. Is *he* to go free, while they lay all the punishment on her . . . so weak and young?'

(*Adam Bede*, Chap. 39, p. 455)

When one looks at Hetty's story Adam's outrage is understandable, for Hetty is hardly an actor in her own drama. Her story is one of passivity rather than action. She lets events take their course. After her seduction she makes only two crucial decisions – the first, to marry Adam, is arrived at not by considered judgement but is 'one of those convulsive, motionless actions by which wretched men and women leap from a temporary sorrow into a life-long misery'. Hetty, says the narrator, is a frail bark tossed on a stormy sea. The second decision, to leave Hayslope and search for Arthur when she realises she is pregnant, is presented as a similar gesture of abandonment, a refusal of responsibility, almost a living form of the suicide which she has just lacked the courage to carry through. In an ominous setting she simply flees into a new dream:

As she sat by the pool, and shuddered at the dark cold water, the hope that he would receive her tenderly – that he would care for her and think for her – was like a sense of lulling warmth, that made her for the moment indifferent to everything else; and she began now to think of nothing but the scheme by which she should get away.

(*Adam Bede*, Chap. 35, p. 412)

On her terrible journey to Windsor, where she believes Arthur's regiment to be, and even more terrible return, she is totally deprived of volition, like a sleepwalker, directed by agencies beyond her conscious control. When she finally reaches the dark pool by which she will later lay her child,

She walked towards it heavily over the tufted grass, with pale lips and a sense of trembling: it was as if the thing were come in spite of herself, instead of being the object of her search.

(*Adam Bede*, Chap. 37, p. 431)

She does not even kill her little baby but abandons it and covers it up in another desperate attempt to blot out reality. In fact, what Hetty is punished for is not her sensuality, as several critics have suggested, but her compulsive dreaming. She and Arthur fall prey to the kind of imagination which Eliot had feared and labelled as 'pernicious' since her girlhood, the seductive power to create an alternative world behind a glass wall which cuts the dreamer off from the rest of humanity. And when Hetty finally sobs out her pitiful story to Dinah it is like an exorcism, the release from a spell, the shattering of the mirror –

At last Hetty burst out, with a sob, 'Dinah, do you think God will take away that crying and that place in the wood, now I've told everything?'

(*Adam Bede*, Chap. 45, p. 500)

Behind the obvious reference to the wailing baby half-buried under the nut-tree echoes the memory of the time when the spell was woven, when Hetty's upturned, tear-stained face led Arthur to kiss her in the delicious, labyrinthine glades of the Chase.

The love story of Hetty and Arthur, which breaks the fundamental taboos of class and must therefore be hidden from their close-knit community, has much in common with the affair of Anthony Wybrow and Caterina in 'Mr Gilfil's Love Story'. In both cases the hidden romance, laden with literary associations, is almost a lesson in the dangers of novel reading, demonstrating the arrogance of introducing romantic fictional plots into ordinary life. Thus in *Adam Bede* Arthur's seduction of Hetty is described as a classical Arcadian idyll which goes wrong, for the real country world cannot contain a false, poetic pastoral. Hetty may begin, as the narrator describes her, in the company of woodland nymphs, but she ends (like Janet Dempster in her husband's delirious eyes) as a type of fatal, petrifying beauty, with 'the same rounded, pouting, childish prettiness, but with all love and belief in love departed from it – the sadder for its beauty, like that wondrous Medusa face, with its passionate, passionless lips'. In its forbidden quality, as well as its rustic setting, their love has a mythic resonance; Arthur does behave with the licence of a god in love with a mortal and Hetty takes on the role of those doomed women who take the play of the gods too seriously. Like Psyche longing to see the face of Eros, her princely lover, she calls down a curse upon herself. While Adam lives too much in the 'solid world of brick and stone' and has to learn the value of intuition and the presence of the mysterious, Hetty and Arthur slide into a world of fantasy.

But is there another way, in which realism and responsibility can be combined with imagination and desire? The resolution is suggested in the person of Dinah. She too is a visionary, but of a different, outgoing kind who seeks out and identifies with the need of others – using what Eliot calls 'sympathetic divination'. Her imagination, like Hetty's, is linked to images of fluidity and moving water, but their source is not a dark land-locked pool but a rushing stream. Defying the opposition of fellow Methodists, she tells the sympathetic Mr Irwine,

'It isn't for men to make channels for God's Spirit as they make channels for the water-courses and say "Flow here, but flow not there.' "

(*Adam Bede*, Chap. 8, p. 134)

She too falls into a kind of trance beyond words:

'it seems as if I could sit silent all day long, with the thought of God overflowing my soul – as the pebbles lie bathed in the Willow Brook. For thoughts are so great – aren't they sir? They seem to lie upon us like a deep flood; and it's my besetment to forget where I am and everything about me, and lose myself in thoughts that I could give no account of, for I could neither make a beginning nor ending of them in words. . . but sometimes it seemed to me as if speech came to me without any will of my own, and words were given to me that came out as the tears come, because our hearts are full and we can't help it.

(*Adam Bede*, Chap. 8, p. 135)

This was also how Eliot experienced her own moments of inspiration. She wrote to Sara Hennell, 'How curious it seems to me that people should think Dinah's sermons, prayers and speeches were *copied* – when they were written with hot tears, as they surged up in my own mind!' (*Letters*, Vol. III, p. 176). Dinah does find words, prompted by the need she sees around her. In her desire to help a fellow-preacher who is ill she is seized by inspiration, 'I felt a great movement in my soul, and I trembled as if I was shaken by a strong spirit entering into my weak body.' We see that her sermons move crowds, but after the opening scene the novel presents her generally in the domestic sphere. Here her actions bring as much comfort as her rhetoric. She soothes, touches, calms, feeds and her physical presence is vital, when she sleeps beside Lisbet or Hetty in the nights of their unhappiness.

George Eliot depicts Dinah not as a bodiless saint but as a warm, sensuous being. The hymn she sings towards the end of the book (which complements Adam's at the beginning) emphasises the lure of feeling over principle, and the struggle between desire and submission to authority:

Speak to my warring passions, 'Peace!'
Say to my trembling heart, 'Be still!',
Thy power my strength and fortress is,
For all things serve thy sovereign will.

(*Adam Bede*, Chap. 50, p. 535)

The marriage of Dinah and Adam seems artistically false to many readers, and I think the discomfort comes, not because it is a casual afterthought, but because it is too neatly symbolic an ending. We are made uncomfortably aware of George Eliot's firm moralism in this vision of sexual harmony, the image which Feuerbach had used as an emblem of the human striving for perfectability. Their union is a kind of sacrament, sealed, as Janet and Tryan sealed their friendship, with a kiss of 'deep joy'. Dinah is the means of her husband's growth to true perception. As he waits for her in the clear sunshine,

Adam's doubts and fears melted under this influence, as the delicate web-like clouds had gradually melted away into the clear blue above him. He seemed to see Dinah's gentle face assuring him, with its looks alone, of all he longed to know.

(*Adam Bede*, Chap. 54, p. 575)

With her help he can penetrate the mystery.

All the central characters in *Adam Bede* acknowledge the pull of forces they do not understand, which seem to overpower their will, which they call 'nature', 'destiny', 'Nemesis' or 'Divine Will'. At times (the women more than the men) they even feel this force physically, like a dragging tide. Their characters and their approach to life determine whether they will tap in to these elemental rhythms and use them for good like Dinah, or whether like Hetty they will be swept away and lost. For the individual need not be overwhelmed. Eliot suggests that although a pattern may be imprinted indelibly by nature, if people see their desires and emotions clearly enough they need not be trapped by their feelings but can subordinate them to other demands from outside – such as loyalty, duty or responsibility to others. (This is the point at which Arthur stumbles and falls.) But even the subordination of egotism to principle as exhorted in Adam's hymn will not lead to right action unless judgement is softened by sympathy, and sympathy can only be learnt by a man if he 'binds his heart strings around the weak and erring and truly shares their suffering'.

Eliot makes it clear that this profound empathy is a gift which comes most naturally to women and is essentially feminine, a distillation of their traditional caring, nurturing role. She does not, of course, associate it with all women – indeed her fiction is full of custom-bound aunts, besotted mothers and heartless wives – but she treats it as an impersonal essence, that quality of 'maternity' extolled in her essays. It is thus a capacity which men may acquire if they live closely with women, or take on feminine roles. From the start the novels are full of 'feminised men' – like Mr Jerome, who is introduced playing lovingly with his small grand-daughter; Mr Irwine, caring for his mother and sisters; the widowed Dr Kenn looking after his small children. Such men are often centres of wisdom. And men can also acquire a maternal sympathy through intense suffering on behalf of a woman, as Mr Tryan does in 'Janet's Repentance' and as Adam does himself: 'Deep, unspeakable suffering may well be called a baptism, a regeneration, the initiation into a new state' (Chap. 42, p. 471). When Hetty stands in the witness box, the general opinion is that she has turned into a hardened criminal:

But the mother's yearning, that completest type of the life in another life which is the essence of real human love, feels the presence of the cherished child even in the debased, degraded man; and to Adam, this pale hard-looking culprit was the Hetty who had smiled at him in the garden under the apple-tree boughs – she was that Hetty's corpse, which he had trembled to look at the first time, and then was unwilling to turn away his eyes from.

(*Adam Bede*, Chap. 43, p. 477)

Hetty, the dreaming child of nature who brought Adam the bitter apples of experience, must be annihilated, banished for ever so that the slow process of his rebirth can begin and he can rejoin the wider community through his 'better and more precious love' for Dinah. Poor Hetty! It makes one think of a sort of spiritual cannibalism – Eliot's humanised love, like Christian salvation, cannot come about without that complex of guilt, rejection, remorse and compassion which make up the notion of 'sacrifice' – and in the disturbing plots of her early fiction the sacrificial victim is inevitably a woman.

CHAPTER SEVEN

THE LIFTED VEIL:
THE LIMITS OF VISION

Three weeks before *Adam Bede* was published in February 1859, Marian and Lewes were investigating the subject of floods, 'looking into the Annual Register for cases of *inundation*' and by the end of March she could promise Blackwood another long novel, 'a sort of companion picture of provincial life'. This was to be *The Mill on the Floss*. But although *Adam Bede* was an instant, outstanding success, reprinting numerous times in different editions, translated into four languages and earning enough to ease the Leweses of financial headaches, the year in which she wrote her new novel had elements of sadness, loneliness and suspicion. Her success, about which she cared intensely, often felt like an anticlimax.

In February 1859 the Leweses had moved into a house of their own, Holly Lodge, Southfields, Wandsworth. As she was always to do, Marian found the whole business of housekeeping, furnishing and finding servants extremely dispiriting, and the house itself soon began to feel too hemmed in and overlooked. It was a bad time. In March, before Marian had time to visit her, Chrissey died of consumption, after writing a final letter which 'ploughed up my heart'. Her heart was also harrowed by more recent attachments. She had been determined to keep her pseudonym a secret and felt deeply betrayed when John Chapman, after forcing a mute acknowledgement from Herbert Spencer, leaked the fact that she had written *Adam Bede* into

London literary circles. Spencer himself seemed coldly jealous of her success, always reporting the criticism he heard and never the praise, yet not reading the novel until eight months after publication. For a long time her letters were full of smarting allusions to false and narrow-hearted friends.

Although she had no wish to expose herself, she was troubled for months by the persistent rumours that *Scenes of Clerical Life* and *Adam Bede* were works written years ago by a Joseph Liggins of Nuneaton, and that Blackwood's had published them without paying him a penny. Blackwood's reaction to this, and to advertisements for a sequel to *Adam Bede*, seemed altogether too tame to the Leweses, who sensed that the publishers were in fact more nervous about the possibility of a real lifting of the veil on George Eliot's identity, a revelation which might affect her reputation and the sales of her books. Although by the end of 1859 she was once more on excellent terms with her loyal publishers, her loneliness was intensified by their hesitation over the Liggins affair. And when she broke the news of her authorship to her oldest friends, the Brays and Sara Hennell, in an emotional scene, their surprise rather took her aback and the moment was further marred by the disappointment of Sara, who had hoped to discuss her own new manuscript on religious philosophy. Instead of relief and pride, the revelation made her feel guilt and shame, her present tactlessness reminding her of past insensitivity. She wrote to Sara:

There is always an after-sadness belonging to brief and interrupted intercourse between friends – the sadness of feeling that the blundering efforts we have made towards mutual understanding have only made a new veil between us – still more the sadness of feeling that some pain may have been given which separation makes a permanent memory. We are quite unable to represent ourselves truly – why should we complain that our friends see a false image? (Letters, Vol. III, p. 90)

Bitterness and isolation, the ferment of a soul which can find no home in the world, the hopeless sense that we can never represent ourselves and others correctly – all these feelings pervade the strange short story which Eliot wrote at the start of this troubled year. *The Lifted Veil* could be an updated version of one of Mary Shelley's Gothic tales in 'The Keepsake' which Bob Jakins brought Maggie Tulliver. In its concern with secrets and doubleness and with the fierce-hearted anger of a murderous wife, it also resembles the new sensation novels with which Mary Braddon and her followers were about to flood the book-stalls. Eliot herself described it as 'a slight story of an outré kind – not a *jeu d'esprit* but a *jeu de melancolie*' (*Letters*, Vol. III, pp. 40–1). Yet although it may represent an aberration in her style (although she always retained a fascination for Gothic melo-drama), the story is related to some of George Eliot's funda-mental preoccupations. For *The Lifted Veil* is all about vision – the use and abuse of foresight, insight and imagination.[1]

In *Adam Bede* Arthur and Hetty are swept into a destructive and self-destructive current because they cannot, or will not, see the results of their actions, preferring to live in a fantasy present and a dream future. Adam, on the other hand, makes what seem quite realistic plans for the future only to be continually tripped up by his inaccurate readings of personality – of Arthur, Hetty, even Dinah. In a similar way in *The Mill on the Floss*, Maggie's misfortunes were to be largely due to her inability to see the end of any story or the consequences of any decisions. In *The Lifted Veil* George Eliot pauses and asks, 'But *is* it really just a question of accurate vision? What would happen to individual choice if people actually could see the future? Would it change their actions? Would it be a blessing, a curse, or a mere irrelevancy? And could there ever be such a thing as perfect insight or would it always be somehow coloured by the medium of perception – the individual personality?'

The Lifted Veil is the fictional memoir of a sensitive, em-bittered narrator, Latimer, written in the month before his death – which he can prophecy to the moment. As a young man he discovers that he has the faculty of seeing into the future and also the ability to hear the inner thoughts of those around him. But he cannot see into the mind of Bertha, who becomes engaged to his brother, and this is part of her fascination.

Eventually, ignoring a vision of how she will hate him later, he takes quick advantage of his brother's sudden death and marries her. They gradually become estranged and when he does see into her heart, he finds only enmity. The denouement confirms his suspicions that Bertha has been conspiring with her maid, Archer. For when Archer dies of fever and Latimer's friend, Dr Meunier, conducts an experiment on her body (hoping to re-animate the corpse through a direct transfusion of his own blood), the dead maid revives to point an accusing finger at Bertha, exposing her plans to poison her husband.

In this Faustian story the hero chooses what he wants now, even though he knows the price will be later misery; for his visions are not of some absolutely determined future, but the future set in motion by the choices he makes. Eliot elaborates the moral by suggesting that what piques our desire most is the unknown: we prefer to live in suspense. Like readers of a novel, even if we know the end we try to forget it and concentrate on the intervening uncertainties of the plot:

So absolute is our soul's need of something hidden and uncertain for the maintenance of that doubt and hope and effort which are the breath of its life, that if the whole future were laid bare to us beyond today, the interest of all mankind would be bent on the hours that lie between.

(*The Lifted Veil*, Chap. 2, p. 43)

Foresight is irrelevant. It is not what we can foresee which is important, but how we live the intervening hours in the light of that knowledge.

The veils which are lifted are those of the future, of human personality, and even of death itself. But the title begs a vital question – who lifts the veil? For Latimer's initial trances are quite involuntary. When he tries to create a vision of Venice to match the hallucination of Prague he fails completely. His vision is a faculty beyond the control of his conscious will. Although allied to the imagination, it is uncontrolled by the intellect. In *The Lifted Veil* and *The Mill on the Floss* the spontaneous imagination is shown as a neutral capacity – its production of pleasing or displeasing images a mere reflection of its possessor's inclinations. But because our innate inclinations are selfish, it is likely to be a power for harm unless controlled by judgement and directed by sympathy for others.

Latimer's visionary power, like the imagination of the artist, is linked by George Eliot to that deep sensitivity, which she defines as 'feminine'. His only memory of love is of his mother's embrace when, as a small child, he was both metaphorically and literally blind, 'the curtain of the future was impenetrable to me, I had a complaint of the eyes for a little while and she kept me on her knee from morning to night'. After her death, his father, 'an unbending, intensely orderly man, in root and stem a banker' can offer no equivalent care. Instead he and Latimer's teacher, Dr Letherall, are determined to correct the boy's over-sensitivity by a dose of scientific education. But, by a nice twist of the plot, George Eliot shows that they were wrong to see science as devoid of imagination, for in the end, through the activities of Meunier, it will be used to break the barriers of normal reality in the most terrifying way.

When Latimer looks back and describes the dominant strain in his personality, he uses the water imagery characteristic of the dreams of Hetty and the visions of Dinah. Letherall assures him that:

'an improved man, as distinguished from an ignorant one, was a man who knew the reason why water ran down-hill'. I had no desire to be this improved man; I was glad of the running water; I could watch it and listen to it gurgling among the pebbles, and bathing the bright green water plants, by the hour together. I did not want to know *why* it ran.

(*The Lifted Veil*, Chap. 1, p. 8)

He turns to water when he seeks to recover the sensation of encircling maternal love, drifting on Lake Geneva embraced by the sky and 'the glowing mountain tops'. This echoes Wordsworth's poem 'The Excursion', but whereas the boy in the poem is active and is frightened by his glimpse of the underlying force and energy of the universe, Latimer is entirely passive, and takes himself as the centre of the natural world. By a cruel irony

Robert Evans – miniature by Carlisle, 1842

Griff House – from Cross, *George Eliot's Life*

Charles Bray

Cara Bray – miniature by Sara
Hennell, 1833

Sara Hennell – watercolour by Cara
Bray, 1833

Herbert Spencer, 1855

Barbara Leigh Smith Bodichon – by Samuel
Laurence

George Eliot, circa 1854

George Henry Lewes – by Rudolph
Lehmann, 1867

Dedication of the manuscript of *Adam
Bede*

Adam Bede – Blackwood illustrated
edition

The Mill on the Floss – Blackwood
illustrated edition

Romola – Frederic Leighton engraving, 1863

George Eliot, 1858

The Priory, Regent's Park

The Heights, Witley, Surrey – from Cross, *Life*

John Walter Cross

George Eliot – by Lowes Cato
Dickinson, 1872

4 Cheyne Walk – from Cross, *Life*

Chapter I.

Men can do nothing without the make-believe of a beginning. Even Science, the strict measurer, is obliged to start with a make-believe unit, and must fix on a point in the stars' unceasing journey when his sidereal clock shall pretend that time is at Nought. His less accurate grandmother Poetry has always been understood to start in the middle; but on reflection it appears that her proceeding is not very different from his; since Science, too, reckons backwards as well as forwards, divides his unit into billions, and with his clock-finger at Nought really sets off in medias res. No retrospect will take us to the true beginning; and whether our prologue be in heaven or on earth, it is but a fraction of that all-presupposing fact with which our story sets out.

Was she beautiful or not beautiful? and what was the secret of form or expression which gave the dynamic quality to her glance & made it an epoch? Was the good or the evil genius dominant in those beams? Probably the evil; else why was the effect that of unrest rather than of undisturbed charm? Why was the wish to look again felt as coercion & not as a longing in which the whole being consents?

She who raised these questions in Daniel Deronda's mind was occupied in gambling: not in the open air under a Southern sky, tossing coppers on a ruined wall with rags about her limbs; but in one of those splendid resorts which the enlightenment of ages has prepared for the same species of pleasure at a heavy cost of gilt mouldings, dark-toned colour & chubby nudities, all correspondingly heavy — forming a suitable condenser for human breath, ~~belonging~~ in great part to the highest fashion & not easily procurable to be breathed in elsewhere ~~at least~~ in the like proportion, at least by persons of little fashion. —

It was near four o'clock on ~~this autumnal day~~ a September day, so that the atmosphere was well-brewed to a visible haze. There was deep stillness, broken only by a light rattle, a light chink, a small sweeping sound, & an

The opening page of *Daniel Deronda*

Latimer's visionary trance reflects his selfish nature rather than his desires, whisking him to arid and alienating landscapes. He finds himself in a city where memory is deadly instead of revitalising, where the light is like the summer sunshine of

a long-past century arrested in its course – unrefreshed for ages by the dews of night, or the rushing rain-cloud; scorching the dusty, weary, time-eaten grandeur of a people doomed to live on in the stale repetition of memories, like deposed and superannuated kings in their regal gold-inwoven tatters. The city looked so thirsty that the broad river seemed to me a sheet of metal.

(The Lifted Veil, Chap. 1, p. 11)

The streets are dominated by blackened statues, 'grim and stony beings' and the citizens too are frozen 'in the rigidity of habit, as they live on in perpetual mid-day, without the repose of night or the new birth of morning'. When he visits the real Prague, Latimer finds a still more ancient symbol of petrification – the 'death in life' revealed by the 'shrunken lights' of the Jewish synagogue, where he shudders as he listens to a reading from 'the book of the Law'. This life dominated by custom and by strict notions of justice and punishment will be redefined in connection with Tom Tulliver, in *The Mill on the Floss*, as characteristic of a 'masculine' approach to life unrefreshed by the feminine springs of sympathy and the imagination.

His second trance introduces the woman who comes to obsess him, Bertha Grant. Again, she represents the opposite of his loving, life-giving mother. Although she springs from a watery world, it is one which contains the promise of death, not birth. She is a spectre of Romantic myth deadly to men, a green-clad figure who, he says,

made me think of a Water-Nixie – for my mind was full of German lyrics, and this pale, fatal-eyed woman, with the green weeds, looked like a birth from some cold sedgy-stream, the daughter of an aged river.

(The Lifted Veil, Chap. 1, p. 16)

Latimer's self-obsession and refusal to engage actively with other people creates visions which are inversions of his desires and embodiments of his fears. We know from the start that he is suspicious, jealous and self-obsessed. The enforced awareness of other people affords him no pleasure, wrings from him no concern – it is like an illness, a ringing in the ears, 'a preternaturally heightened sense of hearing, making audible to one a roar of sound where others find perfect stillness' (Chap. 1, p. 26). His position is the unbearable one which Eliot imagines of hearing 'the roar on the other side of silence' in *Middlemarch*; he has too keen a vision. He lives in constant tension between 'the inward and the outward':

Are you unable to imagine this double consciousness at work within me, flowing on like two parallel streams which never mingle their waters and blend into a common hue?

(*The Lifted Veil*, Chap. 1, p. 32)

This brilliantly evokes the perpetual preoccupation of an artist, and perhaps the fears that Eliot herself felt as she realised the burdens of her own imagination and vocation.[2] But Latimer, stifled by his egotism, can find no outlet either in human contact or in art. The whole story is filtered through the consciousness of a man who, like the selfish Captain Wybrow in 'Mr Gilfil's Love Story' has a literal disease of the heart, *angina pectoris*, and who has 'never been encouraged to trust much in the sympathy of my fellow-men' (Chap. 1, p. 2). Latimer's character should warn us against unquestioning acceptance of his version of reality. He is right, for example, to distrust the patriarchal structures represented by his father or the city of Prague, but he lacks insight into how to change them. He is right too, to see Bertha as threatening, but he lacks the sensitivity to see that the reason for her hostility lies in his own behaviour.

The early descriptions of Bertha – if we read between Latimer's lines – are of a coquettish, sharp-minded woman with an eye for the main chance, a less nervous forerunner of Gwendolen Harleth in *Daniel Deronda*. And just as Gwendolen comes to harbour murderous feelings towards Grandcourt, so Bertha is driven to despair and violence by the unbending desire for domination in the man she thought she controlled. Husband and

wife are like opposing magnetic poles and as Latimer analyses
their mutual repulsion he realises that Bertha is

> haunted by a terror of me, which alternated every now and then with
> defiance. She meditated continually how the incubus could be shaken
> off her life – how she could be freed from this hateful bond to a being
> whom she at once despised as an imbecile, and dreaded as an inquisitor.
>
> (*The Lifted Veil*, Chap. 2, p. 51)

The mental cruelty of Latimer and Grandcourt parallels Dempster's physical violence in 'Janet's Repentance' and the mingled
terror and defiance they arouse in all their wives is very similar.

Latimer rages against his terrible gift but his curse is not in
the faculty itself – even when it reveals unpalatable facts about
society or individuals – but in the way he chooses to ignore
his visions and follow his own desires even when he knows it
will bring unhappiness to himself and others. Gifted with a
'feminine' imagination and sensitivity as a child, he is entirely
lacking in outgoing feminine sympathy (the two do not always
go together). In contrast to men like Adam Bede and Philip
Wakem who, by sharing the suffering of those they love, grow
to a sense of community with the wider world, Latimer narrows
his field of sympathy, until he is left only with his own fear.
Towards the end his visions include dehumanised scenes of
desolated grandeur like Shelley's 'Ozymandias' or Mary
Shelley's apocalyptic novel, *The Last Man*, which oppress him
with the feeling of 'the presence of something unknown and
pitiless. For continual suffering had annihilated religious faith
within me: to the utterly miserable – the unloving and the
unloved – there is no religion possible, no worship but a worship of devils' (Chap. 2, p. 55).

Latimer, the artist who has 'a poet's sensibility without his
voice', is the last of George Eliot's obviously male narrators –
and the only one to be named. The individual men who tell the
stories of the *Scenes* or *Adam Bede*, with their detailed histories
and special accents, give way in *The Mill on the Floss* to a voice
of indeterminate gender, an embodiment of compassionate
memory (although Eliot is still careful to use boyish examples

when appealing to 'our' common experience of childhood games, for example). *The Lifted Veil* is narrated by a man, but one who is 'half-feminine, half-ghostly'. All that makes him a seer is defined as feminine and specifically contrasted to 'masculine' science and law, which concentrate on theory at the expense of experience. *The Lifted Veil* suggests the conflict George Eliot may have found in concealing her own visions behind an impersonation of masculinity – for she had to admit openly now, at least to herself, as she wrote to her old friend D'Albert Durade, 'I have turned out to be an artist – not, as you are, with the pencil and the pallet – but with words' (*Letters*, Vol. III, p. 187).

CHAPTER EIGHT

THE MILL ON THE FLOSS: THE SEARCH FOR A KEY

So many stages of George Eliot's life seem to start and finish with a continental holiday. In July 1859 the Leweses left behind *Adam Bede*, the Liggins rumours and the black mood of *The Lifted Veil* for Switzerland, where Marian stayed in Lucerne while George visited his sons at school. But on their return to Wandsworth their new house, Holly Lodge, still seemed oppressive despite the walks on the Common with her beloved Pug, a gift from John Blackwood. The one ray of light was her friendship with Maria Congreve, daughter of the doctor who had looked after Robert Evans, who now lived nearby with her husband, the Comtist teacher Richard Congreve. Maria's attachment was passionate and long-lasting, typical of the devotion Marian could inspire in younger women, and it comforted her greatly in this dark time.[1]

Gradually, however, she began to feel less cut off and to enjoy being known (at least by close friends and by writers she admired, like Mrs Gaskell) as the author of *Adam Bede*. And when Herbert Spencer at last read her novel, and confessed himself completely overwhelmed by it, that old friendship was resumed. But throughout 1859 her new novel (now called 'The Tullivers') was still in the forefront of the Leweses' minds, even on holiday. In September they visited Radipole, near

Weymouth, where they were shown round a mill, 'the very thing for Polly, who has a mill in her new novel and wanted some details', wrote Lewes; at Dorchester they decided the River Frome was 'too insignificant' for the Floss; at Gainsborough they took a boat on the Trent to the point where it joined the Idle – the perfect meeting of the streams. Over the following winter the book was written and sent off in stages to John Blackwood in Edinburgh. His instant and enthusiastic responses show how deeply he cherished his author and how, carefully tutored by Lewes, he took pains always to encourage and never to criticise. The intimate triangular professional relationship between George and Marian and Blackwood, which had grown up over the *Scenes* and *Adam Bede* was to endure, with a short break over *Romola*, for the next nineteen years.

Blackwood found the novel excellent: 'you are irresistible,' he told Marian. He praised the humour, the pathos, the art, the naturalness, and reported the approval of his brother and his family as they read the sheets coming off the press. But it may be, as this letter suggests, that he did this partly as a tactful way of keeping her alert to the sensibilities of Mudie's female subscribers and the book-purchasing public:

The Major and the rest of the family here who are reading the sheets are enchanted. I am particularly glad to see the way the ladies are taking to Maggie.

No passage in these sheets occurs to me for comment except the description of Mrs Moss as a 'Patient etc. woman'. It is excessively good, but as some might take exception to it, I think I would alter it.

(*Letters*, Vol. III, p. 259)

Gordon Haight, in his notes, tells us that she did alter it, changing the description from 'a patient, loosely-hung, child-producing woman' to 'a patient, prolific, loving-hearted woman'. But she did not take all his advice, and left Mrs Pullet's mouth-rolling account of the dropsy (which Blackwood found rather strong) exactly as it was.

By February 1860, Marian was nearing the end, and Lewes rather gleefully reported her progress to her publisher:

Mrs Lewes is getting her eyes redder and *swollener* every morning as she lives through her tragic story. But there is such a strain of poetry to relieve the tragedy that the more she cries, and the readers cry, the better say I. She is anxious to hear your opinion of the part you have got: although I know you don't like disagreeable and uncomfortable situations.

(*Letters*, Vol. III, p. 260)

Marian was rushing on, partly for the down-to-earth reason that she and George wanted an Easter holiday and planned to be in Rome for Holy Week. Italy was their favourite country, George told Barbara Bodichon, but they had another reason for a swift departure:

As soon as the final 'proof' is corrected we shall fly, not waiting even to see the 'Mill' in its 3 volumes – much less to hear the chorus, pleasant or harsh, which will salute it. This is a comfort. Indeed except to hear of the actual solid fact of sale we would rather be deaf on the side of the Mill; and the next best thing to being deaf is to get out of ear shot.

(*Letters*, Vol. III, p. 270)

On 21 March Marian completed and despatched the last eleven pages of her manuscript. But, as she wrote to Blackwood, whose encouraging letter had helped her through the final pages, 'They were written in a furor, but I daresay there is not a word different from what it would have been if I had written them at the slowest pace'. After 'lying awake in the night and living through the scene again' she had only three slight corrections to make to the account of Maggie's final travail on the flood.

The cry of Latimer in *The Lifted Veil* that no one can understand the pain of 'the double consciousness within me, flowing on like two parallel streams' could have been uttered by Maggie Tulliver – whose waking dreams, in which she makes the world 'afresh in her thoughts' so rarely coincide with what actually happens. Nor does her open-ended, metaphorical, 'feminine' way of looking at life coincide with the practical severity of literal minds, especially that of her beloved brother Tom.

George Eliot makes us feel this conflict through the clash of styles in the novel itself. Although some childhood incidents are treated with comic irony (for example the death of the rabbits or Maggie's omission to share the jam puff), the inner life of brother and sister is conveyed with a poetic intensity and wealth of symbolic reference in marked contrast to the satirical realism used to describe the world they live in, the world of Mr Pullet with his lozenges and musical box, the St Oggs' ladies' bazaar and Mr Deane behind his mahogany desk at the bank. Around the sister and brother she creates a complex world endlessly suggestive of other lives and hidden histories which, if one were to look carefully, would also have their tragedies: Mr Riley's bankruptcy, Mr Wakem's purchase of the mill for his no-good illegitimate son, Mr Stelling's doomed ambitions.

The emotional involvement often seems to over-ride Eliot's declared intention to work as a natural scientist, studying Maggie and Tom as representative of the way provincial narrow-ness 'has acted on young natures' who aspire to a life beyond that of the generation before them. But perhaps it is because we follow their lives so closely and because so much is left un-resolved by its violent conclusion that *The Mill on the Floss* has drawn such an emotional response from generations of readers. From its first publication a series of male critics have longed to possess Maggie and re-write her destiny – Swinburne, Leslie Stephens, F.R. Leavis – and an equal number of women have read into her story their own early rebellions and frustrations. Simone de Beauvoir, describing her reaction at the age of fifteen, expresses feelings shared by many:

About this time I read a novel which seemed to translate my spiritual exile into words . . . Maggie Tulliver, like myself, was torn between others and herself; I recognised myself in her. She too was dark, loved nature, and books and life, was too headstrong to be able to observe the conventions of her respectable surroundings and yet was very sensitive to the criticism of a brother she adored . . . I felt my heart blaze with sympathy for her. I wept over her sorry fate for hours. The others condemned her because she was superior to them; I resembled her, and henceforward I saw my isolation not as a proof of infamy but as a sign of my uniqueness . . . Through the heroine I identified myself with the author; one day other adolescents would bathe with their tears a novel in which I would tell my own sad story.[2]

Most of us, like de Beauvoir, leap from heroine to author. Indeed Eliot was, as she told Barbara Bodichon, mining 'the remotest areas' of her past. The autobiographical element undoubtedly heightens the sense of pain because the exercise forced her to admit that her closeness to her own brother and to her father was not only irrevocably past but that even during childhood, life had not consisted solely in wandering hand-in-hand through fields of daisies. Still 'mining', she writes of Maggie's development in words suggestive of geological strata and hidden fossils, remarking how 'every one of those keen moments has left its trace' and appealing to her readers: 'surely if we could recall that early bitterness, and the dim guesses, the strangely perspectiveless conception of life that gave the bitterness its intensity, we should not pooh-pooh the griefs of our children' (Book I, Chap. 7, p. 123). As Maggie grows from girlhood to adolescence she shows how the nature of this bitterness changes. Immediate pain is replaced by a dull misery, summed up in a scene which recurs frequently in Eliot's fiction, that of a young woman watching by the bed of a sick older man, at once deeply involved and totally estranged:

Maggie in her brown frock with her eyes reddened and her heavy hair pushed back, looking from the bed where her father lay, to the dull walls of this sad chamber which was the centre of her world, was a creature full of eager, passionate longings for all that was beautiful and glad: thirsty for all knowledge: with an ear straining after dreamy music that died away and would not come near to her: with a blind, unconscious yearning for something that would link together the wonderful impressions of this mysterious life and give her soul a sense of home in it.

No wonder, when there is this contrast between the outward and the inward, that painful collisions come of it. A girl of no startling appearance, and one who will never be a Sappho or a Madame Roland or anything else that the world takes wide note of, may still hold forces

within her as the living plant seed does, which will make a way for
themselves, often in a shattering, violent manner.

(*Mill*, Book III, Chap. 5, p. 320)

But of course, despite the personal elements, this is not George
Eliot's 'own sad story', for (as in *Jane Eyre* and *David Copper-
field*) the autobiography is confined to childhood. Maggie, unlike
Mary Ann Evans or Simone de Beauvoir, never grows up to
write a novel, despite her early gift for story-telling. Within the
confines of the narrow provincial world which her creator
escaped, she lives out her drama almost completely internally –
in religious yearning, in longing for beauty, in the desire for
love. When she tries to put her longings into words she be-
wilders or alienates people, while any expression in action –
from cutting her hair to drifting down river with the man she
loves – inevitably ends in disaster and in the fierce disapproval
of 'the world and the world's wife'.

Like Latimer, Maggie is an artist without a voice. But she is
an artist nonetheless, with a responsive imagination. No other
book I know conveys with such physical force the feeling of a
mind reflecting on itself, pounding against the temples in excitement or vibrating 'through every sensitive fibre' in utter despair.
We are, however, not confined by Maggie's viewpoint as we are
by Latimer's: the narration moves in and out of a range of
minds so that we can place her attitude within a spectrum
of approaches, and follow her search for a guide to life.

The position which most radically opposes hers turns out to
be that of the person she cares for most – her brother Tom.
Although their polarity is often described in terms of masculine
and feminine opposition it is more fundamentally that of the
literal and metaphorical ways of looking at life. Any crude
division by gender is immediately confused by the alliances
within the family between Maggie and her father on one hand,
and Tom and his mother on the other. Maggie and Mr Tulliver
both see life as a riddle which has to be interpreted, 'a tangled
skein', a 'thirsty, trackless uncertain journey'.

Part of their difficulty comes from the jarring difference

between the way they want the world to be and the way it actually is. This is why language, which offers a terrible puzzle to Mr Tulliver, is so central to the novel, for it soon appears that it is impossible to describe anything 'accurately', one can only translate it into different terms drawn from different kinds of experience. Both father and daughter escape into a dream world where things *are* simple. When they confuse this with the real world and slip from fantasy into actual enactment of their desires the consequences are disastrous – whether it be Mr Tulliver's attack on Wakem or Maggie's drifting away with Stephen Guest. Their rich imaginations help to cause their downfall.

Maggie's imagination is more creative than her father's and as a child she revels in the multitude of possible worlds it opens up to her. She sees stories everywhere, even in the cockroaches in the yard, and delights in the curious adventures in her books – which so often forecast her own fate (like the witch who either floats and is guilty or drowns and is innocent). But as soon as she tries to make these stories part of her life – for example, by running away to a glorious life with the gypsies – she finds that reality is totally intractable and we realise that her small mind is merely 'the oddest mixture of clear-eyed acumen and blind dreams' (Book I, Chap. 1, p. 167). Both she and her father suffer from a fatal inability to foresee the consequences of their actions, because they can hardly bear to admit that the laws operating in the real world may be at odds with the lives suggested in their imagination. Thus Maggie is sorely bothered by the way Luke, the mill-hand, shakes his head over 'the Prodigal Son in the costume of Sir Charles Grandison' with whom, because of her neglect of Tom's rabbits, she rather identifies:

'I'm very glad his father took him back again aren't you, Luke?' she said. 'For he was very sorry, you know, and wouldn't do wrong again.'

'Eh, Miss,' said Luke, 'he'd be no great shakes, I doubt, let's feyther do what he would for him.'

That was a painful thought to Maggie, and she wished much that the subsequent history of the young man had not been left a blank.

(*Mill*, Book I, Chap. 5, p. 83)

With this Maggie reveals the same flinching from the logic of consequences or the demands of 'plot' as in her inability to continue Scott's *The Pirate*, where the dark beauty Minna is unable to resist the advances of an unreliable lover: 'I went on with it in my own head, and I made several endings; but they were all unhappy. I could never make a happy ending out of that beginning' (Book V, Chap. 1, p. 401). Nor will she finish *Corinne* – for the heroine's achievement as an artist seems nothing to her in the face of her possible unhappiness in love. Ominously, Philip Wakem, who has lent her the books, suggests that she avenge the dark-haired heroines in them by carrying away all the love from her own blonde cousin Lucy.[3] Maggie's anger and dismay at the stereotype is right, just as her frustration at her own constricted life is entirely justified. But Eliot still suggests that it is as dangerous to step over the borders of literature as it is across the threshold of dream. You cannot re-write life as you can create endings for books, but this is what Maggie always wants to do – in direct contrast to Tom:

But if Tom had told his strongest feeling at that moment, he would have said, 'I'd do just the same again.' That was his usual mode of viewing his past actions; whereas Maggie was always wishing she had done something different.

(*Mill*, Book I, Chap. 6, p. 107)

Life is vastly different (although no less painful at times) for those like Tom who see life as a single line, not as a mass of possible options, and to whom correct behaviour is a straightforward matter of following rules. But in Eliot's fiction nothing is ever crudely schematic. Even the most literal-minded characters do at times fall victim to the gap between dreams and reality which besets Maggie and her father. Thus Tom's game with the sword ends in a cut foot, and Mrs Tulliver's approach to Wakem has a result entirely the opposite to what she expected. Their disasters, though, are due to too *little* imagination rather than too much, and they fail as 'fly-fishers fail in preparing their bait so as to make it alluring in the right quarter for want of a due acquaintance with the subjectivity of fishes' (Book III, Chap. 7, p. 341).

In the relationship between Tom and his mother (like that between Lisbet Bede and Adam, or Mrs Holt and Felix), the mother's querulous weakness calls out the son's impatient tenderness. And the rather stupid literalness of the women, which is demonstrated by Mrs Tulliver in the conversation about waggoners and moles which so baffles and frustrates her husband, is transformed into apparent strength in their sons.

Unlike his sister, Tom is rarely worried by the discrepancy between the possible and the real: for him, what he sees, exists. The boy 'with a deficient power of apprehending signs and abstractions' grows into the youth who confronts Philip and Maggie with the declaration, 'I'm not to be imposed on by fine words: I can see what actions mean.' His world, like Adam Bede's, is reducible to measurement and concrete example but it has no place for abstractions, nice arguments or imaginative flexibility. When the value of this kind of knowledge is denied, as it is by Mr Stelling's régime of Euclid and Latin grammar, Tom becomes confused and disoriented. No metaphors come to him to express his misery – he is merely 'in a state of blank unimaginativeness concerning the cause and tendency of his sufferings, as if he had been an innocent shrewmouse imprisoned in the split trunk of an oak tree in order to cure lameness in cattle'. This of course is the narrator's image, not Tom's, and is as much of a comment on Mr Tulliver's sacrifice of his son's natural ability in order to cast out 'Old Harry and the lawyers' as it is on Tom's state of mind.[4]

The very self-conscious use of such imagery throughout the chapter on Tom's schooling also draws our attention to the texture of the book itself, for the medium of the novel is necessarily more in line with the cast of Maggie's mind than of Tom's. Eliot later protested in distress to John Blackwood about a critic who accused her of a disdain for Tom:

As if it were not *my* respect for Tom which infused itself into my reader – as if he could have respected Tom, if I had not painted him with respect; the exhibition of the *right* on both sides being the very soul of my intention in the story.

(*Letters*, Vol. III, p. 397)

But there is no doubt that the fact that his way of thinking is at odds with the style of the book affects the way we judge Tom. *The Mill* is permeated with metaphor – hardly a line passes which does not contain an analogy or a simile or an extension of the character's experience into a different imaginative or intellectual framework. Even the chapter headings offer the reader different models for viewing the world, referring us ironically to theology and social history ('A Variety of Protestantism'), to science ('The Laws of Attraction'), to romance ('The Spell is Broken'), to Bunyanesque parable ('The Valley of Humiliation') and even to comic fable ('How a Hen Takes to Stratagem'). The wider network of allusions to geology, natural history, music, Greek tragedy, the eighteenth-century novel, the poetry of Wordsworth or of Goethe offer a wealth of alternative visions and remind us at the same time of the limited view of the world of St Oggs.

Maggie does have some sense of a variety of viewpoints, but Tom clings to his habitual modes of judgement. Interestingly, when he is confused by his confrontation with a different set of values, Eliot describes him as becoming vulnerable, caring and feminine. For a few brief weeks, says Eliot, the suffering which follows his awareness that there are other ways of seeing makes him 'more like a girl'. But he refuses to learn from his experience, subduing this 'weakness' beneath a sense of his superiority to his sister and his co-pupil Philip. Tom can enjoy stories as much as Maggie, but these are limited to martial tales of determined characters like Robert the Bruce which celebrate the virtues of the world of action. Frightened by what he cannot understand beyond those boundaries, and made uncomfortable by the surfacing of a feminine side to his nature, he crushes habit into rigid rules.

The differences between brother and sister are intensified by the separate spheres of female and male experience. Denied involvement in the world of action – that of business and commerce – Maggie becomes introverted and reflective. She has to fight the shadowy armies within her own soul, while Tom is thrown into the public fray,

> grappling with more substantial obstacles, and gaining more definite conquests. So it has been since the days of Hecuba, and of Hector, Tamer of horses: inside the gates, the women with streaming hair and uplifted hands offering prayers, watching the world's combat from afar, filling their long, empty days with memories and fears: outside, the men in fierce struggle with things divine and human, quenching memory in the stronger light of purpose, losing the sense of dread and even of wounds in the hurrying ardour of action.
>
> (*Mill*, Book V, Chap. 2, p. 405)

Unless there is a marked change in the outward circumstances of men and women's lives, they will never speak the same language.

Outward circumstances, the way they affect women's education and their relation to the culture of a (patriarchal) past are central themes in *The Mill on the Floss*, *Romola*, *Felix Holt* and *Middlemarch*. George Eliot is not so concerned with formal education, about which we learn little, but the ad hoc way in which her exceptional heroines learn both from books and people. Maggie's first books are either part of the cultural past of the artisan class (the Bible and Bunyan), or they arrive (and depart) in a way which reflects the uncertainties of her changing world. Defoe's *History of the Devil*, for example, is bought by her unsuspecting father at a sale: 'They've all got the same covers, and I thought they were all one sample, as you may say. But it seems one mustn't judge by its outside. This is a puzzlin' world.' It disappears again, with the beloved Bunyan, in the sale of their own property which follows her father's bankruptcy. Maggie continues her haphazard browsing in the books that come her way, gleaning ideas from the examples in Tom's school-books and from the novels Philip lends her, because she is excluded from that rigorous 'masculine knowledge' of traditional education. Later her precious Thomas à Kempis arrives, equally unexpectedly, its key passages already marked by another hand, found tucked in amongst the pile of *Keepsakes* which Bob Jakin brings her (after he picks them up in yet *another* sale) in a clumsy attempt to assuage her pain at the loss of the Bunyan and the other family books. Her reading, and especially her manner of reading, offer crucial keys to her predicament.

But Maggie is also taught by daily life, where different educational models are set out in a series of schematic oppositions. She and Tom encounter contrasting groups of people who embody in their actions and judgement not only consciously adopted values and unconscious class prejudices but also whole bodies of knowledge – practical and theoretical – which govern their attitude to life. In *Adam Bede*, characters draw their language and standards of judgement directly from their occupations – farming, cheese-making, carpentry. In *The Mill* these work-linked ways of looking at life are traced with greater intricacy and are securely tied to a slowly evolving, interlocking history. Environment and custom are powerful teachers which, as Eliot was to point out still more clearly in *Silas Marner*, can either channel or obstruct individual development.

The shifting perspective of the novel, and the emphasis on the importance of the milieu she lives in, have the effect of making Maggie's mind like a star in a galaxy at which a telescope is pointed and then withdrawn. She is one individual among many, picked out by the trance-like memory of the narrator who travels back in time, focusing on her inner thoughts and setting her story within the encircling elemental image of the flood (which is at once general and universal, and yet specific to St Oggs), the rushing current which impetuously embraces the incoming tide at the start, and the receding waters of the conclusion.

These restless currents, which we identify with Maggie, seem sometimes to be the pressure of history from without and at others the pressure of desire and imaginative yearnings within. They represent driving forces in the book and, it is suggested, in human nature. But equally strong are the defences which people construct to keep these currents in check, elaborate mental and moral edifices which in their later stages come to seem like 'natural' growths. This is true of the town of St Oggs itself, carrying its history like rings in 'a millennial tree'. Images of building keep pace in the novel with images of flood and the alternation between the two is part of the historical cycle, and part of the reason for our passionate attachment to place, as Mr Tulliver learns in his childhood, when

he had sat listening on a low stool on winter evenings while his father talked of the old half-timbered mill that had been there before the last great floods, which damaged it so that his grandfather pulled it down and built the new one.

(*Mill*, Book III, Chap. 9, p. 352)

A town like St Oggs which 'inherited a long past without thinking of it and had no eyes for the spirits that walked the streets' (Book I, Chap. 12, p. 184), is not so different, Eliot later suggests, from the desolate villages of the Rhône valley which evoke for the passing traveller the lives of unnamed generations: 'part of a gross sum of obscure vitality, that will be swept into the same oblivion with the generations of ants and beavers' (Book IV, Chap. 1, p. 361). These constructed environments have their exact counterparts in the elaborate mental structures which also come to seem natural and which are 'inhabited', to use Eliot's own phrase, by different groups and individuals. One such is the classical education imposed on successive generations of 'gentlemen' by Mr Stelling and his like, which comes to seem unnatural only when its context is inappropriate – like the dams erected instinctively by 'Mr Broderip's beaver', regardless of circumstances. It is made quite clear that this is traditionally the natural habitat of men (unsuitable to the quick and shallow intelligence of girls) and of a particular class of men (Tom is out of his depth socially as well as intellectually). Studying the classics is not absurd in itself, and Greek tragedy will always thrill imaginative students like Philip and Maggie, just as the grammatical rules will satisfy those with 'a taste for abstractions'. But to the new bourgeois merchants like Mr Deane, or even Tom himself with his practical, commercial bent, it appears almost incomprehensible, an elitist anachronism – a survival from another era.

Equally anachronistic, rule-bound and bizarre is the intricate code of Dodson family loyalty, and Mr Deane – one of the new men – clearly approves of the way his wife is gradually detaching herself from her family as the Deane fortunes improve. It is a code whose priestesses are women – in accordance with Eliot's statement in her essay on Riehl that women are the more conservative and custom-bound sex – and it is designed to ensure the preservation of the species. The comic emphasis on the proper form of wills and the correct behaviour at funerals – two principal dogmas – may seem to give it an air of death (like the rules of a 'dead language'), but in fact they are means of ensuring continuation of the creed into an unknown future.

In contrast to the abstraction of the classical culture, the Dodson system is entirely materialistic. None of its adherents could formulate the rules they live by in words, but Mrs Tulliver instantly recognises Tom's Dodson affinity by 'his features and complexion, in liking salt and in eating beans, which a Tulliver never did'. Dress, manner and possessions are of crucial importance and are kept and brought out on special occasions like the china and linen which are Mrs Tulliver's 'household gods'. Gods have to have mystery, however absurd their form and so Mrs Glegg's fuzzy front or Mrs Pullet's medicines all have to be priced, valued and above all locked away. Just as the aristocratic lore of Latin grammar needed a linguistic 'key' (which Maggie quickly found), so this bourgeois materialism needs material keys (which Tom quickly acquires). Keys – literal and metaphorical – jangle through the book, and a fear that they may be confused after her death provides Mrs Pullet with the gloomiest of all prospects for a Dodson, the threat of a posthumous loss of respectability:

'If I should die to-morrow, Mr Pullet, you'll bear it in mind – though you'll be blundering with the keys, and never remember as that on the third shelf o' the left hand wardrobe, behind the night-caps with the broad ties – not the narrow frilled uns – is the key o' the drawer in the Blue Room, where the key o' the Blue Closet is. You'll make a mistake and I shall niver be worthy to know it. You've a memory for my pills and draughts, wonderful – I'll allays say that of you – but you're lost among the keys.'

(*Mill*, Book VI, Chap. 12, p. 577)

It can be no coincidence that on the same page the simple sympathetic Lucy feels that 'her nature supplied her with no key to Tom's'.[5] Lucy, like other naturally responsive characters in the book – Aunt Gritty or Bob Jakin – judges people individually and not by rules of class or form. But Dodson-type people are locked into artificial, inflexible structures and feed upon prejudices because they 'can get no sustenance out of that complex, fragmentary, doubt-provoking knowledge which we call truth'.

Dodson materialism and classical idealism are equally prone to reduce knowledge and morals to a set of formulae. *The Mill on the Floss*, like *Silas Marner*, is a plea for a more flexible system of ethical judgement. One should need vision, not 'keys', as Dr Kenn reflects when he thinks of Maggie's plight:

The great problem of the shifting relation between passion and duty is clear to no man who is capable of apprehending it: the question, whether the moment has come in which a man has fallen below the possibility of a renunciation that will carry any efficacy, and must accept the sway of a passion against which he had struggled as a trespass, is one for which we have no master key that will fit all cases. The casuists have become a by-word of reproach; but their perverted spirit of minute discrimination was the shadow of a truth to which eyes and hearts are too often fatally sealed: the truth that moral judgements must remain false and hollow, unless they are checked and enlightened by a perpetual reference to the special circumstances that mark the individual lot.

All people of broad, strong sense have an instinctive repugnance to the men of maxims.

(*Mill*, Book VII, Chap. 2, pp. 627–8)

In the chapter 'A Voice from the Past', trying to seek solace from Tom's old books, Maggie takes one of these 'Men of Maxims', Aldrich's *Logic*, down by the river 'where the water-fowl rustled out on her anxious, awkward flight – with a startled sense that the relation between Aldrich and this living world was extremely remote for her' (Book IV, Chap. 3, p. 380).

The cultural tradition which does, at first, seem to embody the living world is that of imaginative literature and art. In the course of the book Maggie progresses from the old English inheritance of the artisan classes – *Pilgrim's Progress* (whose imagery informs the story, for she is Christiana without a Greatheart), Defoe and Jeremy Taylor – to the Romantic literature of the near past – Scott and Byron and George Sand – until she is checked by reading the renunciatory quietist philosophy of Thomas à Kempis.

It is at this point that we realise that Eliot's distrust of Maggie's new reading is not solely because it feeds her dream-worlds at the expense of her contact with others. It is because it too represents a specific kind of historical accretion, just like Stelling's classics and the Dodson funerals. It is a product of a wealthy leisured society which has no room for 'emphatic faith', and whose charm disguises the fact that it depends for its existence on the exploitation of the invisible mass:

condensed in unfragrant deafening factories, cramping itself in mines, sweating at furnaces, grinding, hammering, weaving under more or less oppression of carbolic acid – or else, spread over sheepwalks, and scattered in lonely houses and huts on the clayey or chalky corn-lands, where the rainy days look dreary. This wide national life is based entirely on emphasis – the emphasis of want.

(*Mill*, Book IV, Chap. 3, p. 385)

Philip, Maggie and Lucy (like George Eliot herself) are part of the first generation of tradespeople and artisans to have access to this culture. Stephen Guest belongs unequivocally to the world of 'claret and velvet carpets'. This is why Eliot mocks him and distrusts him. While never underestimating his attraction (nor his suitability) for Maggie, Eliot confronts the fact that in accepting him and the life he offers, Maggie would cut herself off from her roots and from the 'wider national life' of the common people.

In many ways the new generation have been set adrift: Stephen is out of place on the wharf, Philip uncomfortable in the lawyer's office – what will their future be? Unless they become artists like Philip they are in danger of becoming dilettantes or even art objects, like Arthur Donnithorne admiring himself in his mirror. The attraction of culture might be so strong that it could replace the duties of real life altogether: ' "Poetry and art and knowledge are sacred and pure," insists Philip, ' "But not for me – not for me," said Maggie, walking more hurriedly, "Because I should want too much" ' (Book V, Chap. 1, p. 402).

In a way this is what happens: she is seduced by culture. Philip describes his love for Maggie in terms of a painter's inspiration, while her own gradual drift into Stephen's arms is a cultural as well as sexual passage which takes place to the music of Purcell, Bellini's *Sonnambula* and Arne's songs for *The Tempest*. The language of music allows them to evade responsibility:

One other thing Stephen seemed now and then to care for, and that was, to sing: it was a way of speaking to Maggie – perhaps he was not distinctly conscious that he was impelled to it by a secret longing, running counter to all his self-confessed resolves, to deepen the hold he had on her. Watch your own speech and notice how it is guided by your less conscious purposes, and you will understand that contradiction in Stephen.

(*Mill*, Book VI, Chap. 3, p. 583)

When he kisses Maggie's arm we see her flesh as antique sculpture 'which moves us still as it clasps lovingly the time-worn marble of a headless trunk', and this scene of agonised desire takes place in a conservatory, a supreme Victorian expression of nature turned into art:

'How strange and unreal the trees and flowers look with the lights among them,' said Maggie, in a low voice. 'They look as if they belonged to an enchanted land and would never fade away:– I could fancy they were all made of jewels.'

(Mill, Book VI, Chap. 10, p. 560)

Despite its intense eroticism, the scene is sinister, cut off as firmly as the barren rule-bound systems from the living world.

Maggie finds no model here or elsewhere to show her how to live. Her primary experience is of lonely struggle. This is why she longs so to be passive, and for a moment on the boat with Stephen she allows herself to believe that she is:

Maggie listened – passing from her startled wonderment to the yearning after that belief that the tide was doing it all – that she might glide along with the swift, silent stream and not struggle any more. But across that stealing influence came the terrible shadow of past thoughts; and the sudden horror lest now at last the moment of fatal intoxication was close upon her, called up a feeling of angry resistance towards Stephen.

'Let me go!' she said, in an agitated tone, flashing an indignant look at him and trying to get her hands free. 'You have wanted to deprive me of any choice.'

(Mill, Book VI, Chap. 13, p. 591)

In reality it is she who has decided she cannot bear to go on choosing. In *The Mill*, as in *The Lifted Veil*, Eliot suggests that the impulse to dream and to live in the imagination is closely related to the need for love, 'the strongest need in poor Maggie's nature' (Book I, Chap. 5, p. 89). Both are expressions of a desire, not for knowledge, but for complete identification with another person or a different world: the different experiences offered by Tom's outdoor adventures, Philip's culture, Stephen's sensuality. The greater the polarity of worlds, the greater the desire. Maggie's craving for love carries her, just as her imagination does, always away from the role her society expects her to play. Although her loves are 'true' and authentic expressions of her needs and her response to the mystery of others, in society's terms they remain hopelessly, insolubly wrong. For Maggie is never *free* to choose – she is caught in the structures into which she was born. As the narrator repeats, those are *living* structures, social bonds made up of chains of people, linked by complex ties. This is what Maggie's father finds when he cannot bear to solve his debt by ruining his sister Mrs Moss, and it is the theme of the impassioned conversation between Stephen and Maggie which takes place, significantly, in the lanes near the Moss farmhouse. When Stephen insists that their pledges to Lucy and Philip are 'unnatural' and must be broken, Maggie pleads that 'Love is natural – but surely pity and faithfulness and memory are natural too' (Book VII, Chap. 3, p. 571).

As different groups of people appeal to 'nature' as a justification, the very term becomes riddled with uncertainty. And just as nature is contradictory, unpredictable and full of dissonances, so within the individual spirit, desire and social duty can exist in cycles of perpetual conflict, like the cycles of floods and building, or the warring armies and ever-rising enemies who populate Maggie's mind.

Instead of a Hetty balanced by a disciplined and self-sacrificing Dinah, *The Mill on the Floss* has a single heroine, a single divided soul. It is hard to see her suffering in terms of the fruitful sacrifices of the earlier books, although her rejected lover Philip grows in vision as Adam does, and feels that 'this gift for transferred life which has come to me in loving you, may be a new power to me' (Book VII, Chap. 3, p. 634).

But Philip's gain almost pales into insignificance beside Maggie's dilemma. For despite her return to Thomas à Kempis Maggie never escapes her confusion or reaches any clear philosophical or moral certitude. Perhaps, as some critics have suggested, the dark heroines cried out too loud for vengeance, or Eliot's own unrecognised desire for her brother Isaac[6] created 'powerful authorial desires' which pushed the story beyond the limits of plot in much the same way as the river overflows its banks. Certainly Eliot wrote the last few chapters with intense emotion and in the violent conclusion both the law of consequences and the demands of the foregoing plot are swept away with passionate and unnerving violence.

It seems to me, however, that the ending, and indeed the entire fragmentary, dislocated form of the book which jumps from social comedy to romantic drama to overwhelming tragedy, is entirely appropriate to Eliot's understanding of her heroine. Maggie is a soul adrift, a chaotic personality, rich in imagination, weak in judgement, full of desire, yet inhibited by guilt and by loyalty. The book feels as though it were packed with action, but in fact the drama is all internal. Maggie achieves nothing, and even her drift down river with Stephen is the result of refraining from choice. She carries nothing through to a conclusion, not even her own desires, and yet one feels that with a different kind of courage and honesty she *could* have admitted her passion for Stephen, confronted Lucy's pain and outfaced St Oggs. George Eliot makes us see, however, that this was not possible because Maggie is doubly trapped, by her own nature and by her position in society at that particular moment in history. She is thwarted at every turn – not only in the craving for education which is out of her proper feminine sphere, but also in her search for romance and marriage, the routes through which women traditionally *should* achieve fulfilment.

The inner chaos of Maggie's mind, her sudden abandonment of responsibility in the face of passion and her hopeless attempts to regain equilibrium are mirrored in the incoherence of the book, with its wild sweeping away of probability and literary realism. At the end, even language fails. Maggie and Lucy meet and part in a flurry of broken statements and unanswered questions. Even in her final refusal of Stephen's desperate 'Come!', appealing to the memory of what it felt 'to be within reach of a look – to be within hearing of each other's voice', Maggie cannot rise above this welter of questions and unfinished phrases:

Surely there was something being taught her by this experience of great need; and she must be learning a secret of human tenderness and long suffering that the less erring could hardly know? 'O God, if my life is to be long, let me live to bless and comfort –'

(*Mill*, Book VII, Chap. 4, p. 649)

But here the flood water laps about her knees.

In the cataclysmic ending the confusion persists. Maggie goes to save Tom, but pulls him to his death. Before they perish it is he who attains vision and for whom the veil is lifted. The sudden perception of the strength of Maggie's love

> came with so overpowering a force – such an entirely new revelation to his spirit, of the depths in life, that had lain beyond his vision which he had fancied so keen and clear, that he was unable to ask a question.
>
> (*Mill*, Book VII, Chap. 5, p. 654)

Together they are hurtled back into childhood, Tom to the threshold of speech, Maggie to pure sensation:

> at last a mist gathered over the blue-grey eyes, and the lips found a word they could utter: the old childish – 'Magsie' – Maggie could make no answer but a long, deep sob of that mysterious wondrous happiness that is one with pain.
>
> (*Mill*, Book VII, Chap. 5, p. 655)

The material world and the complex structures which divided them are finally broken up as 'huge fragments, clinging together in fatal fellowship, made one wide mass across the stream'. They are killed by the chaos made by solid buildings uprooted in the flood. Their death is not an evasion or a defeat, or a unification of two halves of a divided personality. It is an affirmation that the two currents of consciousness which we all experience to a greater or lesser degree and which the imaginative artist experiences so intensely – the streams of inner reflection and outer perception – can only finally flow together at a deep level beyond the reach of language.

A moment of inarticulate communion, in which suffering and ecstasy, pleasure and pain meet, occurs again and again at the climaxes of Eliot's novels. Its effect is troubling and disturbing because it is always so physical and mystical at the same time, suggesting – like some idealist philosophies – that it is only in extreme situations that we truly experience selfhood. Sensation transcends all surrounding circumstances until there is nothing left but *me*, feeling. Yet it is the very opposite of 'I think, therefore I am', a definition of the self which separates one individual from another, for while thoughts are differentiated the intense mingling of emotional and physical sensation is the common experience of all humankind. The death of Maggie and Tom Tulliver is an epiphany, the extreme example of Eliot's long-held belief, which she could not yet see how to encompass in life:

Speculative truth begins to appear but a shadow of individual minds, agreement between intellects seems unattainable and we turn to the *truth of feeling* as the only universal bond of union.

(Letters I, p. 162)

CHAPTER NINE

SILAS MARNER:
SPRINGS OF RENEWAL

After correcting the rushed final proofs of *The Mill on the Floss* the Leweses set off in March 1860 to Italy, where the idea for *Romola* was conceived. After a leisurely holiday they came back to England via Switzerland, bringing back with them George's son Charles who soon, with Anthony Trollope's help, began a career in the Post Office. It was partly to make life more convenient for Charles that the Leweses left Richmond (which they had never liked), and moved into town at the end of September. They stayed for three months in Harewood Square, before taking a three year lease on 16 Blandford Square.

Once in the city they could not avoid being drawn more into London society. Barbara Bodichon was a summer neighbour at 5 Blandford Square, but spent the winters with her husband, the French doctor Eugène Bodichon, in Algiers. Trollope, Spencer and old acquaintances of *The Westminster Review* days like Clementia Taylor soon came to call. But it was here that Marian formulated the rule 'of *never* paying visits', as she told Clementia, a rule which not only saved her embarrassment but also effectively reinforced her self-banishment. She consciously felt herself to be in exile, not only from society but also from her past, driven from old ties and places both by her literary ambitions and her love for Lewes. At the end of their life together, in *Impressions of Theophrastus Such*, she painted a portrait which seems to reflect her own condition:

My system responds sensitively to the London weather-signs, political, social, literary . . . 'I belong to the Nation of London'. Why? There have been many voluntary exiles in the world, – and . . . probably . . . some of those who sallied forth went for the sake of a loved companionship, when they would willingly have kept sight of the familiar plains, and of the hills to which they had first lifted up their eyes.

(Impressions, p. 52)

Her journal for 28 November 1860 records her mixed feelings, despite her happy domestic life and growing prosperity:

Since I last wrote in this journal I have suffered much from physical weakness accompanied with mental depression. The loss of the country has seemed very bitter to me, and my want of health and strength has prevented me from working much – still worse, has made me despair of ever working well again. I am getting better now by the help of tonics, and I should be better still if I could gather more bravery, resignation and simplicity of striving. In the meantime my cup is full of blessings: my home is bright and warm with love and tenderness, and in more material vulgar matters we are very fortunate. I have invested £2,000 in East Indies Stock, and expect shortly to invest another £2,000, so that with my other money, we have enough in any case to keep us from beggary.

(Letters, Vol. III, p. 360)

Hard-earned money was to figure large in her next story. For her exile also ensured her privacy to write and for the past two months she had been hard at work – not on her planned historical novel *Romola*, but on a country tale which, in the same journal entry, she said had 'thrust itself between me and the other book'. In her city depressions she said, 'I felt a new creature as soon as I was in the country': now the return to a rural setting gave her, as well as her hero, a chance to be reborn. *Silas Marner* was completed by 10 March 1861, and published three weeks later.

In *Silas Marner* George Eliot again explores mysterious laws woven into the fabric of daily life; how intuition can grasp such laws when they seem to defy reason, and how love can intensify inner vision and integrate the isolated individual into a wider community. Consoling John Blackwood, who found the opening chapters 'sad, almost oppressive', she wrote that he would not find it sad in the end 'since it sets – or is intended to set – in a strong light the remedial influence of pure, natural human relations. The Nemesis is a very mild one.' She explained that she had begun by feeling that the most appropriate form for Silas's inner drama would be metrical, but eventually chose prose because in poetry 'there could not be an equal play of humour' (*Letters*, Vol. III, p. 382). The end result is both poetic and prosaic, for the precise structure and rich imagery mesh perfectly with a sharp-eyed ironic presentation of class, of historical circumstances, social traditions and quirks of individual character. The reader is led effortlessly from realistic incident and speech to symbolic meaning and moral teaching.

The words 'mysterious', 'vague' and 'dreamy' reverberate through *Silas Marner* and Eliot always wrote of its composition as having an almost involuntary origin: 'a sudden inspiration that came across me in the midst of altogether different meditations' (*Letters*, Vol. III, p. 392), 'a story of old-fashioned village life which has unfolded itself from the very millet-seed of thought' (*Letters*, Vol. III, p. 371). But even as she wrote she knew that industrial problems were creeping across that old-fashioned Warwickshire countryside. Letters from the Brays brought news of the decline in the ribbon trade and the unemployment of many weavers, which filled her with distress. The industrial crisis was very different to that in the period of her novel – which stretches from about 1795 to 1820, when the rise of the factory system was sweeping away the small groups of urban artisans. But the sense of insecurity is the same – the workers in *Silas Marner* streaming out of their factory next to the prison yard in a foul-smelling city are still cut off from 'natural human relations'.[1]

The novel is, however, far from a nostalgic hymn to the lost innocence and organic bonds of a vanishing rural society. In many ways it deliberately emphasises the bad aspect of recent history for both town and country; when corn prices were kept high by the Napoleonic wars so that town paupers starved; when a breakfasting squire could toss his deer-hound enough bits of beef to make 'a poor man's holiday dinner'; when an abandoned mother could turn to opium and bring up her child in squalor in one of the prosperous market towns of 'merry England' without anyone coming to her aid, and could die in a ditch without raising more than a passing comment. Molly Farran vanishes 'from the eyes of men', an almost invisible victim of their economic and sexual power. Her death is the pivot of the book's values, just as it is the centre of the story of individual moral choice for Silas and Godfrey Cass.

In an interesting way *Silas Marner* re-writes the central crisis of *Adam Bede*. Molly and Hetty are both seduced by dreams of marriage to men of substance and status, but Molly's final bitterness is material rather than emotional: '*He* was well off; if she had her rights she would be well off too.' Although Godfrey marries Molly, it makes no difference: she is still reduced to misery and like Hetty, wanders across the countryside in a vain search for the father of her child, in a state of wilful self-annihilation. Her fate is a mirror-image of Hetty's: the illegitimate baby dead in the hole beneath the bush and the mother who survives in misery are replaced by Molly, dying below the overhanging furze, and Eppie crawling through the snow to a life of love. In each case the mother's suffering allows the hero to achieve a new emotional life – Adam through sharing Hetty's suffering, and Silas through accepting Molly's child. But the final message is more positive than that of either *Adam Bede* or *The Mill on the Floss*. As her epigraph from Wordsworth insists, the survival of the child is a 'gift' from Mother Earth to 'declining man' at the year's turn. It brings hope for the future.

So Molly's snow-covered sleep is a necessary sacrifice which allows Silas to awake from his own emotional hibernation:

the unwept death which, to the general lot, seemed as trivial as the summer-shed leaf, was charged with the force of destiny to certain

human lives that we know of, shaping their joys and sorrows even to
the end.

(Silas Marner, Chap. 14, p. 178)

The leaf is part of a rhythmic cycle, an untaught harmony which
George Eliot invokes in the sequence of the seasons, in the work
of the countryside whose flowing rhythms of flailing or winnow-
ing contrast with the harshness of Silas's loom and 'the mockery
of its alternating noises', and in the folk songs, fiddling and
carols of the untaught local musicians. The structure of the book
resembles a country dance, with its meetings, partings and
exchanges. A musical patterning enters the prose itself at solemn
moments. We hear it in Godfrey's bitter acceptance, 'I wanted
to pass for childless once, Nancy – I shall pass for childless now
against my will', and in Dolly's evocation of the mystery of life
when she affirms Silas's crucial decision:

'Ah,' said Dolly, with soothing gravity, 'it's like the night and the
morning, and the sleeping and the waking, and the rain and the harvest
– one goes and the other comes, and we know nothing how nor where.'

(Silas Marner, Chap. 14, p. 179)

To Silas the unwept death is a 'blessing' which is sent to him,
just as the theft of his money is a 'blessing' in disguise. It forces
him into a new way of living which is not only the opposite of his
reclusive years in Raveloe but also the opposite of the way he
had been taught to live. Describing Silas's upbringing in the
narrow sect based at Lantern Yard, and the role it played as the
'fostering home of his religious emotions' Eliot writes:

A weaver who finds hard words in his hymn-book knows nothing of
abstractions; as the little child knows nothing of parental love, but only
knows one face and one lap towards which it stretches its arms for
refuge and nurture.

(Silas Marner, Chap. 2, p. 63)

The analogy is based on contrast – Silas's real spiritual growth
comes not from the 'hard words' of his 'brethren' and the

'unquestioned doctrine' of the minister but from his own response to a child's demand for 'refuge and nurture'. The harsh justice of Lantern Yard involves the same sort of rigorous, unbending standards that are associated with Adam's initial attitude to his father, with Tom Tulliver's attitude to Maggie and with the rigid Judaism of the law in *The Lifted Veil*. In offering a foster home to Eppie, Silas replaces these with self-sacrificing tolerance:

So Eppie was reared without punishment, the burden of her misdeeds being borne vicariously by father Silas. The stone hut was made a soft nest for her, lined with downy patience.

(Silas Marner, Chap. 14, p. 189)

This is the kind of softness that we associate with the stereotype of maternal love, as with Milly Barton, and its nature is made clearer and stripped of conventional sentiment because it is attached to a man. As Dolly Winthrop says with her down-to-earth, pursed-lip gravity, we have to forget stereotypes:

'I've seen men as are wonderful handy wi' children. The men are awkward and contrairy mostly, God help 'em, but when the drink's out of 'em, they aren't unsensible, though they're bad for leeching and bandaging – so fiery and unpatient. You see this goes first, next the skin,' proceeded Dolly, taking up the little shirt, and putting it on.

'Yes,' said Marner docilely, bringing his eyes very close, that they might be initiated in the mysteries.

(Silas Marner, Chap. 14, p. 180)

The scene is comic but its import is serious. Patterns based on the opposition of masculine and feminine characteristics give powerful support to the ethical teaching of *Silas Marner*. But they are not simplistic attributes attached to particular men and women so much as suggestive images of opposing attitudes to life. They even creep into conventional descriptions of landscape and, by implication, describe the societies which flourish there. The itinerant weavers who wander like lost children, 'remnants of a disinherited race', seek to make new lives in the sheltered lanes 'deep in the bosom of the hills'. Silas himself is like those exiles who lose touch with their past in a new land 'where their mother earth shows a new lap' and he hides his bruised spirit in the hidden village 'nestled in a snug well-wooded hollow'.

George Eliot also gives Silas earlier memories and allegiances which have been suppressed by his religious education, of a time when he was cared for by his mother and in turn cared for his little sister after his mother's death. There is no mention of a father. We feel that he is one who could be initiated into female mysteries – and that these 'natural' mysteries may well be in opposition to the abstract Calvinist teaching of his church. The abstract doctrine of Lantern Yard stopped him from investigating the meaning of the material world, just as it interpreted his cataleptic trances as spiritual signs rather than physical states:

> as with many honest and fervent men, culture had not defined any channels for his sense of mystery, and so it spread itself over the proper pathway of inquiry and knowledge. He had inherited from his mother some acquaintance with medicinal herbs and their preparation – a little store of wisdom which she had imparted to him as a solemn bequest – but of late years he had had doubts about the lawfulness of applying this knowledge, believing that herbs could have no efficacy without prayer, and that prayer might suffice without herbs: so that his inherited delight to wander through the fields in search of foxglove and dandelion and coltsfoot, began to wear to him the character of a temptation.
>
> (*Silas Marner*, Chap. 1, p. 57)

When he arrives in Raveloe his skill with herbs and his cure of Sally Oakes's dropsy (which he recognises from his mother's own illness) leads to an invitation to take on the mantle of the local Wise Woman – an even more fundamental female role than the one he eventually adopts – and one which would set him up in opposition to the official male medical line, just as his adoption of Eppie sets him up in opposition to 'his betters' and to the official claims of legal paternity. Dr Kimble was 'always angry about the Wise Woman' and, as we later learn, Kimble is an integral part of the old Cass–Osgood patriarchy: 'time out of mind the Raveloe doctor had been a Kimble' (*Silas Marner*, Chap. 11, p. 154). Silas resists the temptation, for he has no desire to help his neighbours on a false basis. It is not until much later, when Eppie's wanderings force him out into the lanes and fields again, that he regains his love for his herbs. They become part of his own healing, knitting together his broken spirit and soothing his wounded memory.

In *Silas Marner* plants and gardens take their place in a suggestive debate about nature and culture. Silas spends many years in the wilderness of the stone pits, among the dewy brambles and rank tufted grass, before he looks at the hedge-rows again in terms of their social use. But Eppie wants to take the taming of nature further. As she grows she feels they have everything they could wish for except a garden. Her ideal garden will enclose the wild furze bush where her mother died, sur-rounded by perpetually regenerating bulbs, but will also bring in the familiar cottage herbs and the lavender of the big house. Aaron, a gardener, will help her and their plot will be like a sampler of good husbandry, free from the waste and want which characterised the old Raveloe, for 'nobody need run short o' victuals if the land was made the most on'. Eppie's plans, full of a generous profusion, are carefully contrasted to the geometrical formality of the neatly swept walks, the 'dark cones and arches and wall-like hedges of yew' (Chap. 17, p. 212) at the White House where Nancy and Priscilla talk of childlessness and dis-appointment in marriage.

Silas's own spirit is a wasteland taught to blossom again – and as we might expect from her earlier works Eliot suggests both its desiccation and renewal through images associated with water, which she links explicitly to his response to that maternal world of 'useful nature'. His capacity for feeling is illuminated by the way he treasures the pieces of his broken water jug, but as his loom becomes the centre of the world, the natural springs dry up within him – he grows inhuman and the piles of coins, con-versely, take on a human face, as he,

felt their rounded outline between his thumb and fingers, and thought fondly of the guineas that were only half-earned in his loom, as if they had been unborn children – thought of the guineas that were coming slowly through the coming years, through all his life, which spread far away before him, the end quite hidden by countless days of weaving. No wonder his thoughts were still with his loom and his money when he made his journeys through the fields and lanes to fetch and carry home his work, so that his steps never wandered to the hedge banks and the lane-side in search of the once familiar herbs; these too belonged to the past, from which his life had shrunk away, like a rivulet that has sunk far down from the grassy fringe of its old breadth into a little shivering thread, that cuts a groove for itself in the barren sand.

(*Silas Marner*, Chap. 2, p. 70)

When his final emotional prop, the gold, is taken away, he has no way of responding to the 'simple way of life and its comforts' with which Dolly tries to cheer him:

The fountains of human love and of faith in a divine love had not yet been unlocked and his soul was still the shrunken rivulet, with only this difference, that its little groove of sand was blocked up and it wandered confusedly against dark obstruction.

(*Silas Marner*, Chap. 10, p. 140)

Eppie's arrival unlocks the fountains, for 'there was love between the man and the child and love between the child and the world'. But as Silas turns outwards towards the community, so Godfrey Cass looks increasingly inward. Appropriately enough, Godfrey's concentration on his work, his farm, leads him to drain his land and when the pool at the Stone Pits is reduced in its turn to a shrunken rivulet, it reveals the skeleton of his brother Dunsey and the spectre of his own guilt, as well as the weaver's now unwanted treasure.

The tale of the two men, Silas Marner and Godfrey Cass, the foster father and the biological father (but which is the 'natural' father?), builds upon contrast and coincidence with such skill that in the end the coincidences of the plot seem like concrete links in universal chains of cause and effect. Both men lose their mothers in childhood and are at the mercy of tyrannical father-figures – one religious, the other secular. Both are accused of misappropriating their 'father's' money and just as

Silas's unforgiving minister casts him out of the community so Squire Cass threatens to cut Godfrey out of his will. When we meet them, both are obsessed by money – Silas by the growing pile of gold earned from his work, Godfrey by the desperate lack of funds caused by his waywardness (he has collected the rent from one of his father's farms and handed it over to Dunsey, who is blackmailing him over his secret marriage).[2] Both, we are told, were originally warm, affectionate men, but by the time the story opens they are inward-looking and embittered, trapped by their own pasts – Silas by memories of being an innocent victim, Godfrey by guilt – and both are deceived by 'brothers' they trust. The connections concentrate at the crises at the heart of the novel in Dunsey's theft of Silas's money and Silas's adoption of Godfrey's child.

Eppie tumbles from Molly's arms into the snow 'with a peevish cry of "Mammy" ' and finds solace on Silas's hearth. By the time Godfrey rushes from the New Year Ball to confirm his terrible fears, she is already attached to her new protector. She can 'make no visible, audible claim' on her father and the two men are therefore tested by the way they respond to an inarticulate plea in the shock of the moment. Silas, momentarily confusing the golden hair with his lost treasure, feels an instant identification with the 'lone thing', followed by the sense that the child, who is so like his own little sister, can link him with his lost, far-off past. But Godfrey can only see a threat to his future, and slips easily into the 'prevarication and white lies' which allow him to justify the denial of paternity. He consoles himself with a false assurance of altruism, of doing the best thing not only for himself but for Nancy and for the child: 'he would never forsake it; he would do everything but own it.' The event fills Silas with awe 'at the presentiment of a Power presiding over his life', while Godfrey explains Molly's death and the weaver's action as the operation of the self-vindicating gambler's deity, Chance.

Their reactions are conditioned by their background and their class as much as by their individual circumstances. While the villagers offer instant support and almost too much advice to

Silas and his orphan, Godfrey (who has just come from the New Year Ball at which the relative status of landlord, cottager and servant are made only too clear) knows that if he acknowledges his child he would lose all claims to respectability – and would probably lose Nancy Lammeter as well. At that moment respectability and Nancy seem more important than formal, or moral claims.

But sixteen years later, when the most important thing seems to be the re-possession of his daughter, Godfrey resorts to the very claims he had foregone. Both fathers, like poor Molly, have a sense of their 'rights'. The debate which surrounds the word 'right' in the novel is carefully elaborated, as one would expect from a writer who confessed 'a weakness for those indications of the processes by which language is modified' (*Letters*, Vol. III, p. 432). 'It's come to me – I've a right to keep it,' is Silas's first response – an appeal to a naïve, customary claim like 'finders keepers'. This is subtly amended when he answers Godfrey's questions, when he accepts that there may be competing claims of blood and law but also appeals to an obscure poetic sense of what is 'right' and fitting:

'Why, you wouldn't like to keep her, should you – an old bachelor like you?'

'Till anybody shows they've a right to take her away from me,' said Marner. 'The mother's dead, and I reckon it's got no father: it's a lone thing – and I'm a lone thing. My money's gone, I don't know where, and this is come from I don't know where. I know nothing – I'm partly mazed.'

(*Silas Marner*, Chap. 13, p. 176)

When Dolly Winthrop supports his decision, she extends the possible meanings of the term still further, declaring, 'You'll have a right to her, if you're a father to her and bring her up accordingly . . . if you'd do the right thing by the orphin child.' Here the sense of an absolute privilege vanishes, to be replaced by the idea that a 'right' has to be deserved and will always involve a corresponding duty. Legality is replaced by morality, and by a sense that there is some underlying pattern to human behaviour, a fundamental 'right'.

The debate re-opens sixteen years later. When Eppie inexplicably rejects Godfrey's magnanimous offer of adoption, he jumps at once to his 'rights' which he now justifies under the authority of both 'nature' and 'duty':

'But I've a claim on you, Eppie – the strongest of all claims. It's my duty, Marner, to own Eppie as my child, and provide for her. She's my own child: her mother was my wife. I've a natural claim on her that must stand before every other.'

(*Silas Marner*, Chap. 19, p. 230)

Nancy shares her husband's view, sticking to her code that blood-relationships must have a superior claim, although she acknowledges the bonds built up in the intervening years. The shifting use of 'natural' to describe both biological and social links is very similar to the argument in *The Mill on the Floss*, when Maggie opposes Stephen Guest's claim on her love by appealing to the belief that memory, loyalty and duty are 'natural' too. Nancy, interestingly, moves the argument on by suggesting that Godfrey's parental right must imply Eppie's filial duty:

'What you say is natural, my dear child – it's natural you should cling to those who've brought you up,' she said, mildly; 'but there's a duty you owe to your lawful father . . . When your father opens his home to you, I think it's right you shouldn't turn your back on it.'

(*Silas Marner*, Chap. 19, p. 234)

Eppie's reply, like Silas's original choice, is dictated by strong feeling, based on memory, habit and an impulse to care which transcend the notion of mere duty, and an intuitive sense of belonging:

'I can't feel as I've got any father but one,' said Eppie, impetuously, while the tears gathered. 'I've always thought of a little home where he'd sit i' the corner, and I should fend and do everything for him: I can't think o' no other home. I wasn't brought up to be a lady, and

I can't turn my mind to it. I like the working-folks, and their victuals and their ways. And,' she ended passionately, while the tears fell, 'I'm promised to marry a working-man, as'll live with father, and help me to take care of him.'

(Silas Marner, Chap. 19, p. 234)

Her fierce class loyalty supports the view implicit in the whole book that organic social bonds are far more likely to develop among the rural working population than among their 'betters' who cling to an individualistic ethic of 'rights' which is open to self-interested interpretation. As we find it explored in this novel, the concept of rights loses out as an ethical notion by contrast with the concept of 'nature'. Arguments based on rights (unless refreshed by the appeal to a deeper standard of what is 'right') come to seem like a deep and horrible travesty of morality. The systems of rights are so formal, whether upheld by law or by constitutions, that it is as if they did not exist before they were 'granted' or 'enacted'; rights cannot be foundational in the way that those complex unstated obligations are which grow from shared experience.[3]

A general political extension of the moral argument develops from Eliot's depiction of the Cass family throughout the book; the squire's attitude to his tenants, Godfrey's neglect of Molly, Dunsey's cruelty and greed. Through them Eliot's criticism of the 'lawful father' who presses his claims and rights as 'natural' extends to the inherited patriarchal structure of English society as a whole and to the system of rights and privileges which justify traditional authority. As in *The Mill on the Floss* she argues that the rigid rules of law should be set aside in favour of moral 'laws' which take account of individual circumstances. Mr Macey's puzzled discussion in 'The Rainbow' as to what makes the 'glue' in the marriage contract (is it the ritual, the words, the feeling or the signing of the register?) is just one aspect of the book's inquiry into the mechanism of social cohesion, the search for a new, more flexible (and more 'maternal') ethic.

Eppie's speech is designed to persuade us that this 'right' way of living can be discovered only through actually living with people and sharing their lives (which in Raveloe is expressed by the sharing of food). Like true parenting, moral understanding comes from feeling with, rather than analysing or theorising about human lives. Not for nothing is Silas short-sighted, the most crucial events occurring when he is in a trance, staring vacantly with 'wide but sightless eyes'. Although as Eppie grows he acquires a less vague, 'more answering gaze', it is the confidence to trust in the inner vision which is so hard to articulate and 'bring to the tongue's end' which this, George Eliot's most poetic novel, finally celebrates.

CHAPTER TEN

ROMOLA: DAUGHTER TO MOTHER

Although the gestation of George Eliot's novels seems slow and her production small compared to many other prolific Victorian writers, it is quite astonishing how quickly a new novel flashed into her mind after the one before. The initial ideas for *Romola* and *Daniel Deronda*, for example, took seed on the holidays taken as soon as Marian had put down her pen after *The Mill on the Floss* and *Middlemarch*, apparently completely exhausted. Thus in 1860, after spending Easter in Rome and some time exploring Naples and the Calabrian coast, the Leweses sailed north again for Livorno and Florence. There, on 21 May, George wrote in his journal:

This morning, while reading about Savonarola it occurred to me that his life and times afford fine material for an historical romance. Polly at once caught at the idea with enthusiasm. It is a subject which will fall in with much of her studies and sympathies; and it will give freshness to our stay in Florence.

(*Letters*, Vol. III, p. 295)

As it seems that the prompting for *Romola* came directly from George Eliot's husband, it is a nice irony that its main theme should be the way a passionate intellectual woman responds to being told what to do all her life by men, and ends by shaking herself free altogether to become the matriarchal head of a household of women, shaping a boy of the next generation of men according to *her* beliefs.

Marian confided to John Blackwood that she wanted to keep the idea for the book secret as 'It will require a great deal of study and labour.' She was right. The next three years (briefly interrupted by the writing of *Silas Marner*) were to be largely devoted to research into the history, politics, dress, food, language, beliefs and slang of the Florentine Republic. On a second trip to Florence the following year Lewes tried hard to persuade her that it was imagination and not accurate scholarship which brought characters to life. 'Why is it that Shakespeare makes us believe in his Romans?' he asked her. But back in England the research piled up, unrelieved by the vivid memories which fed her Midland novels. As John Blackwood explained it to his wife, 'Her great difficulty seems to be that she, as she describes it, hears her characters talking, and there is a weight upon her mind as if Savonarola and friends ought to be speaking in Italian, instead of English' (*Letters*, Vol. III, p. 427). Poor Lewes gave up his attempts to restrain her and turned to his own work, which included a long article on rabies: 'She is buried in the middle ages and I am yapping away among mad dogs' (*Letters*, Vol. III, p. 435).

During these months of intense work she and Lewes also had other things on their minds, particularly the future of Lewes's boys: Charles seemed settled but Thornton failed his Civil Service exams because, he said, he wanted to 'go and fight Russians in Poland'. He was eventually persuaded (by Barbara Bodichon) to try game-hunting in Natal instead, while the good-natured Bertie was packed off to learn farming in Scotland. The duties of parents to children on the threshold of adulthood was to be one of the underlying concerns of her novel.

It reflects her immediate life in other ways as well. Some of the heroine's strength, and some of the intense questioning of the position of women, may have been influenced by Marian's growing closeness to the independent and warm-hearted Barbara who almost certainly provided the physical model for the tall, red-haired Romola. And *Romola* is also part of another contemporary debate, this time about nationalism – particularly Italian nationalism – which was of current concern to a British public watching with deep involvement the moves towards the unification of Italy in the late 1850s and early 1860s. The political and the personal merge in the novel's exploration of the nature of freedom, the meaning of trust, the utopian idea of love as a governing principle and the 'social mission' of woman.

In many ways *Romola* is Eliot's most striking exposition of the role of women. It is more thoughtful than the early, angry chapters of *The Mill on the Floss* and its slowly wrought arguments are followed through to a logical and positive conclusion. Romola herself is educated and outspoken, able to consider the possibility of surviving on her wits as a learned woman; she is a practical philanthropist, an efficient nurse and a good teacher, and has sufficient authority to challenge political and religious leaders and to keep an angry crowd at bay. In the elaborately patterned plot she climbs from enclosed unawareness to a life of confident altruism, while her husband Tito falls from careless selfishness into a morass of deceit and death. As she progresses from stage to stage her story becomes a parable of the way men (in Victorian England rather than Renaissance Florence) define women – as daughter, wife, mother or 'guardian angel' – and the way women can free themselves from these stereotypes.

The main events in *Romola* take place between 1492 and 1496 when the Medici rule was briefly replaced by a republic led by the friar Savonarola. The personal drama of Romola and Tito is set against a background of great events and public rituals – from the wearing of a good luck charm to the huge set pieces such as the feast of St Giovanni or the Trial by Fire of Savonarola. And because it is set in an age when allegory was a popular medium, in both literature and public display, George Eliot is able to use the layered meanings of metaphor in an unusually direct and fruitful way.[1]

Like nineteenth-century England, Romola's Florence is in a period of ferment, exploration and transition. It needs a new principle of social and spiritual organisation. The inheritance of the classical past is impotent and broken, like the fragments in the library of Bardo, Romola's father, which include 'a beautiful feminine torso; a headless statue, with an uplifted muscular arm wielding a bladeless sword; rounded, dimpled, infantine limbs severed from the trunk, inviting the lips to kiss the cold marble' (Chap. 5, p. 93). The medieval tradition is equally disconnected: in the church of the Nunciata wedged in between the statues of the great are 'detached arms, legs, and other members, with here and there a gap where some image had been removed for public disgrace, or had fallen ominously, as Lorenzo's had done six months before. It was a perfect resurrection-swarm of remote mortals and fragments of mortals' (Chap. 14, p. 200).

Who can make anything of these ghosts of the past? Only the artist Piero di Cosimo, who interprets them anew with living models – Tito as the Tempter, Romola as Ariadne/Antigone, Bardo as Oedipus. George Eliot took care in her choice of artist, for the real Piero was famous for his prophetic mythological paintings and the description of his studio (based on Vasari) emphasises that he, alone of all the city dwellers, has access to nature, with a hidden door opening on to a secret 'wild garden'.[2] Piero is an artist/magician and his intuition (ignored by his contemporaries) is the one unclouded vision that the book affords us.

But although he can direct our judgement he cannot tell us *how* to live – and this is what Romola seeks. Like Maggie, she feels a desperate need for a 'thread' to lead her through the labyrinth. The novel contains terrifying pictures of the vertigo which fills people when they lose the line they cling to: Baldassarre, for example, the adoptive father whom Tito has betrayed and who is now questioning whether he can ever 'lay hold of the slippery threads of memory? Could he, by striving, get a firm grasp somewhere, and lift himself above these waters that flowed over him?' (Chap. 30, p. 342). Many characters share his fundamental anxiety, 'like that of an insect whose little fragment of earth has given way, and made it pause in a palsy of distrust' (Chap. 30, p. 333), and the heroine herself is only too aware of inner uncertainty:

Romola's trust in Savonarola was something like a rope suspended securely by her path, making her step elastic while she grasped it; if it were suddenly removed, no firmness of the ground she trod could save her from staggering, or perhaps from falling.

(*Romola*, Chap. 45, p. 465)

But until she learns that strength must come from within she continues to place her trust in the ropes that men hold out to her – or bind around her.

Unlike Piero none of the men she submits to can see Romola's true nature. When the reader first encounters her she is reading aloud the story of how Pallas Athene/Minerva blinded Tiresias because he saw her bathing naked, but granted him the gift of prophecy on the intercession of his mother Chariclo. Against this verbal tapestry of female wisdom, male intrusion, interceding motherhood and the dangers of sexual knowledge stands the figure of Romola, full of 'proud tenacity and latent impetuousness'. It is an astonishing introduction.

Romola herself links Tiresias with her father Bardo who, though blind, carries the image of Minerva, the goddess of wisdom, in his soul. But here, as so often, she is wrong. It is she who responds to the meaning of the passage; her father is only worried about its surface, the accuracy of the text and the 'grammatical falsities'. Unlike Tiresias he has no understanding of women at all and, like the more kindly Mr Brooke in *Middlemarch*, is led by 'blind' prejudice against the 'wandering, vagrant propensity of the feminine mind'. He accepts her aid as poor compensation for the loss of his son to the Dominican friars. Such is the authority of the father and the love of the daughter that she not only concurs in his low estimate but values her scholarship and even her sexual and romantic life, not as routes to her own satisfaction, but as ways of tending her father's needs:

'But I will study diligently,' said Romola, her eyes dilating with anxiety. 'I will become as learned as Cassandra Fedele. I will try and be as useful to you as if I had been a boy, and then perhaps some great scholar will want to marry me, and will not mind about a dowry; and he will like to come and live with you, and he will be to you in place of my brother . . . and you will not be sorry that I was a daughter.'

(*Romola*, Chap. 5, p. 100)

Her distress does touch Bardo, but his response only reveals more clearly his entrenched idea of women in general and his insensitivity to this woman in particular:

'I said not that I could wish thee other than the sweet daughter thou hast been to me. For what son could have tended me so gently in the frequent sickness I have had of late?'

(*Romola*, Chap. 5, p. 100)

Bardo is caught in the meshes of his own egotistical scholarship, like Casaubon in *Middlemarch*, trapped in the dream of a great work in which he had 'desired to gather, as into a firm web, all the threads that my research had laboriously disentangled' (Chap. 5, p. 97). Romola can only be his true daughter by denying part of herself: she tends him with that mixture of piety, pity and weariness which Maggie Tulliver experienced by the bedside of her deluded father. Yet for a long time duty to the father remains her fiercest loyalty; she leaves her husband because he disperses Bardo's library after his death, and she breaks with her mentor Savonarola because he executes Bernardo, the godfather who has come to stand in Bardo's place.

The irruption of Tito into their closed, airless world is like a flash of sunlight: her 'astonishment could hardly have been greater if the stranger had worn a panther-skin and carried a thyrsus' (Chap. 6, p. 105). She responds immediately to him as a Dionysiac liberator, springing her free into the world of sense. In describing this next stage of Romola's life George Eliot explores an idea which was important to her yet which remained problematic. She believed that to be a complete woman involved acknowledgement of one's sexual being, yet she saw that as long as relations between men and women were of unequal power, and were obscured by a false romantic ideology, sexual love could be more of a trap than a liberation. Furthermore, the sexual independence of a daughter is often perceived as a threat to the father who demands submission to his will.

The two conflicting impulses in Romola's life, towards pleasure and self-renouncing duty, are embodied in the conflict between her attraction to Tito and the fear injected into her by the warnings and prophetic dreams of her brother, Fra Luca,[3] in whose voice we hear again the harsh judgement of Tom Tulliver as Maggie awakens to sensual life with Stephen Guest (and perhaps also the outrage of Isaac Evans at the affair between his sister and George Henry Lewes). Romola asks if women can ever combine duty and desire:

Or was there never any reconciling of them but only a blind worship of clashing deities, first in mad joy and then in wailing? Romola for the first time felt this questioning need like a sudden uneasy dizziness and want of something to grasp; it was an experience hardly longer than a sigh, for the eager theorising of ages is compressed, as in a seed, in the momentary want of single mind.

(*Romola*, Chap. 17, p. 238)

Romola's combination of inner integrity with powerful physicality is immediately sensed by Tito:

he felt for the first time, without defining it to himself, that loving awe in the presence of noble womanhood, which is perhaps something like the worship paid of old to a great nature-goddess who was not all-knowing but whose life and power were something deeper and more primordial than knowledge.

(*Romola*, Chap. 9, p. 145)

Yet once he possesses her his awe is replaced by the desire to master her independent spirit in the way that he dominates Tessa, the peasant girl with whom he is already having a clandestine affair. The irony is that Tessa is no sensual creature, but an innocent who craves protection. It is Romola who throbs with desire, who knows that she could become a 'demon' and who sees herself as a bacchante.

Both Tito's women receive their first embraces from him while their faces are wet with tears. 'My Romola! My goddess!'

he murmurs – but he is relieved by her vulnerability and her ignorance of the fact that he has cheated and disowned his adoptive father, Baldassarre. Tito is quick to step into the role of Bacchus but, to the careful reader, he gives himself away. When he commissions Piero to make and decorate a special casket for him, he brings together two stories – one where Bacchus avenges himself on the pirates who have kidnapped him by making ivy and vines grow over their rigging, and the other where he rescues Ariadne on the isle of Naxos. The allegory conceals Tito's own betrayal of Baldassarre who had been captured by pirates, and presents Romola as another prize of his treachery: the casket will be used to conceal the crucifix of Fra Luca, the voice of conscience.

George Eliot brilliantly conveys Romola's lonely disappointment as Tito turns increasingly to intrigue – and to Tessa. And just as she had denied her own needs in her role as daughter so now the loss of love fills Romola with such terror that she colludes in her own humiliation:

Romola was labouring, as a loving woman must, to subdue her nature to her husband's. The great need of her heart compelled her to strangle, with desperate resolution, every rising impulse of suspicion, pride and resentment; she felt equal to any self-infliction that would save her from ceasing to love. That would have been like the hideous nightmare in which the world had seemed to break away all round her and leave her feet overhanging the darkness.

(*Romola*, Chap. 27, p. 313)

Tito's secret guilt weakens the magnetism between them as the soft warm skin of the lover is replaced by the hard chainmail he wears under his cloak for fear of Baldassarre's revenge. Eventually the smiling lover is unmasked as the brutal husband: 'it was time for all the masculine predominance that was latent in him to show itself.' The couple are locked in combat and neither can easily escape: Tito 'had locked-in his wife's anger and scorn, but he had been obliged to lock himself in with it' (Chap. 32, p. 352). His determination to master his wife is 'secretly throttling and stamping out' his gentler nature; and Romola's reserve cannot stem her flood of anger.

Like Bardo, Tito has spun a web of selfishness to trap himself. Since his marriage to Tessa, 'It seemed to him that the web had gone on spinning itself in spite of him, like a growth over which he had no power.' The imagery of physical growth is particularly apposite to his situation, and quite early in the story George Eliot tells us that actions are also uncontrollable growths (like Tito's illegitimate children) which will lead inevitably to exposure:

But our deeds are like children that are born to us; they live and act apart from our own will. Nay, children may be strangled, but deeds never: they have an indestructible life both in and out of our consciousness; and that dreadful vitality of deeds was pressing hard on Tito for the first time.

(*Romola*, Chap. 16, p. 219)

But at this mid-stage in the story Romola, by contrast, has no issue – either of children or deeds. Her marriage is barren in every sense and as she looks at her wedding dress buried in an old chest and remembers her early passion she weeps:

the woman's lovingness felt something akin to what the bereaved mother feels when the tiny fingers seem to lie warm on her bosom, and yet are marble to her lips as she bends over the silent bed.

(*Romola*, Chap. 36, p. 389)

The accent of real grief in this passage brings home to us the fact that she is left with nothing but the sepulchral effigy of her dead hopes.

The life of the affections is not enough and she must seek a wider role. Trying to flee from Florence in the disguise of a lay sister, and planning to live as an independent woman scholar in Venice, Romola is turned back at the gate by Savonarola. Her first instinct is rebellion – but the priest subdues her by appealing, not to her religious feeling, but to the sacredness of social ties and duties which are enforced from birth simply by virtue of being part of a human community. He equates good with obedience to a divine law, rather than with the assertion of the individual will, and implies that for women obedience should come more naturally because they are dependent beings who – unlike their brothers – can have no special vocation. In the end, in a moment of intense emotion, Romola submits to the familiar voice of male authority:

'Father, I will be guided. Teach me! I will go back.'

Almost unconsciously she sank on her knees. Savonarola stretched out his hands over her; but feeling would no longer pass through the channel of speech, and he was silent.

(*Romola*, Chap. 41, p. 436)

Once again she is in an attitude of 'yearning passivity' before a man.

Two years later ('in her place', as the ironic chapter heading tells us) she is among the crowds watching the tabernacle of the Madonna dell' Impruneta, and the 'miraculous hidden image' of the Pitying Mother, enshrouded by 'veils and curtains and mantles', directs us to her own work as a 'visible Madonna' caring for the sick and starving. Eliot writes thoughtfully about her philanthropy (a role denied to Maggie Tulliver), which brings Romola close to the lives of some of the great Victorian women like Florence Nightingale or Octavia Hill. Her conclusion is respectful but exceedingly conservative – enshrining the notion of domestic feeling and duty above any professional or individual pride in a valuable job, and suggesting that women turn to public work because their private life is unsatisfactory rather than out of desire for a career or anger against conditions which could be altered:

She had no innate taste for tending the sick and clothing the ragged, like some women to whom the details of such work are welcome in themselves, simply as an occupation. Her early training had kept her aloof from such womanly labours; and if she had not brought to them the inspiration of her deepest feelings, they would have been irksome to her. But they had come to be the one unshaken resting place of her mind, the one narrow pathway on which the light fell clear . . . All that ardour of her nature which could no longer spend itself in the woman's tenderness for father and husband, had transformed itself into an enthusiasm of sympathy with the general life.

(*Romola*, Chap. 44, p. 463)

But as Romola's work in the community teaches her tolerance, she finds herself recoiling from the 'denunciatory exclusiveness' of Savonarola. Her disillusion is compounded by the further collapse of her domestic life, for in the streets of Florence she encounters and helps Tito's father, wife and son and discovers the personal and political secrets he tried so hard to hide. When she realises with a shock that she had hoped Tito *was* married to Tessa so that she could be legally free, she is driven to meditate on the conflicting perspectives of

outward law which she recognised as a wide-ramifying obligation, and the demands of inner moral facts. . . . The law was sacred. Yes, but the rebellion might be sacred too. It flashed upon her mind that the problem before her was essentially the same as that which had lain before Savonarola – the problem where the sacredness of obedience ended, and where the sacredness of rebellion began.

(*Romola*, Chap. 56, pp. 552–3)

The conflict between her 'personal tenderness' and his 'theoretic conviction' comes to a crisis when he executes her godfather Bernardo, despite her intercession. She realises she cannot go on. Although it is woven of faith and social concern, Savonarola's system too is a mass of 'tangled threads' (Chap. 61, p. 586). At this, her lowest point, Romola again puts on the robe of the lay-sister in a despairing rejection of her own identity:

Why should she care about wearing one badge more than another, or about being called by her own name? She despaired of finding any consistent duty belonging to that name. What force was there to create for her that supremely hallowed motive which men call duty, but which can have no inward constraining existence save through some form of believing love?

(*Romola*, Chap. 61, p. 586)

She consigns herself to fate, setting herself adrift on the Arno. The terms in which her self-abandonment is described are so close to that of Maggie's sexual drifting that we realise it is not death which she really desires but an escape into the world of sensation untroubled by the perplexities of choice. The symbolic episode which follows, as she is borne down the Arno to a village emptied by the plague, describes a spiritual rebirth. Romola joins that band of Eliot's orphans who are deprived of belief and trust and are burdened by a dream of their childhood and by 'memories of human sympathy which even in its pains leaves a thirst that the Great Mother has no milk to still'. But when she lands in the 'green valley' (a secret cleft in the land like that which shelters Silas Marner in Raveloe) she finds that 'instead of bringing her to death' her boat 'had been the gently lulling cradle of a new life'. In this novel the woman does not die to regenerate a man, or drown in the flood of her own confused desires, but is roused to a new life in her own right. Like Silas she is called to life again by the cry of a child. She cannot wake the dead but she can feed the living. She may not be a spectral Madonna as the villagers first believe but she can stand in when needed for the 'Great Mother': ' "Now we will carry down the milk," said Romola, "and see if anyone wants it" ' (Chap. 68, p. 649).

This over-idealised interlude is, Eliot would have us believe, 'like a new baptism'. As in *Silas Marner* the rural community, even though it contains suffering and superstition, heals the pain born in the city and shows 'the simplest relations of the human being to his fellow men'. Romola too adopts an orphan, a Jewish child called Benedetto ('the blessing') whom she entrusts to the villagers when she leaves. But her integration into the community through a maternal role is different from that of Silas because, in a way no reader can shirk, it meets an explicit emotional desire. When Romola hunts for Tessa and the children whom she will foster in Florence, it is the first time in the book that we are told she is really doing anything out of her own need, and not out of affection or duty:

She never for a moment told herself that it was heroism or exalted charity in her to seek these beings; she needed something that she was bound specially to care for; she yearned to clasp the children and to make them love her. This at least would be some sweet result, for others as well as herself, from all her past sorrow.

(*Romola*, Chap. 70, p. 656)

Free from the direction of men she is able to identify completely with the traditional role of women, but also to widen it so that it embraces culture, learning, art and strength as well as affection and self-denial.[4]

In her own way Romola has exchanged a way of life based on obedience and custom for one directed by love and the recognition of need. She might even take for her own the motto of Comte's 'religion of humanity', '*l'Amour pour principe, l'Ordre pour base et le Progrès pour but*'. As Rosemary Ashton has written, 'If any of her works may be called 'positivist' it is *Romola*'.[5] Ashton shows how the principal influences on Romola's development – the medieval fanaticism of Savonarola, the sceptical humanism of Bardo and the practical demands of the community – embody Comte's three historical stages, the theological, metaphysical and positivist. But the influence of Comte is even more pervasive. Romola's progress seems at first to demonstrate some of the central tenets of his social philosophy: the belief that a new ethical system could flourish if love rather than law guided moral judgements, the insistence that such love must spring from the heart and not the intellect and that social love could eventually triumph over self-love by 'a slow and difficult training of the heart'. In Comte's utopian theory, as in Eliot's fiction, the symbols of harmony are the bonds of loving marriage and family relations, and the desirable social end is a general 'substitution of duties for rights'. Enriched by an awareness of history which gives a sense of continuity with previous generations, humanity could aspire to an ideal state of social cooperation.

Romola explores the way such ideas might work within a single life, but it subjects them to fierce criticism and makes us understand that the 'slow and difficult training of the heart' has to be accompanied by a rigorous questioning of *all* bonds, social and familial, especially the binding obligations which men lay on women and which are so often used as a kind of moral blackmail. The book questions and re-formulates Comte's analysis of the mission of women.

In the 'religion of humanity' first expounded by Saint-Simon in his *Nouveau Christianisme* and then formalised by Comte, women played a crucial role. Like the priests, they were held to be in closer touch with the mysteries of nature and to be ideally suited as moral guides because of their innate gentleness. In the theories of other Saint-Simonians their role was even more exalted: Enfantin, for example, said that God must be a dual-sex being and for a new era to begin a female Messiah or "Mother" had to be found to complement the Father. Now George Eliot never took these ideas seriously as theology and both she and Lewes looked askance on the institution of the 'Church of Humanity', despite Lewes's key role in promoting interest in Comte's work and the fact that the Church was organised in Britain by their friend from Wandsworth days, Richard Congreve. But the notion of the woman priestess and mother caught her imagination. It tied in closely with her own views on the symbolic importance of the feminine nurturing role which had been slowly developing since her evangelical youth when she had responded so warmly to works like Martin's *Education des Mères*. 'Maternal influence', declares Martin, 'is an influence which is exerted on the heart, which through the heart may direct the mind, and which, in order to save and regenerate the world, only requires to be properly directed.'[6]

This teaching is not dissimilar to that of Comte, who believed that within the domestic sphere that was woman's world each man had three guardian angels – mother, wife and daughter. But as a mature novelist Eliot could not accept these theories without considerable qualification – in showing Romola as 'daughter', 'wife' and 'mother' Eliot paints the picture from the other side, and in her impassioned outburst about the absence of guardian angels in the modern world and the necessity of relying on stumbling human beings she demolishes any simplistic idea that a single woman or priest can carry the total burden of responsibility for others.

She could also see only too clearly the hidden assumption of male superiority which lay behind the evangelical teaching and lurked within Comte's apparent glorification of women as repositories of feeling. Comte never accepted women as the intellectual equals of men, believing that their brains were at a lesser stage of development. His views are exposed in his fascinating correspondence with J.S. Mill in 1843 where he suggests that women had remained closer to nature and that 'the female sex is constituted in a kind of state of radical infancy that makes it essentially inferior to the corresponding organic type'. The true Comtean woman is not Romola, but the baby-faced Tessa, hardly someone one would automatically trust with the future direction of the human race. When George Eliot gives Tito some good Comtean arguments against removing Tessa from her peasant background, she manages to pinpoint the male self-interest of the whole theory through the particular selfishness of her hero:

> he was determined, if possible, to preserve the simplicity on which the charm depended; to keep Tessa a genuine contadina, and not place the small field-flower among conditions that would rob it of its grace. . . . By this means, Tito saved Tessa's charm from being sullied; and he also, by a convenient coincidence, saved himself from aggravating expenses that were already rather importunate to a man whose money was all required for his avowed habits of life.
>
> (*Romola*, Chap. 34, p. 371)

It is in his interest, in every sense, to keep his 'natural' woman in her place.

How, asks Eliot, can such theories encompass the educated women, the Romolas who spring like Athena from the brains of scholars? Comte's correspondence with Mill shows how he had deliberately rejected the feminist arguments of 'exceptional' women such as Mary Wollstonecraft even though they made a great impression on him: 'I set my mind irrevocably against any such assault on my sympathies'.[7] He then goes on to argue against the possibility of women achieving 'direction or execution' in any sphere outside the home, pronounces that it is a 'final advantage' for women to be saved from education, and declares that the female sex has never and will never produce any worthwhile art, music or poetry.

In *Romola* Eliot met the challenge of Comte's conservatism and of her own. For she too believed in love and the moral symbolism of the maternal role – but did this mean that she must celebrate mindless domesticity? When she had written of Mary Wollstonecraft and Margaret Fuller, she had applauded their insistence that some women should follow unconventional paths – be sea-captains if they so desired. In *Romola* she solves her dilemma by one bold step; she takes the maternal mission away from the docile wife and mother of the evangelical family, away from the 'specialised' morally superior but intellectually inferior womanhood idealised by Comte, and hands it over instead to the single, sensually aware but childless woman, an educated Madonna who, having learned from experience, has freed herself from the domination of men and is prepared henceforth to think for herself.

CHAPTER ELEVEN

FELIX HOLT, THE RADICAL: PERSONAL AND POLITICAL

In May 1863 Marian and Lewes began to hunt for a new house, since the lease on Blandford Square was running out. Eventually – feeling very extravagant – they bought The Priory, North Bank, on the Regent's Park Canal. It was a solid, dignified house and was decorated for them by the designer Owen Jones, who fitted it with new carpets and curtains and swept out all their old furniture. They moved in on 5 November, in considerable chaos; the piano tuner was sick all over the new drawing-room wallpaper (specially designed for them alone), Marian was ill and her purse was stolen by a workman. But all was arranged by the 24th, when they held a housewarming party for their old friends, to coincide with Charles's twenty-first birthday. Marian was greatly relieved when it was all over as she confessed to Maria Congreve:

Before we began to move, I was swimming in Comte and Euripides and Latin Christianity: *now* I am sitting among puddles, and can get sight of no deep water. *Now* I have a mind made up of old carpets fitted in new places, and new carpets suffering from accidents; chairs, tables and prices; muslin curtains and downdraughts in cold chimneys. I have made a vow never to think of my own furniture again, but only of other people's.

(*Letters*, Vol. IV, p. 116)

She really wanted to get down to work, and in the following summer she did, not on a new novel but a verse drama, *The Spanish Gypsy*, which was finally completed and published in 1868. The play tells the story of Fedalma, who turns her back on a noble and devoted lover in order to carry out the wider role decreed by her dying father, that of a gypsy princess and 'mother' to her people. The idea came to her, she said, while she and George were on holiday in Venice in May of 1864, and she was struck by a Titian painting of the Annunciation:

A young maiden, believing herself to be on the eve of the chief event of her life, marriage, – about to share in the ordinary lot of womanhood, full of young hope, has suddenly announced to her that she is chosen to fulfil a great destiny, entailing a terribly different experience from that of ordinary womanhood. She is chosen not by any momentary arbitrariness, but as a result of foregoing hereditary conditions: she obeys.[1]

Curiously Fedalma's independence is, therefore, linked not to a *rejection* of maternity, but to its most absolute symbol, the Virgin Mary. In this reading, the Annunciation foretells a spiritual, symbolic motherhood like that of Romola when she appears as 'a Visible Madonna'. When she was writing *Romola*, Marian was deeply engrossed by the demands of mothering Lewes's sons and, in her early forties, may have been confronting the results of her decision not to have children herself. Fedalma (like Alchirisi in *Daniel Deronda*) is an exceptional woman who chooses a particular public vocation at the cost of domestic life. And it *is* a cost.

The other great theme of *The Spanish Gypsy* is the pressure of inheritance and the clash between 'hereditary entailed Nemesis and the particular individual lot', also the subject of Eliot's next novel, *Felix Holt*. Eliot defines this clash as the essence of tragedy: 'Sometimes, as in the Oresteia, there is a clashing of two irreconcilable requirements, two duties, as we should say in these times. The murder of the father must be avenged by the murder of the mother, which must again be avenged.' These are suggestive words when you notice how *Romola*, in which all the 'fathers' are killed off one by one, is followed by *Felix Holt*, in which the adulterous, clinging mother is punished, and the father figures – in the persons of the Puritan clergyman Rufus Lyon and Felix Holt himself – are partially vindicated. Very often Eliot's novels fall into such balancing pairs, as if the residue of an argument had lingered unresolved in her mind.

But in her notes, when she wants to be specific about how inheritance can lead to individual tragedies, she returns to the subject of 'the renunciation of marriage, where marriage cannot take place without entailing misery on the children' and quotes as the determining conditions of a woman's life examples of inherited characteristics: 'she may be a negress, or have other marks of race repulsive in the community where she is born, etc. One may go on for a long while without reaching the limits of the commonest inherited misfortunes.' For the gypsy in *The Spanish Gypsy* and the Jew in *Daniel Deronda*, the social stigma of race is a harsh reality: thinking of Eliot's own life and options brings to mind another such stigma, that of illegitimacy. But actually these notes are misleading; these negatives are not the reason for Fedalma's renunciation of marriage. Although her destiny is affected by her race she chooses singleness because of what *she* feels she must do, not because of any fears for her children.

The first attempt at writing *The Spanish Gypsy* proved impossibly hard and in the winter of 1864 Marian sank into a slough of depression, feeling smothered by her poem which was 'sticking in the mud', in 'a swamp of misery'. Both she and Lewes were ill, and after weeks of headaches, biliousness and lethargy, she simply recorded in her diary, on 21 February 1865, '*George has taken my drama away from me.*'

Her letters often give an impression of difficulty, illness and uncertainty. But during this time, to the outward eye, the Leweses were flourishing. Their family affairs seemed settled, especially when Charles married Gertrude Hill in March 1865, and after their move to The Priory they became drawn into wider and grander society. In 1864 they became friends with the Lehmann and Benzon families, whose series of linked marriages had brought the wealth of German and British steel magnates into the orbit of the English intellectual world. During the following year the artists and scholars they met through the Lehmanns mingled on Sunday afternoons with the writers Lewes knew in his work, like T.H. Huxley, Walter Bagehot, Frederic Harrison. Although he gave up his editorial consultancy to *The Cornhill* in 1864, he immediately took on a similar role for George Smith's new magazine *The Pall Mall Gazette*, and soon (much to Marian's anxiety) agreed to edit another new journal, *The Fortnightly Review*.

While George dined out everywhere and enjoyed himself immensely, Marian was happier to remain at home, limiting her social life to visits from the women she trusted, like Barbara Bodichon, and to dinners with particular friends like Tom and Anthony Trollope at which there was 'a good deal of pleasant talk, or rather shouting'. Yet her journal admits her sense of purposelessness compared to the busy Lewes. 'About myself I am in deep depression, feeling powerless. I have written nothing but beginnings.' Four days later, on 29 March, comes the brief entry, 'I have begun a novel.'

Felix Holt took only fourteen months to write, following the usual pattern of a slow beginning and confident second stage, collapsing into doubt and anxiety before a feverish rush through the final pages. As she told Cara, 'I finished writing on the last day of May, after days and nights of throbbing and palpitation – chiefly I suppose from a nervous excitement which I was not strong enough to support well. As soon as I had done and read the last page to George, I felt better' (*Letters*, Vol. IV, p. 267). And Lewes confirmed this in his journal: 'Yesterday Polly finished *Felix Holt*. The sense of relief was very great and all day long suffused itself over our thoughts. The continual ill health of the last months and her dreadful nervousness and depression, made the writing a serious matter' (*Letters*, Vol. IV, p. 265). Within ten days the novel was on sale under the imprint of her old publisher, John Blackwood, who was delighted to meet the price of £5,000 for the copyright, which had been turned down by George Smith, the publisher of *Romola*. By publication day the Leweses had escaped to the Continent, to fall into a life of relaxation at the German Spa of Schlangenbad, 'an indolent, dreamy fragmented, *far niente* place' where 'the baths are incomparable luxuries – water as clear as crystal and as soft as milk' (*Letters*, Vol. IV, p. 284).

Felix Holt, like *Romola*, traces the efforts of a young woman to find 'a clue of principle amid the labyrinthine confusions of right and possession' (*Felix Holt*, Chap. 42, p. 524). The hard quest is one which the heroine, Esther Lyon, feels she would gladly give up 'if something would come and urge itself strongly as pleasure'. Desire and duty tussle within her after she is roused by her encounter with Felix Holt, whose 'radical' criticism of her ladylike ambitions dislodges her sense of her own rightness.

The fundamental note of *Felix Holt* is one of dislocation. The novel probes into people who are haunted by division – either because the life they lead conceals a secret or harbours a dream which bears no relation to their present situation or because they are torn by a conflict of values. As Esther grows aware of values other than her own she feels that her personality is on the verge of disintegration. What does Felix want her to do?

Did he want her to be heroic? That seemed impossible without some great occasion. Her life was a heap of fragments, and so were her thoughts: some great energy was needed to bind them together.

(*Felix Holt*, Chap. 15, p. 264)

This reminds us of the piled fragments of classical and Christian culture in the studios and churches of Romola's Florence. At the crisis of the novel even the natural world seems to fall apart from lack of a cohesive force – the very sunlight, one of the most potent images in the book, shines athwart, aslant and is 'fragmented' by shadow. When Esther comes to walk the corridors of the 'well-upholstered Utopia' of her girlish dreams, as heiress to Transome Court, she finds she is still in a labyrinth, not at one with herself, but 'a woman whose heart was divided and oppressed'. Like Latimer, Maggie Tulliver and Romola she feels she is living on two levels at the same time, one public and one private, and being driven by two separate currents of feeling which can somehow never flow together.

Moving between Malthouse Yard and Transome Court, and choosing between Felix and Harold, Esther is poised between two fundamentally different ways of approaching life. At the same time the society she lives in also trembles on the brink of a momentous choice. For although Eliot presents a world 'governed by forces', pitiless general laws of natural and social evolution, her interpretation of determinism does not free people from the burden of choice. Sometimes they would like to think it does, and all they can see is the relentless tide hurrying them on: ' "Oh," said Mrs Transome, with low toned bitterness, "I must put up with all things as they are determined for me" ' (Chap. 36, p. 457). But actually 'all things' have sprung from the choices she herself made in her youth – a far more terrifying idea. The law of consequences in fact increases personal responsibility, for our actions can set off a chain of reactions as inexorable as those described by a law of physics, and this chain stretches far beyond our own lives because society is a complex interlinked body and not a random collection of individuals. In the words of old Mr Nolan, sage of 'the Marquis of Granby', 'It's all one web, sir. The prosperity of the country is one web' (Chap. 20, p. 304).

The novel thus focuses on a moment of choice; but it also insists that behind each choice lies the pressure of previous decisions and the cumulative weight of years. The burden of 'inheritance' is expressed genetically in *Felix Holt* through a stress on 'blood'; it is seen to operate materially through the inheritance of estates and formally through the elaborate workings of the law. But there is also a cultural inheritance, and here, Eliot says, we *can* choose – although particular cultural expressions may be associated with other lines of inheritance such as class or religion, as they are in the literature of English Dissent or European Romanticism, and in the aristocratic portraits of Reynolds and Lely.

Felix Holt is largely about the way revelations from the past can help people make choices for the future. This is shown in the lives of individuals whether they endlessly brood over their own past, remorsefully or nostalgically, like Mrs Transome or Rufus Lyon, or discover they own a wholly unexpected history, like Esther and Harold. But it is also demonstrated in the life of society, and the story therefore becomes a contribution to a contemporary issue. Written in 1865 during the debates before the Second Reform Act, it is set in 1832, the era of the First Reform Act. Treby is based on Nuneaton where, as a schoolgirl of thirteen, Mary Ann Evans had witnessed the riots and deaths which accompanied the first election after the extension of the franchise. As in *Romola*, private and public stories are linked. Esther and the voters of England are both asked to choose between a sudden leap to material power through 'mechanical' means (the technical law of entail and the extension of the franchise) or a gradual growth to spiritual power through education of the feelings.[2]

The sense of dislocation which comes to trouble Esther will also threaten the country as a whole, and it is forecast in the author's brilliant and disturbing introduction. It opens like a nostalgic celebration of old England. But as George Eliot asks us to imagine the stage-coach travelling across the Midlands, from the liberal wildness of the hedgerows into a mosaic of farmland and market towns, mines and canals, she moves us into a landscape imbued with menace:

under the low grey sky which overhung them with an unchanging stillness as if Time itself were pausing, it was easy for the traveller to conceive that town and country had no pulse in common.

(*Felix Holt*, Introduction, p. 80)

As the focus narrows to Transome Court behind its screen of trees, also apparently immune to change, we learn that it is actually undermined by law suits; by the unexpected radicalism of its heir, and by the wasted lives of the old people within it. The suggestion of hidden political conflict slides into a disclosure of inaudible personal misery, for the 'vibrations that make human agonies are often a mere whisper in the roar of hurrying existence'.

Before the story even opens, all superficial and static appearances are placed under suspicion. Through the tracking movement of the introduction we learn that truth lies in process, in the way that events outrace 'blind climbing hopes'. We cannot escape the cycle of generation nor can we evade the past even in the restless depths of the personality where 'the red warm blood is darkly feeding the quivering nerves of a sleepless memory that watches through all dreams' (Introduction, p. 84). Within a chapter these quivering nerves are identified with the arrogant, demanding Mrs Transome, hiding 'a woman's keen sensibility and dread, which lay screened behind all her petty habits and narrow notions, as some quivering thing with eyes and throbbing heart may lie crouching behind withered rubbish' (Chap. 1, pp. 106–7). Mrs Transome's tragedy is her own, yet her identification with aristocratic tradition and imperiousness – 'she liked that a tenant should stand bareheaded below her as she sat on horseback' – allows her painful predicament to carry the weight of political allegory as well.

For this is a very public novel with a constant cross-reference between individual and social histories, where the climactic events take place literally before a host of witnesses and are constantly assessed by a commenting audience. But as in Eliot's first story 'Amos Barton', the gossip of provincial public opinion tells a false story – since it mutters only of visible behaviour. Its voice speaks counter to the voice of the narrator and to the suggestive whispers of metaphor which direct us to deeper truths. The guiding metaphors in *Felix Holt* work through dialectical contrasts: of sickness and healing; spring growth and autumn decay; gardens and wilderness; wandering and homecoming. They also comment on the action through reference to other 'stories' such as the Arabian Nights, the Christian myths of paradise and the fall, or the classical legends of Ariadne and the Minotaur in the labyrinth, Cupid seeking Psyche on the mountaintop, Hecuba weeping in the shades of hell. 'These things are parables', as the narrator reminds us.

Eliot's favourite metaphor of sight expresses a central argument. As in *Silas Marner* and later in *Middlemarch*, she contrasts inner vision with apparent short-sightedness in the peering Rufus Lyon or the squinting bust of Fuller and compares the 'vision' of dream and prophecy with realistic foresight. But her main point in *Felix Holt* is that the moral vision must be able to follow movement as well as to recognise basic characteristics. Personalities and societies, just like natural forms, develop by almost invisible processes which combine predictable growth with sudden apparently wayward changes of direction. Thus Felix thinks he knows himself, but 'very close and diligent looking at living creatures, even through the best microscope, will leave room for new and contradictory discoveries' (Chap. 22, p. 327).

We must never be satisfied that we can see clearly – a point Eliot makes again in a similar application of microscopic vision to the matchmaking Mrs Cadwallader in *Middlemarch*, who seems to be standing still but is actually like a water creature creating little vortices of movement which sweep her unfortunate victims towards her. The important thing is to be able to trace these almost undetectable processes and so to be able to read the 'writing . . . made on the face by the slow months of suppressed anguish' (Introduction, p. 84). Unless you look closely you might think that the victim was the pursuer and vice versa; it is only the patterns of movement which reveal the patterns of power.

Retracing past processes may be the best way to project ahead. As Felix says, 'we are saved by making the future present to ourselves'. A second familiar pattern which gives form to the plot of *Felix Holt*, as it had done to that of *Adam Bede*, *Silas Marner* and *Romola*, and which also provides a potent metaphor of historical continuity and change is that of generation, birth and parenthood. 'I'll lay hold of them by their fatherhood,' Felix says, when he wants the Sproxton miners to look to the future through the education of their children rather than through trying to influence a parliamentary election. But George Eliot then extends her metaphor to examine separation from the parent. Mrs Transome and Mrs Holt must learn that the sons they worshipped as babies and blithely assumed would cherish them in return may grow away from them. They are not static – Harold is not the same as his portrait and Felix is not a statue despite 'his little toes and feet like marbil'. It is dangerous to see the future as the extension of personal desires, as Mrs Transome discovers:

all the while the round-limbed pet had been growing into a strong youth, who liked many things better than his mother's caresses, and who had a much keener consciousness of his independent existence than of his relation to her: the lizard's egg, that white rounded passive prettiness, had become a brown, darting, determined lizard. The mother's love is at first an absorbing delight, blunting all other sensibilities; it is an expansion of the animal existence; it enlarges the imagined range for self to move in: but in after years it can only continue to be joy on the same terms as other long-lived love – that is, by much suppression of self, and power of living in the experience of another. Mrs Transome had darkly felt the pressure of that unchangeable fact. Yet she had clung to the belief that somehow the possession of this son was the best thing she lived for; to believe otherwise would have made her memory too ghastly a companion.

(Felix Holt, Chap. 1, p. 98)

Sometimes devotion to children cloaks selfish desire, a fact which the sons – politicians who profess to care for the next generation – must also recognise.

Felix and Harold are both 'hungry, much-exacting souls' who want to impose their will on the future. Felix does admit the egoism of his idealism: 'It is just because I'm a very ambitious fellow, with very hungry passions, wanting a great deal to satisfy me, that I have chosen to give up what people call worldly good' (Chap. 27, p. 363). In his own way he is as arrogant as the materialistic Harold, and so both of them are doomed to failure: Harold loses the election and Felix loses control of the crowd. They have to learn two things: that the people they seek to control have minds of their own (like children), and that they cannot operate independently but must accept their dependence upon others. Thus Felix must accept Esther's love, and Harold must accept that he is Jermyn's son and feel 'the hard pressure of our common lot, the yoke of that mighty resistless destiny laid upon us by the acts of other men as well as our own' (Chap. 49, p. 587).

Relations between the sexes, like parent–child relationships, are also symbolic expressions of political attitudes throughout *Felix Holt*. Felix's lack of insight into the subtle, slow way in which ordinary people apply politics to their own lives, his assumption of superiority and his belief in his own independence are reflected in his attitude to women and their 'petty desires':

That's what makes women a curse; all life is stunted to suit their littleness. That's why I'll never love, if I can help it; and if I love, I'll bear it, and never marry.

(*Felix Holt*, Chap. 10, p. 212).

Harold is equally nervous of feminine influence: 'I hate English wives; they want to give their opinion about everything. They interfere with a man's life, I shall not marry again.' He prefers to control the women he encounters, to reduce them to decorative pieces like 'a grandmamma on satin cushions' or a possession bought in the market place. But, as both men find, women are as unpredictable as the 'common people' – they ignore them at their peril.

The true radical in the book is Rufus Lyon who stands in the tradition of the divines and democrats of the commonwealth – the 'Root and Branch men', Levellers and Diggers.[3] Eliot chides him for his trust in the 'old political watchwords' but she sees that these illusions are the outcome of a generous faith in human nature. His ideal of freedom is not individualistic but communal and is identified with harmony, that common pulse of which *Felix Holt* so passionately mourns the lack. When he corrects Felix for his iconoclastic fire, which may 'dazzle others in the labyrinth', he takes his argument directly from the preceding conversation about the problems which beset the Malthouse Yard choir:

You yourself are a lover of freedom, and a bold rebel against usurping authority. But the right to rebellion is the right to seek a higher rule, and not to wander in mere lawlessness . . . I apprehend that there is a law in music, disobedience whereunto would bring us in our singing to the level of shrieking maniacs or howling beasts: so that herein we are well instructed how true liberty can be nought but the transfer of obedience from the will of one or of a few men to that which is the norm or rule for all men. And though the transfer may sometimes be but an erroneous direction of search, yet is the search good and necessary to the ultimate finding.

(Felix Holt, Chap. 13, p. 242)

Rufus's political ideal of freedom depends on the same sub-mission of self of which he has proved capable in private life. His instinctive generosity to the destitute Annette Ledru and her child reminds one forcibly of Silas Marner:

Searching with his short-sighted eyes, he perceived someone on a side-bank; and approaching, he found a young woman with a baby on her lap. She spoke again, more faintly than before –
'Sir, I die with hunger; in the name of God take the little one.'

(Felix Holt, Chap. 6, p. 164)

His love for Annette, 'a blind French Catholic', makes him question the strict laws of salvation of Calvinist doctrine, and forces him to step back on the threshold of a promising career as a preacher. But it also opens the way to growth, as 'religious doubt and newly awakened passion had rushed together in a common flood (Chap. 6, p. 163). Annette does not die in order for Rufus to be reborn, but the notion of sacrifice and of transferred life lingers on into this later novel, in the same way that Lyon's buried past affects the 'present' story. The closest parallel from Eliot's early books is 'Mr Gilfil's Love Story', where the Anglican clergyman's spiritual growth also came from his devotion to a foreigner disappointed in love who withers and dies like a plant in strange air. For Annette, 'the three years of life that remained were but a slow and gentle death. Those three years were to Mr Lyon a period of such self-suppression and life in another as few men know' (Chap. 6, p. 173). He carries this self-suppression into his relationship with Esther; and the daughter's interpretation of her mother's story helps her in turn to give up material wealth and embrace the loyalties of her adoptive father. The emotional radicalism of *Felix Holt* thus finds its central expression in the suppression of egotism through an intense relationship with another person. It makes the Victorian ideology of feminine submissiveness a basis for a genderless ideal of a harmonious society, in contrast to the theory-bound, individualistic 'male' ethic at the base of many superficially different approaches to life – Harold's materialism, Felix's cultural exclusiveness, Jermyn's law or Lyon's Calvinism.

While she never suggests that egotism is limited to the male sex (the 'masterful' men are matched by women who think of themselves as 'queens' and 'Empresses'), George Eliot does show that men and women exert this power in different ways: men in the world of action, women in personal relationships. Both sexes are deluded about the extent of their personal power. Men think they can manipulate events; but do not realise that in this particular chess game they have to reckon not only with their opponents, but also with the devious, stubborn wills of some of their pieces. Women think they can manipulate emotions, but do not realise that these very emotions can be turned against them. Mrs Transome's despairing relationship with Jermyn and with Harold is doubly pathetic because the feelings she invested are not returned and she is left a mere spectator of her own suffering, crying out that 'a woman's love is always freezing into fear' and 'God was cruel when he made women'.

The book alerts the reader to male hostility towards an un-ruly, dangerous element in women which threatens to overturn their plans. Once again Eliot uses men's attitude towards women as an index of the brutality which informs a patriarchal society structured on class and capital; a connection made clear by Esther's dilemma in Chapter 43. Harold has invited her to live at Transome Court, since he has discovered that she is the rightful heir and now contemplates marrying her to restore his fortunes. (His personal choice also reflects his radical politics –

the attempt of a morally bankrupt and illegitimate aristocracy to wed the common people, the new heirs to power). As she watches 'the masculine ease with which he governed everybody' she is forced to contrast the social power, material wealth and 'natural' assumptions of superiority of the landed gentry to the 'strong visions' of Felix Holt and her father. When she is embarrassed by the ungainly Mrs Holt, who comes to plead for Felix, she feels within her that 'there had been a betrayal'. Yet Harold's apparent sympathy for Felix swings her mood back again, for it seems a flattering acknowledgement of her 'power' over him and she 'quite forgot the many impressions which had convinced her that Harold had a padded yoke ready for the neck of every man, woman, and child that depended on him' (Chap. 43, p. 538).

The only way Esther can 'place' Harold in the flirtatious conversation that follows is in literary terms, as she tries to fix him in his correct genre. She dismisses him as unsuitable for a tragic or even a romantic hero, but settles at last for a character from genteel comedy – until the whole literary illusion is shattered by Harold's admission, intended to reassure Esther that she alone rules in his heart, that 'Harry's mother was a slave, was bought in fact.' The playing with genre is far from frivolous, for *Felix Holt*, like *The Mill on the Floss*, is concerned with the way people explain life to themselves; and one of the ways they do this, as the coachman makes clear in the Introduction, is through 'stories'. The novel itself exploits various genres to make particular points – a comedy of humours, a morality play, a satire on the arrogance of 'Maximus' and 'Augustus', a heraldic bestiary, Greek tragedy.[4]

The women are especially prone to see life through the lens of books, and Mrs Transome's silver-spoon anecdotes come to seem to Esther 'like so many novelettes'. Both women learn false ideals from the Romantic reading of their youth (and it is worth noting that each book they read is another sign-post to submerged meaning – when Esther reads Chateaubriand's *René* or Fénelon's *Télémaque* they underline her own escapism, with wandering, imprisonment on enchanted isles and final homecoming), and their stories are themselves comments on 'women's literature'. Esther reverses the ending of many of the 'Silly Novels' when she turns her back on the worldly reward which should accompany her 'correct' moral choice. Yet in a more profound sense her story is a true romance, true at least to Eliot's view (and own experience) that 'love makes us choose what is difficult, not what is easy'. On the other hand Mrs Transome's story resembles those of popular sensation novels which so often describe the downfall of a subversive woman who has transgressed the sexual code. The frisson comes from the thought that if the angel in the house is, in fact, a demon in disguise, might not all the accepted structures be rotten at the core and fall before the uncontainable desires of restless women or ambitious men? The corridors through which Mrs Transome wanders like a ghost are as silent and smothering as the heavily draped chamber in the asylum where the queen of all sensation heroines ends her days in *Lady Audley's Secret*.[5] But the 'deafening down of the pillows' cannot drown the cries of their hungry souls.

At a critical stage in her sentimental education Esther recognises that books no longer retain any appeal, for she is being forced to apply her feminine habit of reading, and writing, fiction to herself: 'her life was a book which she herself seemed to be constructing – trying to make character clear before her, and looking into the ways of destiny'. Instead she ruminates on the Transome family portraits which George Eliot uses throughout (as she had done in 'Mr Gilfil's Love Story') to comment on aristocratic tradition and, by comparing portraits with mirrors, to make ironic contrasts between past and present, surface and depth, stasis and change. When Harold finds Esther before an eighteenth-century portrait of Lady Betty Transome he is struck by the resemblance: '"Don't move, pray," he said on entering, "you look as if you were standing for your own portrait."' But Esther does move, rejecting identification with Lady Betty who, she says, 'looks as if she had been drilled into that posture and had not enough will of her own ever to move again unless she had a little push given to her.'[6] Esther has been given a 'little push' by Felix and is now aware of the danger of being reduced to an object of art.

The young heroine walks away from Transome Court with its wealth of painting and sculpture into the onward-driving bourgeois world of the novel. There she lives out her romance which, George Eliot would have us believe, can be every bit as subversive as Mrs Transome's 'sensational' adultery had been. When Esther rises to her feet at Felix's trial she embodies the revolutionary power of 'feminine' passion to overturn rigid law:

When a woman feels purely and nobly, that ardour of hers which breaks through formulas too rigorously urged on men by daily practical needs, makes one of her most precious influences: she is the added impulse that shatters the stiffening crust of cautious experience. Her inspired ignorance gives a sublimity to actions so incongruously simple, that otherwise they would make men smile. Some of that ardour which has flashed out and illuminated all poetry and history was burning today in the bosom of sweet Esther Lyon. In this, at least, her woman's lot was perfect; that the man she loved was her hero; that her woman's passion and her reverence for rarest goodness rushed together in an undivided current. And today they were making one danger, one terror, one irresistible impulse for her heart. Her feelings were growing into a necessity for action, rather than a resolve to act.

(*Felix Holt*, Chap. 46, p. 571)

Here are all the familiar symbolic oppositions which were formulated years before in *The Lifted Veil*, now presented in such grandiose language that they topple into uncharacteristic cliché. Female passion, purity, fluidity and irrationality associated with the creative imagination confront male habit, rigidity, rationality and legality. But in *Felix Holt* they are bound inseparably to the notion of women as a relative sex whose lot is made by the love they choose, in marked contrast to the stress on independence in *Romola* and *The Spanish Gypsy*. The passage above is 'radical' in the sense of claiming a vital role for an innate femininity, but it is alarmingly conservative (and regressive in the body of Eliot's work) in associating this influence solely with marriage and domesticity. In *Middlemarch* and

Daniel Deronda she moves away from such direct statements towards a more provisional, more finely qualified stance and it is interesting to note that when she came to revise her works for the Cabinet edition she removed the first few lines of the above passage.

Esther's outburst in court is the grand occasion which allows her to be 'heroic' and it is depicted not only as a moment of total psychic unity, but also as one in which the individual woman merges into an idealised essence of womanhood. Furthermore, it brings a similar unity to Felix, for it is the moment he dreamed of when he wondered if it would ever be possible to measure 'the force there would be in one beautiful woman whose mind was as noble as her face was beautiful – who made a man's passion for her rush in one current with all the great aims of his life' (Chap. 27, p. 364). Sexual harmony and moral harmony are one.

But Esther's victory is provisional; a glimpse of light in a book whose overall mood is one of darkness and loss of control. We have been made to see the animal or the shrieking maniac beneath the veneer of civilisation and the novel is punctuated from start to finish by the words 'hate', 'anger', 'temper', 'shock', 'terror', 'trembling' and 'fear', and with images of electric shocks, branding, scorching, eels skinned alive, knives drawn across soft flesh. *Felix Holt* expresses personal and political uncertainties so acute that they become physical sensations felt along the bone from the opening image of the body of the nation with its erratic pulse to the breaking heart of Esther when her brave speech seems to have been in vain:

Her heart swelled with a horrible sensation of pain; but, alarmed lest she should lose her self-command, she grasped Mrs Transome's hand, getting some strength from that human contact.

(*Felix Holt*, Chap. 46, p. 574)

Even when we learn that she has inspired the burghers of Treby to petition for a pardon this is overshadowed by Harold Transome's traumatic recognition, at the same meeting, that the hated Jermyn is his father. The narrative thus undercuts Esther's achievement and she in turn now has to give Mrs

Transome strength to endure. At the end, Felix, Esther and their son are banished to a good life in some nameless town. The image which lingers is not the vague promise of their happiness but the sharply drawn picture of two women who could so easily have been mother and daughter, comforting each other for the pain they experience on behalf of the men they love, and we are left feeling that stoicism, sympathy and endurance are the essential qualities required for personal, and for political, survival.

CHAPTER TWELVE

MIDDLEMARCH: AGAINST SIMPLICITY

In the early summer of 1866 the Leweses dallied on the Continent, while at home reviews poured out in praise of *Felix Holt*. But it was to be three years before Marian wrote fiction again and the intervening time – a time of widening public fame and bitter personal tragedy – was one in which she increasingly turned to her poetry. Her first task was to re-write *The Spanish Gypsy*. A trip was planned to the south of France and Barcelona, for George's health, as soon as Christmas was over. From Paris, where Mme Mohl introduced them to Renan and other scholars, they travelled down to Biarritz and there 'with snow on the ground' Marian confided her dream of pressing still further south to the sun of Granada. 'The idea quite fired me,' Lewes wrote in his journal, and at once they went out and bought 'a Spanish conversation book and grammar' to practise as they walked on the beach. The Spanish excursion, vividly described in their letters, was a real adventure, but by March they had had enough and trekked homewards across Spain and France in a series of endless train journeys: 28 hours to Madrid, 23 hours to Biarritz, 17 hours to Paris. Where were the feeble constitutions now?

Inspired by her travels Eliot spent most of the next few months on her drama, which was eventually published in June 1868. During 1868 and early 1869 she fretted about 'beginnings', made lists of projects for both poetry and prose and travelled abroad and in England, visiting a new infirmary in Leeds, inspecting the Benzons' iron works in Sheffield and reviving early memories by a trip to the Derbyshire dales which she had visited with her father in her teens. At home at The Priory the open Sunday afternoons were beginning to acquire their shrine-visiting aspect. Instead of the old circle round the fire, callers now ranged from admirers from abroad to members of aristo-cratic circles who had been attracted to the Positivist movement, like Lady Airlie and her sisters, Lady Amberley and Rosalind Howard, who swept Lewes off to candelabra-lit dinners, recep-tions and garden parties – the world of *Daniel Deronda*. Lewes's sociability fascinated many visitors and a young American, Charles Eliot Norton, left a detailed and snappy description of a Sunday in 1869:

Lewes received us at the door with characteristic animation; he looks and moves like an old fashioned French barber or dancing master, very ugly, very vivacious, very entertaining. You expect him to take up his fiddle and begin to play . . . all the action of his mind is rapid, and it is so full that it seems to be running over.

His partner was less immediately impressive:

Indeed one rarely sees a plainer woman, dull complexion, dull eyes, heavy features . . . Her manner was too intense, she leans over you till her face is close to yours and speaks in very low and eager tones; nor is her manner perfectly simple. It is a little that, or it suggests that, of a woman who feels herself to be of mark and is accustomed, as she is, to the adoring flattery of a coterie of not undistinguished admirers.[1]

But she was still charismatic enough to make another young American, Henry James, declare, 'Yes, behold me, literally in love with this great horse-faced blue-stocking.'[2]

As with all the metamorphoses of her life, Eliot seems to have willed herself into the role of sybil. But there is a sense of strain which raises the question: what was the meaning of these per-formances? Was Lewes really a showman making the most of a marketable commodity, deliberately building up an image of the wise woman? Or were his efforts a form of recompense, an attempt to make the spectacle of the famous writer erase that other much talked-of curiosity of the 'strong-minded woman' who ran off with a married man? Today, as much as in Victorian society, the open adoption of an unconventional liaison turns private lives into public property; everyone feels free to speculate about the relationship in a way they never would about a conventionally married couple. Both Lewes and Eliot felt this intensely, and it can be felt in the webs of gossip and rumour which the 'world and his wife' weave in her novels. We know that despite her goodness, if she had stayed, Dorothea Brooke would always receive the sideways glances of the Middlemarchers for her odd marriages, first to a sick scholar old enough to be her father and then to a dilettante with a foreign name young enough to be his son: 'Those who had not seen anything of Dorothea usually observed that she could not have been "a nice woman", else she would not have married either the one or the other.'(*Middlemarch*, Finale, p. 896).

The plight of women, 'nice' or not, preoccupied her greatly at this time, and her analysis was helped by the strengthening women's movement. The 1860s saw the emergence of the campaigning 'Langham Place Group', of which Barbara and Bessie Parkes were prominent members, and the growth of *The Alexandra Magazine*, to which Marian subscribed, which had been founded as *The Englishwoman's Journal* in 1857, and later became *The Englishwoman's Review*. The decade was also marked by the petition to the House of Commons in 1866, Mill's Amendment to the Suffrage Bill in 1867, and the foundation of Girton College. Marian's letters return constantly to the subject and contain several thoughtful statements of her position.[3] To John Morley in 1867 she wrote that, while 'as a fact of mere zoological evolution, woman seems to me to have the worse share in existence' there are moral advantages to be gained from the physical inequality, notably the greater capacity for love (*Letters*, Vol. IV, p. 364). In response to Clementia Taylor's appeals for help in the suffrage campaign, she replied that while she sympathised with the desire to see 'women educated equally with men, and secured as far as possible along with every other

breathing creature from suffering the exercise of any unrigh-
teous power', she did not agree that much could be achieved
'from a particular measure' (*Letters*, Vol. IV, p. 366).

Yet against these well known and rationally argued statements
of caution we can set others in which her ambivalence is so
marked that it reads not like an intellectual qualification but a
plain emotional muddle. In one such letter to Mrs Senior she
explained that her doubts about the Girton campaign sprang not
only from a sense of hidden complications and a dislike of the
kind of assertive, striving women involved, but also from an
unspecified inner fear:

There is no subject on which I am more inclined to hold my peace and
learn, than on the 'Woman Question'. It seems to me to overhang
abysses, of which even prostitution is not the worst. Conclusions seem
easy so long as we keep large blinkers on and look in the direction of our
own private path . . . I have been made rather miserable lately by
revelations about women, and have resolved to remain silent in my
sense of helplessness.

(*Letters*, Vol. V, p. 58)

Middlemarch is very much about the dangers of the blinkered
private path and the abyss beneath. In July 1870 she wrote to
Mrs Robert Lytton an equally troubled letter about the restriction of women to the world of 'love' (which she revealingly
describes as bringing cares as the acquisition of property does):

We women are always in danger of living too exclusively in the affections; and though our affections are perhaps the best gifts we have, we
ought also to have our share of the more independent life – some
joy in things for their own sake. It is piteous to see the helplessness of
sweet women when their affections are disappointed – because all their
teaching has been, that they can only delight in study of any kind for
the sake of a personal love. They have never contemplated an independent delight in ideas as an experience which they could confess without
being laughed at. Yet surely women need this sort of defence against
passionate affliction even more than men.

(*Letters*, Vol. V, p. 106)

How much of her own learning, from childhood on, had been a defence against passionate affliction? We will never know. Certainly the solidity of her achievement and fame was a bulwark not only against gossip but against her own self-doubt. As Oscar Browning notes, 'She describes herself at this time as a bundle of unpleasant sensations, with a palpitating heart and awkward manners, and professes a large charity for people whe detest her.'[4] She was constantly sending notes propitiating people in case she had seemed impulsive or uncharitable when they last met. Outside her fiction she played desperately safe. And within her fiction her stress on social bonds, and the very realism of her narrative, are all the stronger because of the sense of the abysses beneath.

The sense that the life of affections could be a passionate affliction was brought home in 1869 by a private tragedy. Thornton Lewes had fallen seriously ill in Natal with a spinal disease and his father at once sent money for his journey to England. In May, two days after they returned from the Continent, he reached The Priory, incredibly thin and in considerable pain. It was a Sunday afternoon and a hopeful young visitor, Henry James, had arrived on the doorstep, 'infinitely moved' to find the great authoress in such distress, and to find himself comforting Thornie until Lewes returned with some morphia and James could dash off to fetch their doctor, Sir James Paget. Paget's diagnosis was not promising, and the next months were overshadowed by Thornie's gradual decline. Marian nursed him constantly, helped, as so often, by the 'real practical sympathy' of Barbara Bodichon who came twice a week to sit with Thornton so that she could rest. In August Marian wrote to John Blackwood, 'Sons are heavy hostages to the powers at work in our lives' (*Letters*, Vol. V, p. 51). By then he was partially paralysed and soon it was clear he would never recover. He died in Marian's arms on 19 October.

For a while, Lewes said, he thought she would never get over it, and she herself wrote in her journal, 'This death seems to me the beginning of our own' (*Letters*, Vol. V, p. 60). She expressed her grief in poetry, especially in 'The Legend of Jubal', but as she spent the winter watching George suffer and grieve, she found it impossible to turn to other work. In the spring the Leweses fled England for the distractions of Europe, travelling to Berlin, then on to Prague and Vienna and back to Salzburg. But George was still not well and in the summer of 1870, in search of better health for him, they visited Harrogate and Whitby before returning to Park Farm, Limpsfield, where they had retreated after Thornie's death. There Marian wrote *Armgart*, her remarkable dramatic poem about a great opera singer whose voice suddenly fails. Armgart had been playing Orpheus, a woman singing the part of a man, the supreme artist who believes his art can raise the dead, but when her gift vanishes she loses all sense of identity –

> Oh I had meaning once,
> Like day and sweetest air. What am I now?
> The millionth woman in superfluous herds.
>
> (*Poems*, p. 113)

Armgart is chastised for her longing to stand out from the mass of ordinary womanhood, but the strength of the writing makes us sympathise with her knowledge that it is her artistry, her exceptional nature, which gives meaning to her life.

That summer Marian doubted whether her own gifts endured. Her novel of provincial life – about the young doctor Lydgate and the Middlemarch families of the Vincys, Garths and Featherstones – crept on, but very slowly. Not until December 1870 when she began to experiment with a story called 'Miss Brooke' and thought she might combine the two fictions, did she really start to feel her way. By the following spring and summer when they took a cottage at Shottermill in Surrey, she was able to work easily. This letter to Maria Congreve, written on 14 August, gives a wonderful glimpse of the settled routine of those summer days:

We enjoy our roomy house and pretty lawn greatly. Imagine me seated near a window, opening under a verandah, with flower-beds and lawn and pretty hills in sight, my feet on a warm water-bottle, and my writing on my knees. In that attitude my mornings are passed. We dine at two; and at four, when the tea comes in, I begin to read aloud. About six or half-past we walk on to the commons and see the great sky over our head. At eight we are usually in the house again, and fill our evening with physics, chemistry, or other wisdom if our heads are at par; if not, we take to folly, in the shape of Alfred de Musset's poems, or something akin to them.

(*Letters*, Vol. V, p. 177)

Her voice had returned. After that the writing went fast, although a fierce attack of illness (perhaps colitis) made her lose a precious two months' work when they returned to London. Lewes had negotiated a new publication scheme for the book, which was clearly going to be unusually long, and Blackwood brought it out in eight books which appeared between December 1871 and Christmas 1872. Avid readers awaited each instalment. Letters poured in from France, Germany and America and the plight of Dorothea figured large in private correspondence. Surely innumerable women and men over the past hundred years have shared the response of one of those first readers, Emily Dickinson: 'What do I think of *Middlemarch*?' she wrote in answer to a cousin's query . . . 'What do I think of glory?'[5]

If *Middlemarch* is glorious, it is about glory in the shade, burning souls dampened by the suffocating atmosphere of the English Midlands. So much is suggested by the title, with its connotations of compromise and mediocrity, of a narrow strip of territory between boundaries. Yet the society of Middlemarch is far from homogenous. The townsfolk are acutely aware of degrees of rank, subtleties of status and nets of kinship (acknowledged or not) and enter with gusto into the perpetual small-scale confrontations between Whig and Tory, church and chapel and land and business, or between doctors who believe in 'weakening' and others who believe in 'strengthening' remedies. Eliot presents all these with an ironic care. But her real interest is in the deeper conflict between those who accept or are at least reconciled to the constraints of Middlemarch, and those like Dorothea Brooke and Tertius Lydgate who aspire to a life which extends beyonds its limits.

The delicate meshing of one life with another in a complex community and the way that the natural balance of this small world is threatened by an energetic invasion of new ideas is one of the great themes of the novel. The text is sprinkled with references to inventors and explorers, whose names would mean little to the people of Middlemarch. But the feeling which prompts new ideas is more important still, as she was to explain in *Daniel Deronda*:

> even strictly-measuring science could hardly have got on without that forecasting ardour which feels the agitations of discovery beforehand, and has a faith in its preconception that surmounts many failures of experiment. And in relation to human motives and actions, passionate belief has a fuller efficacy. Here enthusiasm may have the validity of proof, and, happening in one soul, give the type of what will one day be general.
>
> (*Daniel Deronda*, Chap. 41, p. 572)

Middlemarch is the testing ground for Eliot's emotional elitism, her belief that the only effective power for personal and historical change is the power of feeling accompanied by insight (the recognition that everyone has their 'equivalent centres of self'). Its chief interest is therefore not with ordinary people but with 'great souls' who stand out as oddities because of their strength of feeling or, to use her own favourite word, their ardour. In the foreground stand two exceptional people (who quickly gain a reputation as cranks) who have recently arrived in the town, bringing with them ideas and ideals received abroad. Dorothea Brooke whose 'mind was theoretic and yearned by its nature after some lofty conception of the world which might frankly include the parish of Tipton and her own conduct there' is paralleled by Tertius Lydgate, preoccupied with research into the theory of a 'primitive tissue' which might link all human conditions and equally determined on professional reform. Both are doomed to frustration – defeated not only by Middlemarch society but by their own myopia. They cannot see where they step, as Dorothea's sister Celia points out. But they also cannot see what we, the readers, know from the start – that their greatest strength (and potentially their greatest weakness) is not their 'theoretic bent' but the way they let their judgement be swayed by their sympathies. The separate yet linked fates of Lydgate and Dorothea also offer a new model within Eliot's fiction for the way that men and women may feel about each other, a model of sisterhood which begins to express at a more abstract level the way that masculine and feminine qualities should complement, rather than contrast with, each other in society and within individual personalities.

Their stories are ones of defeat, or only partial victory. But although the town seems to win, and does expel its invaders, the course of events is never presented as wholly determined – people do make their own choices against the backdrop of history. (It is interesting that, however much they may fret, cajole, bully or plot – like Mrs Cadwallader – the older generation have virtually no influence upon the decisions of the younger.) The movement of history is not felt so immediately as in earlier novels – the town seems more stable, not threatened by images of catastrophe like the bankruptcies and floods of *The Mill on the Floss*, the Florentine wars of *Romola* or the riots of *Felix Holt*. The forceful transitions of the age enter instead as accidents which contribute to individual lives. We feel the current of great events running through the novel like the main stream of a river, but what we experience are the eddies near the bank on which we are placed as readers.

Yet, as in *Felix Holt*, we are made aware – by devices such as Dorothea's Puritan ancestry or Mr Brooke's random collection of pictures – that present attitudes are the result of past choices. When she is in Rome on her honeymoon with Mr Casaubon, Dorothea finds the weight of history in the art and buildings almost unendurable. The only people who can make sense of the profusion of styles are the allegorical painter Naumann (like Piero di Cosimo in *Romola*) and his friend, Casaubon's nephew Will Ladislaw. Will tells Dorothea that he came to terms with the city when he found that it 'made the mind flexible with constant comparison and saved you from seeing the world's ages as a set of box-like partitions without vital connection'. One of the pleasures (and penalties) of reading a book whose chief aim is also to abolish 'box-like partitions' – between ages, between people, between passions – is that it seems arbitrary to separate one story, or one aspect, from another. For the most engrossing aspect of *Middlemarch* is the way in which the stories are related so that different points of view are brought to bear upon each other and separate lives become inextricably intertwined. While our attention is absorbed in the fate of Dorothea, Fred and Mary, Lydgate and Rosamund, we come to feel that in some strange way the shifting and linking of their viewpoints and the ways they choose their understanding of the world have themselves become the subject of the novel. Their stories are inseparable – and the total combination is like a kaleidoscope which falls into different shapes depending on which organising pattern we choose.

Middlemarch dramatises the fact that in our lives there are many stories, each of which can have a different 'language'. These stories overlap, and can even compete so that we can almost watch ourselves taking part in our own dramas. Thus Lydgate, obsessed with Rosamund, knows what is happening but cannot stop himself:

He had two selves within him apparently, and they must learn to accommodate each other and bear reciprocal impediments. Strange, that some of us, with quick alternate vision, see beyond our infatuations, and even while we rave on the heights, behold the wide plain where our persistent self pauses and awaits us.

(*Middlemarch*, Chap. 15, p. 182)

Eliot's previous novels had always demonstrated division and complexity of view. In *Felix Holt*, the hero and heroine had longed for their passion for abstract principles to flow together with a sexual passion. They were uncomfortable because they felt two possibly opposing passions at once. This is a dilemma which Eliot develops in *Middlemarch* where she deliberately challenges the fictional convention which determines that 'passion' is only analysed romantically. The suggestion is that although plots may depend upon the 'lust' for power, the 'greed' for money or the 'thirst' for revenge, we rarely take these words at their face value and actually depict the physical excitement and emotional intensity of such desires as, for example, Casaubon's longing for the key to all mythologies. Even Joshua Rigg, an unknown outsider, can completely change the fate of the townsfolk because of his private dream:

The one joy after which his soul thirsted was to have a money-changer's shop on a much frequented quay, to have locks all around him of which he held the keys, and to look sublimely cool as he handled the breeding coins of all nations.

(*Middlemarch*, Chap. 53, p. 564)

This echoes Silas Marner, brooding over his coins as if they were unborn children. Such passions bring with them the same jealous possessiveness as romantic or parental love and George Eliot frequently suggests that the drive which is found in sex and procreation can inform an asexual ambition. So why, she asks, do we never tire of 'telling over and over again how a man comes to fall in love with a woman and be wedded to her, or else be fatally parted from her' yet are comparatively uninterested in an intellectual passion like Lydgate's? For:

In the story of this passion, too, the development varies: sometimes it is the glorious marriage, sometimes frustration and final parting. And not seldom the catastrophe is bound up with the other passion, sung by the Troubadours.

(*Middlemarch*, Chap. 15, p. 173)

This false separation is not only a literary problem – indeed, as Barbara Hardy has pointed out, it causes endless trouble to the inhabitants of Middlemarch.[6]

Yet men and women make different sorts of blunders. They are victims of the ideology which decrees that men and women should have different specialities, the women emotional, the men intellectual. Thus women, in accordance with the Romantic dictate, 'Man's love is of his life a thing apart, 'tis woman's whole existence', tend to blur the distinction between personal attachments and impersonal aims, or at least to see one as a means of achieving the other. Dorothea confuses her desire for learning with a feeling for Casaubon, and Rosamund Vincy mistakes her social aspirations for an attraction to Lydgate. Ironically, both are also deluded in their belief that their husbands *can* gratify these other needs – or any needs at all in Casaubon's case. Men, on the other hand, believe that the serious 'male' business of life is something which cannot possibly be affected by a personal relationship. Yet Lydgate sees his intellectual passion corroded by the slide into compromise and debt which follows his marriage to Rosamund, and Casaubon transfers his anxiety about his historical work into a feverish resentment and jealousy of his young wife – the latter being the more bearable sort of pain.

The men make the more fundamental error in believing that they can keep their work, their religious practice or their politics in a separate compartment. The most moving victim of this mistake is the banker Bulstrode, who believes he can obliterate (and even justify) his sins of omission in the past by his virtuous public actions in the present. But his split reasoning is frequently echoed by other men: not even Lydgate can be entirely unconscious of irony when he pronounces:

'a man may work for a special end with others whose motives and general course are equivocal, if he is quite sure of his personal independence, and that he is not working for his private interest – either place or money.'

(*Middlemarch*, Chap. 46, p. 507)

No one can claim independence of this kind. They have to recognise the way they are led by unacknowledged desires – Will Ladislaw, for example, works for Mr Brooke not because he approves of his politics but because he loves his niece. They also have to accept that their actions form part of a chain and are inescapably affected by the strength of the other links. Eliot thus makes fun of stereotypes of men and women, while using her analysis to make general points about the muddles that can arise when we are inadequately aware of our own emotions. This is one way in which this curiously sly, androgynous book – which illuminates with uncanny credibility the dark mental corners of both men and women – is shaped by Eliot's thinking on the subject of definitions of women.

The influence of her feminist analysis permeates the novel in many other ways. First, as in *Felix Holt*, our judgement of a man's general approach to life (ethical, political or religious) is often directed by what he thinks about women; while women reveal themselves in the way they see their own position. All too often they show the same dangerous tendency to simplify and to compartmentalise. Part of George Eliot's aim is, in contrast, to celebrate diversity, to pick out the cygnet among the ducks, and to deny the existence of a norm. She makes this clear when she writes in the Prelude of the puzzle set by idealistic women who can find no outlet for their ambitions:

Some have felt that these blundering lives are due to the inconvenient indefiniteness with which the Supreme Power has fashioned the natures of women: if there were one level of feminine incompetence as strict as the ability to count three and no more, the social lot of women might be treated with scientific certitude.

(*Middlemarch*, Prelude, pp. 25–6)

What she strives after in *Middlemarch* and *Daniel Deronda* is a mode of perception which is at once accurate, like the microscope, and can yet contain contradiction and ambiguity, like the imagination, and a language which can adequately embody such refined perception. On several occasions she suggests that it is not outward events so much as the internal language we use to interpret experience which creates our universe. Thus:

Miss Brooke argued from words and dispositions not less unhesitatingly than other young ladies of her age. Signs are small measurable things, but interpretations are illimitable.

(*Middlemarch*, Chap. 3, p. 47)

And Lydgate's experience shows that people can be signs themselves as well as interpreters:

For surely all must admit that a man may be puffed and belauded,
envied, ridiculed, counted upon as a tool and fallen in love with, or at
least selected as a future husband, and yet remain virtually unknown –
known merely as a cluster of signs for his neighbours' false suppositions.

(*Middlemarch*, Chap. 15, p. 171)

Middlemarch asks us to compare different ways of interpret-
ing life – by balancing against each other the descriptions
provided, for example, by gossip, science, religion, biology and
physics, poetry and art. (One indicator of Dorothea's potential
for spiritual growth is her openness to new languages, whether
it be Greek, or the 'strange language' of Renaissance art.) And
the testing ground for all these languages is invariably 'the
nature of woman,' a subject which all male Middlemarchers feel
competent to pronounce on, yet on which they always end by
admitting defeat. Mr Brooke declares for certain that women are
too 'flighty' and can't think (whenever they attack his own
hopeless vagueness), but ends by labelling them as incomprehensible to the ordinary rational man: 'In short, woman was a
problem which, since Mr Brooke's mind felt blank before it,
could be hardly less complicated than the revolutions of an
irregular solid.' Sir James Chettam condescendingly decides that
Dorothea would make a good wife and that he could always
control her tendency to impose her own ideas:

Why not? A man's mind – what there is of it – has always the
advantage of being masculine – as the smallest birch tree is of a higher
kind than the most soaring palm – and even his ignorance is of a
sounder quality. Sir James might not have originated this estimate; but
a kind Providence furnishes the limpest personality with a little gum or
starch in the form of tradition.

(*Middlemarch*, Chap. 3, p. 44)

Within pages he is rendered speechless by her decision to marry

Casaubon, but soon turns to her sister Celia who, as his mother says, 'is more docile and fonder of geraniums'.

Within the novel stereotypes vary from Casaubon's ideal of a self-sacrificing help-meet (parodied by the Middlemarch wisdom of Mr Trumble who says a man should 'always marry a nurse'), to the romantic dreams of Lydgate. His fate would be comic if its consequences were not so tragic, for it reveals how little he knows about himself, as well as how little he knows about women. He happily disconnects himself from one half of womankind while falling a hopeless victim to the other. His judgement, which he expresses so epigrammatically, is hopelessly superficial: 'Plain women he regarded as he did the other severe facts of life, to be faced with philosophy and investigated by science' (Chap. 11, p. 121), for he cannot see the beauty of the 'plain' Dorothea or Mary Garth. He claims to learn from his experience with the actress Laure but, despite his insistence that from henceforth he will take a strictly 'scientific' view of women, he remains blind to any connection between his science and his private life. There is wonderful comedy in the way he leaves his 'frogs and rabbits to some repose under their trying and mysterious dispensation of unexplained shocks', only to watch Laure casually murder her husband on stage; or returns to his laboratory, after being so skilfully manipulated by Rosamund that he is 'melted like a jelly-fish without knowing it', to check on an experiment in 'maceration' (Chap. 27, p. 305). Lydgate sees his romance with Rosamund as a fairy tale or an 'Arabian Night' and ignores the other side of the romantic myth, where women are *femmes fatales* who lure men to destruction.

If the men are the dupes of simple stereotypes, so are the women. Dorothea, seduced by reading the lives of Milton and Pascal, believes that truth lies solely 'in the province of masculine knowledge'; Rosamund, immersed in French novels and Byronic verse, sees Lydgate as 'a man whom it would be delightful to enslave'. Their error is made clear by Mary Garth who is free from such illusions. For although she too reads widely, from Shakespeare to Scott and George Sand, when Fred comes out with the cliché that 'It is always some new fellow who strikes a girl', she makes fun of people who take their analyses of sexual behaviour from literature and, moreover, only from one kind of plot:

'Let me see,' said Mary, the corners of her mouth curling archly; 'I must go back on my experience. There is Juliet – she seems an example of what you say. But then Ophelia had probably known Hamlet a long while. . . . Waverley was new to Flora MacIvor; but then she did not fall in love with him. And there are Olivia and Sophia Primrose, and Corinne – they may be said to have fallen in love with new men. Altogether, my experience is rather mixed.'

(*Middlemarch*, Chap. 14, p. 167)

Not surprisingly, it is in the Garth household, where Mrs Garth teaches the children while up to her elbows in dough, that the issue of female equality will be argued explicitly – not by Mary but by the younger children Ben (who is happy in the superiority of muscle-power) and Letty ('who argued much from books'). But we are told that their dispute takes place long after the story finishes, for active feminism in Middlemarch would be an anachronism. The narrator looks back from the debates of the 1860s to the dilemma of women in the 1830s who lacked the arguments to back up their sense of unease. This dilemma is encapsulated towards the end of the novel when Dorothea decides to help Lydgate face out the ugly rumours that he may have helped Bulstrode to get rid of the blackmailer Raffles by funding his work at the hospital. Her decision brings out all the prejudices of Brooke and Chettam against women's independent action. Even Mr Farebrother, who does under-stand the healing power of feminine sympathy, advises caution, while Celia plainly recommends that she should let Sir James think for her:

'He lets you have your plans, only he hinders you from being taken in. And that is the good of having a brother instead of a husband. A husband would not let you have your plans.'
'As if I wanted a husband!' said Dorothea. 'I only want not to have

my feelings checked at every turn.' Mrs Casaubon was still undisciplined enough to burst into angry tears.

'Now, really, Dodo,' said Celia, with rather a deeper guttural than usual, 'you *are* contradictory: first one thing and then another. You used to submit to Mr Casaubon quite shamefully: I think you would have given up ever coming to see me if he had asked you.'

'Of course I submitted to him, because it was my duty; it was my feeling for him,' said Dorothea, looking through the prism of her tears.

'Then why can't you think it your duty to submit a little to what James wishes?' said Celia, with a sense of stringency in her argument. 'Because he only wishes what is for your own good. And, of course men know best about everything, except what women know better.'

Dorothea laughed and forgot her tears.

'Well, I mean about babies and those things,' explained Celia. 'I should not give up to James when I knew he was wrong, as you used to do to Mr Casaubon.'

(Middlemarch, Chap. 72, p. 792)

Alas, how can Dorothea win? Behind the humour of this exercise in logic (and the old joke about letting men make all the important decisions and the women the minor ones like the children's education) lies a serious point. Celia, a skilled pragmatist, divides life neatly into zones of influence, but for Dorothea life is more complicated. Duty is not a matter of rules or form, but of *feeling*. Feeling alone gives rise to principles. She acts towards Lydgate, as Esther acted at Felix Holt's trial, out of a sense of inner necessity rather than from a carefully argued position. She remains an innocent, a kind of inspired idiot, and 'childlike' is the word Eliot uses to describe her at her moments of greatest influence. Her basic impulses are usually right, but what she has to learn in order to avoid mistakes is not to oversimplify, to sort out the different *kinds* of feelings which sweep through her so that she can distinguish between selfish desire and identification with the needs of others.

Eliot makes the point general by linking her heroine to two contrasting images of passionate women: Ariadne and Antigone. The first is the embodiment of loving self-sacrifice and physical awakening; the second of rebellious struggle and sisterly loyalty. Both figures had great attraction for Eliot and she had combined them before, in *Romola*.[7] The two images fuse in *Middlemarch* when Dorothea is in Rome and is spotted by Naumann, who calls Ladislaw to come and look at her as she stands where 'the reclining Ariadne, then called the Cleopatra, lies in the marble voluptuousness of her beauty'. Naumann, struck by the contrast between her Quaker-like dress and the sensuous statue, demands that Will should see her as 'antique form animated by Christian sentiment – a sort of Christian Antigone – sensuous force controlled by spiritual passion' (Chap. 19, p. 221).

Ladislaw objects to the reduction of a living creature to the fixity of a work of art. He demands for Dorothea the right which Esther claimed in *Felix Holt* when she refused to be identified with the aristocratic portraits of Transome Court; the right to be an actor, not an object, and to speak for herself.

Will turns this into an argument for ranking literature above the plastic arts:

Language gives a fuller image, which is all the better for being vague. After all, the true seeing is within; and painting stares at you with an insistent imperfection. I feel that especially about representations of women. As if a woman were a mere coloured superficies! You must wait for movement and tone. There is a difference in their very breathing: they change from moment to moment. This woman whom you have just seen, for example: how would you paint her voice, pray? But her voice is much diviner than anything you have seen of her.

(Middlemarch, Chap. 19, p. 222)

But Naumann is also partly right, for the use of allegory gives a universal relevance to a single image (without it we might be lost in particularities) and Eliot often avails herself of this subtle form of generalisation. The Ariadne–Antigone contrast also illuminates her ideas about the 'revolutionary' potential of female passion. The real name of the Ariadne statue is not known to Dorothea or to the two men, but it is known to the reader, who can interpret the references with the advantage of history (like the feminist import of the book as a whole).

Dorothea had wanted to help her husband out of the labyrinths of his scholarship (as Ariadne helped Theseus). Although she failed, because he would not accept her help, the second part of the story still applies – just as Theseus abandoned his bride on Naxos, so Casaubon abandons Dorothea in Rome in favour of his musty libraries (his other passion). He abandons her in other ways as well, nervously rejecting every physical overture and emotional advance as evidence of her behaving in 'a most unaccountable, darkly feminine manner'. The pain of Dorothea's rejected tenderness and the loneliness of their mutual misunderstanding in Italy and back in England is hauntingly real. That it is not an isolated experience is illustrated by the semicomic plight of Rosamund, who is certainly loved physically, when Lydgate fails to live up to her social expectations:

She felt that she was beginning to know the pangs of disappointed love . . . Poor Rosamund lost her appetite and felt as forlorn as Ariadne – as a charming stage Ariadne left behind with all her boxes full of costumes and no hope of a coach.

(*Middlemarch*, Chap. 31, p. 334)

In Rome Casaubon even shies away from taking Dorothea to see the frescoes of Cupid and Psyche, 'probably the romantic invention of a literary period'. Little does Casaubon know that, as Bacchus/Cupid rescued Ariadne, so a deliverer will appear for Dorothea in the person of Will, the absolute embodiment of light and change. Even 'the little ripple in his nose was a preparation for metamorphosis. When he turned his head quickly his hair seemed to shake out light, and some persons thought they saw decided genius in this coruscation. Mr Casaubon, on the contrary, stood rayless' (Chap. 21, p. 241). Like Tito, another Bacchus figure seizing Romola from the dark library of her father, Will gradually frees Dorothea's imprisoned sensuality, first by making her appreciate the rich art of Rome and then by winning her love. For Dorothea, as for Maggie Tulliver and Romola, this is a necessary stage in her growth. She has to become an Ariadne before she can become an Antigone: sensuous force controlled by spiritual passion.

Naumann can feel this spiritual passion just as he can deduce her hidden sensuality. Sophocles' Antigone (the most admired classical heroine of European Romanticism) had been a potent symbol for Eliot even before she reviewed a text of the *Antigone* in March 1856, at the very start of her career as a novelist.[8] For Eliot the significance of the play lay in the way that 'impulses of affection and religion' led Antigone to disobey Creon's proclamation against the burial of her beloved brother Polynices; 'the impulse of sisterly piety which allies itself with reverence for the Gods, clashes with the duties of citizenship; two principles, both having their validity, are at war with each' (*Essays*, p. 263).

There are no neat equations in Eliot's novels, which are rich in their fluctuating assessments of conflicting duties. But each heroine at some point feels herself to be an Antigone, when inner promptings conflict with the 'legality' of rules. Interestingly, in her own life, and in much of her fiction, the brother (in *The Mill on the Floss*) or his mentor (Savonarola in *Romola*) is the Creon figure who insists on the value of rigid codes. The brother rejects the love she offers and sides with society against her, making the conflict of loyalties even worse.

But in the years immediately preceding *Middlemarch*, George Eliot had brooded much on the brother–sister relationship, and had written her 'Brother and Sister Sonnets'. Recapturing summer days by the canal at Griff, they show all the tensions of her childhood relationship with Isaac and yet suggest that this experience of separate beings growing side by side *should* be an education in sympathy, even for the brother:

> Thus boyish Will the nobler mastery learned
> Where inward vision over impulse reigns,
> Widening its life with separate life discerned,
> A Like unlike, a Self that self restrains.
>
> (*Poems*, p. 205)

As she wrote to John Blackwood, 'life might be so enriched if that relationship were made the most of, as one of the highest forms of friendship'. After the writing of the sonnets, the hard, bitter sons and brothers vanish from her fiction. They are

replaced in *Middlemarch* by Mr Farebrother (the name is significant) or by good-natured, teasing Fred Vincy, and in *Daniel
Deronda* by the gentle Hans Meyrick, Mordecai Cohen and Rex
Gascoigne. Yet there is always a wry awareness of the way that
these brothers take precedence, in education, in the way they are
free to go out into the world, even in the food they eat.

Middlemarch is imbued with the idea of sisterhood, but it is a
sisterhood where women lead the way and it is often combined
with a lover-like tension. Ariadne and Antigone mingle. The
idea of the sister is there in the slow growing love of Fred and
Mary Garth; in the way Dorothea, like the sister who remains at
home, directs Will's passage in the wider world, and in the bond
between Dorothea and Lydgate, alike and yet separate – the
dreaming girl slightly jealous of the boy's chance to put into
practice the plans which she cherishes. Dorothea's instinctive
appeal to their companionship, as children of their age, is felt by
the bewildered Lydgate in her cry for his help at the time of
Casaubon's fatal illness:

For years after Lydgate remembered the impression produced in him
by this involuntary appeal – this cry from soul to soul, without other
consciousness than their moving with kindred natures in the same
embroiled medium, the same troublous fitfully-illuminated life.

(*Middlemarch*, Chap. 30, p. 324)

It is the defeat of his kindred soul which makes Dorothea finally
speak out, as Antigone stood fast after her brother's death, but
also as Esther speaks out at Felix's trial.

This is no 'buried meaning' but something which George
Eliot herself makes clear in the Prelude and in the Finale to her
book. St Theresa does not set out alone but is 'the little girl
walking forth one morning with her still smaller brother'. Both
children are turned back by domestic reality. The last page
returns to the lost ideal of sisterhood, which can be seen as the
pattern for women's achievement: 'A new Theresa will hardly
have the opportunity of reforming a conventual life, any more
than a new Antigone will spend her heroic piety in daring all for
the sake of a brother's burial: the medium in which their ardent

deeds took shape is forever gone' (Finale, p. 896). The mention of St Theresa and convents reminds us that sisterhood, unlike the Victorian norm of sexual love, can be a very flexible, open model. It is another way that *Middlemarch* escapes the trap of simplicity. Antigone had a sister too, and Sophocles' play opens with an appeal to sisterly feeling (although Ismene, like Celia, cannot follow her sister in her rebellion). Dorothea's most heroic action is a gesture of sisterhood towards both a man and a woman, when she goes to plead Lydgate's cause with his wife, even though she is racked by jealousy because she believes Rosamund is having an affair with Will. Her decision to do this follows a miserable dark night of the soul and is presented in appropriately mythic, ritualistic terms:

And what sort of crisis might not this be in three lives whose contact with hers laid an obligation on her as if they had been supplicants bearing the sacred branch? The objects of her rescue were not to be sought out by her fancy: they were chosen for her. She yearned towards the perfect Right, that it might make a throne within her, and rule her errant will.

(Middlemarch, Chap.80, p. 846)

Immediately afterwards she opens her eyes in the pearly dawn on an elemental scene: 'on the road there was a man with a bundle on his back and a woman carrying her baby; in the field she could see figures moving – perhaps the shepherd with his dog.' She knows that she can no longer remain a spectator, but must participate in the 'involuntary, palpitating life' of humanity.

Despite her talent for sympathy Dorothea has always felt out of place, a bemused spectator:

The dream-like association of something alien and ill-understood with the deepest secrets of her experience seemed to mirror that sense of loneliness which was due to the very ardour of Dorothea's nature.

(Middlemarch, Chap. 34, p. 360)

In the scene with Rosamund, which takes her across social as well as personal barriers, she finds, at the deepest level, that she can feel with someone completely different from herself. She discovers in herself the mysterious power which flowed through Dinah when she preached in *Adam Bede*, and through Esther in court. The strength of her feeling streams over all the 'obstructions' and fears in Rosamund's mind, and the waves of sorrow and emotion carry them over the boundaries of speech, to that wordless kiss which stamps the crises of George Eliot's fiction from 'Janet's Repentance' to *Daniel Deronda*. Rosamund 'could find no words, but involuntarily she put her lips to Dorothea's forehead which was very near her, and then for a minute the two women clasped each other as if they had been in a shipwreck' (Chap. 81, p. 856).[9] John Cross's life of George Eliot supplies a fascinating insight into this scene; the sense of a powerful force coming from without, the removal of alienation and the mysterious loss of self in another is both its subject and a description of what Eliot herself felt while writing it. Dorothea's passion is, therefore, at one with the sympathetic imagination of the artist.[10]

After the scene with Rosamund a second emotional storm soon follows, as Dorothea and Will stand in the library with the thunder and rain battling melodramatically outside:

'Oh, I cannot bear it – my heart will break,' said Dorothea, starting from her seat, the flood of her young passion bearing down all the obstructions which had kept her silent – the great tears rising and falling in an instant: 'I don't mind about poverty – I hate my wealth.'

(*Middlemarch*, Chap. 83, p. 870)

In *The Mill on the Floss* Maggie's youthful passion had swept her and her brother to death, the fragments of the broken wharves along the banks of the river bearing down upon them. At the end of *Middlemarch*, despite its regretful negatives, the channels of Dorothea's feeling bear her influence on in a complicated 'incalculable' pattern – dispersed but not destroyed by barriers and obstructions of a society run by men – as the Euphrates was diverted when Cyrus built his imperial city. She is called back into the ranks of ordinary womanhood but, as a fictional character, she will always retain her own strong identity; she may be 'only known in a certain circle as a wife and mother', but in the memory of readers she remains the powerful model of a passionate sister, defiant of authority. Denied a vocation by her age she must remain potential. The negatives of the ending are, like photographic negatives, the shadow of a positive. For in the end what we are asked to recognise in Dorothea, and in all 'great-souled women', is not their achievement but their capacity, the incalculable quality which can survive even the direst historical constraints. Evading all 'scientific' definitions and sloughing off the labels of property and prejudice, their spirit can be conveyed only through myth and poetry, the only languages which suggest the true measure of female power.

CHAPTER THIRTEEN

DANIEL DERONDA: THE FRONTIERS OF SELF

September 1872 found the Leweses on the Continent again, for they left as soon as they had read the proofs of Book VIII of *Middlemarch* to relax in the German spa towns of which they had become so fond. From Homburg Marian sent Blackwood the Finale to her great novel and, almost simultaneously, wrote a letter anticipating the start of her next: *Daniel Deronda*. Writing to Mrs Cross, whom she had met in Rome in 1869, she described her reaction to the gaming rooms of the Kursaal, which she had visited with their friends the Baron and Baroness Castletown, their daughters Mrs Wingfield and Lady Murray and Lady Murray's diplomat husband. Although the company she was in was distinguished, the Kursaal itself was a vision of horror:

The air, the waters, the plantations are all perfect – 'only man is vile'. I am not fond of denouncing my fellow-sinners, but gambling being a vice I have no mind to it stirs my disgust even more than my pity. The sight of the dull faces bending round the gaming tables, the raking-up of the money and the flinging of the coins towards the winners by the hard-faced croupiers, the hateful, hideous women staring at the board like stupid monomaniacs – all this seems to me the most abject presentation of mortals grasping after something that can be called a good, that can be seen on the face of this earth . . . Hell is the only right name for such places.

(Letters, Vol. V, p. 312)

Monomania, egotism, desperate grasping, obsession – all would be explored in *Daniel Deronda*. And in Homburg, as it was to do in the novel, her terrible sense of danger focused on one young woman – Byron's great-niece Geraldine Leigh. Lewes recorded in his journal how 'feverish and excited' Miss Leigh looked as hundreds of pounds slipped from her, and Marian wrote to Blackwood: 'It made me cry to see her fresh face among the hags and brutally stupid men around her' (*Letters*, Vol. V, p. 314).

Her concern may have been intensified by the responsibility she now felt towards several younger women who looked to her as a confidante and mentor. They included Elma Stuart, who showered her with letters and gifts and when she died, was buried beside her in Highgate cemetery. Elma's tombstone is inscribed 'whom for 8½ blessed years George Eliot called by the sweet name of "Daughter" '. But, as Haight points out, Elma was not the only 'spiritual daughter'.[1] Marian had been used to arousing intense emotions in women since her youthful friendship with Maria Lewis. Her correspondence with Sara Hennell, Cara Bray, Barbara Bodichon and Maria Congreve, her friend of Wandsworth days, bear witness to the strength of these relationships. All these friends were strong, accomplished women and so were her more recent, younger admirers. They included Georgie Burne Jones, Emilia Pattison, now a distinguished art historian, Mrs Ponsonby, a stylish figure at Court, and the remarkable Edith Simcox, a scholar of renown and a determined feminist, trades unionist and educational campaigner.

Marian enjoyed the role of mother for the tenderness it allowed her to express, as she explained apologetically to Emilia Pattison in 1869:

I feared after you had left us that I had allowed myself an effusiveness (of that dumb sort which is the more apt to come when one has not full opportunity of speech) beyond what was warranted by the short time we had known each other. But in proportion as I profoundly rejoice that I never brought a child into the world, I am conscious of having an unused stock of motherly tenderness, which sometimes overflows, but not without discrimination.

(Letters, Vol. V, p. 52)

Beyond Marian's maternal warmth and personal charm, she embodied for this group a vision of possible achievements outside the normal limits and constraints imposed on women's lives. Her influence was therefore, on the whole, inspiring. But with her talent for drawing forth people's most intimate feelings she also found herself constantly playing the part of patient listener, receiving hidden fears and insecurities. Something of her impatience, as well as her sympathy, with the dependency of her spiritual daughters is expressed in the picture that *Daniel Deronda* shows of the disabling side of mother-fixation, the need for daughters, and sons, to take responsibility for their own lives. In the novel Gwendolen, Daniel and Mirah are driven in different ways by reliance on the idea of the 'mother' only to find that, in reality, their mothers are weak, rejecting or dead – absent presences in their lives. Real help comes from friends, brothers or lovers, who force them to examine their own needs.[2]

Marian's impatience comes across very clearly in Edith Simcox's vivid memoir when she describes a scene shortly after Lewes's death, when Marian felt bound to check Edith's fervour by gently explaining:

that she cared for the womanly ideal, sympathised with women and liked for them to come to her in their troubles, but while feeling near to them in one way, she felt far off in another – the friendship and intimacy of men was more to her. Then she tried to add what I had already imagined in explanation that when she was young, girls and women seemed to look on her as somehow 'uncanny' while men were always kind.[3]

Admittedly this explanation was forced out of her when Edith was trying to burn 'holes in her cheeks' with kisses, but it remains true that, apart from Barbara, she kept slightly aloof from her women friends however much she valued their affection.

The adulation which followed the success of *Middlemarch* was almost too overwhelming and from 1872 the Leweses retreated frequently to the Continent, and to the English countryside, looking busily for a country house of their own. Now accepted into society by virtue of her fame, Marian became increasingly irritated by the arrogance of the English upper classes, so evident in the growing concentration on Empire. Her dismay was fostered not only by her long-standing championship of European culture, especially German and French literature, but also by her new interest in Hebrew studies which followed her friendship with Emmanuel Deutsch, a Silesian scholar and emigré whom she first met in 1866. Deutsch, a gentle invalid much loved by many of the London intelligentsia, had become fired (like Mordecai) with the dream of a Jewish homeland in the Levant. He died on his second visit to the Middle East in Alexandria in 1873.

That same summer of 1873 found Marian developing her plans for her new novel, which she had begun to sketch out the previous winter. When she heard of Deutsch's death she was already busy with close research into Jewish history, and her careful work ensured that the sympathetic picture of Jewish culture was to win the support of Jews throughout the world. As she knew it would, it was also to alienate many British readers, especially when contrasted with the completely satirical portrait of English landed society. But part of her aim, as she told Harriet Beecher Stowe, was precisely to shatter this British complacency:

not only towards the Jews, but towards all oriental peoples with whom we English come in contact, a spirit of arrogance and contemptuous dictatorialness is observable which has become a national disgrace to us. There is nothing I should care more to do, if it were possible, than to rouse the imagination of men and women to a vision of human claims in those races of their fellow-men who most differ from them in customs and beliefs.

(*Letters*, Vol. VI, pp. 301–2)

The prejudice against and ignorance of a culture which was fundamental to their own alleged beliefs she felt to be 'a sign of the intellectual narrowness – in plain English, the stupidity, which is still the average mark of our culture'.

Her research into Judaeism took her to the synagogue at Mainz in the summer of 1873 and was balanced by a search for the correct location for her English characters the following year. In September 1874 the Leweses visited the grand Wiltshire houses of Bowood, Lacock Abbey, Corsham Court and Savernake Forest, scenes which were to provide the landscape in which Gwendolen and Deronda were to feel such outsiders. Once the scene was set her writing progressed smoothly. It was, however, broken by bouts of extreme pain from the kidney stone which had troubled her since 1874, and which returned with great severity in March and May of 1875. She was often prostrated with pain, taking opiates and hot baths, cared for lovingly by Lewes. In June he found them a peaceful house for the summer, The Elms, near Rickmansworth, and here they settled down to long mornings of work, followed by drives and walks. But a further great sadness came their way when they learnt that Bertie had died of tubercular fever in Natal.

Over the winter and spring Marian wrote on. Lewes was working on a further volume of his own innovative psychological study, *Problems of Life and Mind*, but he dealt as usual with all her business and publishing arrangements. As with *Middlemarch*, the first books of *Daniel Deronda* were published before the end was written and the novel appeared in eight parts between February and September 1876. The last words were written on 8 June. That same afternoon the packing was done and, after calling on Blackwood, who found her looking 'pale and tired in her carriage at the door', Marian and Lewes set off once more across the Channel, such a significant frontier in their lives.

Daniel Deronda is a novel about boundaries – their usefulness in ordering chaos, their danger in restricting freedom – and about the ambivalence we feel about crossing thresholds. It is an enormously bold, multi-layered book which plays even with the traditional ordering of time in fiction. In telling the story of a man and a woman, Daniel Deronda and Gwendolen Harleth, whose quite separate lives touch and influence each other's destiny, Eliot dramatises her theme at a variety of levels – from the physical frontiers of nations and the social limitations of law and custom, to the bridge between reality and fantasy and the precarious borderlines within the individual psyche. The acts of novel-writing and reading themselves become ways of abolishing frontiers, as Eliot enters with equal sympathy into the minds of both sexes and incorporates all her readers, with all their differences, in her generous authorial 'we'. In the end the novel asks questions about the subjectivity of experience, and questions how, if we all inhabit our own worlds, we can cross the boundaries which separate soul from soul and make general rules which will allow us to act for the best in the future.

To represent the conflict between the human need to label and control and the threat this ordering poses to tolerance and understanding, George Eliot makes subtle use of the imagery of 'masculine' and 'feminine' characteristics which she had first formulated in *The Lifted Veil*. At its most formulaic the opposition is this: masculine equals hard, arid, rigid, rule-bound, individualistic, 'scientific'; while feminine equals soft, fluid, flexible, tolerant, self-suppressing and 'poetic'. The continuity of these patterns in Eliot's fiction is illustrated by the way that Prague, the shade-less landscape dominated by stone statues of symbolic fathers in *The Lifted Veil*, reappears in *Daniel Deronda* as the 'scorching' city from which Mirah flees from her real father, the aptly named Lapidoth.

But in this last novel, as in *The Lifted Veil*, or in *Silas Marner* and *Felix Holt*, Eliot avoids a crude equation of masculine and feminine characteristics by making her 'good' feminine character a man – Daniel Deronda himself. His feminine receptivity is contrasted to the 'bad' feminine character of Gwendolen, warped by her education and by the ideology of women which it enshrines. Furthermore, the greatest impersonation of female power in *Daniel Deronda*, the opera singer Alchirisi, is also the most masculine in her insistence on individual rights and her insulation from the claims of law and community. In such ways does the novel itself fight to escape the narrow structures of false stereotypes and easy definitions.

In *Daniel Deronda* the reader is always asked to look at people and events from new angles, and to embrace a 'wider vision' of life. Indeed one of its most dizzying, difficult, exhilarating features is the variation in perspective and scale. It is George Eliot's boldest attempt to track intimate private history to the almost unconscious depths of personality and yet relate it at the same time to the general experience of men and women, to the worldwide sweep of historical progress and to the universal suggestiveness of art, folk-tale and myth. The opening epigraph acknowledges the difficulty of the attempt, for it directs us to the arbitrary nature of any story-telling, whether it be in the language of science, 'the strict measurer', or 'his less accurate grandmother', poetry, and it points to the artificiality of time itself as a way of ordering experience. Although 'Man can do nothing without the make-believe of a beginning', we are always, she suggests, *in medias res*.

The epigraph to Chapter 16, which describes the 'make-believe' of Daniel Deronda's youth, makes similar disturbing switches between the intimate and the universal:

Men, like planets, have both a visible and an invisible history. The astronomer threads the darkness with strict deduction, accounting so for every visible arc in the wanderer's orbit; and the narrator of human actions, if he did his work with the same completeness, would have to thread the hidden pathways of feeling and thought which lead up to every moment of action, and to those moments of intense suffering which take the quality of action – like the cry of Prometheus, whose chained anguish seems a greater energy than the sea and sky he invokes and the deity he defies.

(*Daniel Deronda*, Chap. 16, p. 202)

Again and again in the course of the novel we are swung between microscopic attention to detail and huge vistas. The way that the Meyrick family in their crowded cottage can yet see the 'star of the Great Bear' from their back window is like the way that the books the Meyrick girls read can give glimpses across centuries, as Kate says of *Histoire d'un Conscrit*: 'It is a bit of history brought near us with a strong telescope. We can see the soldiers' faces: no, it is more than that – we can hear everything – we can almost hear their hearts beat' (Chap. 18, p. 239).

By these contrasts the novel poses a question which must beset us all at some time – how can it be, when space and time make the individual as insignificant as a dot on a page, that a personal event like an unhappy marriage can be so overwhelming as to blot out the sun? We feel this with an oppressive weight when Gwendolen is trapped by Grandcourt. She has married him despite her moral qualms because she believed he could free her widowed mother, her sisters and herself from financial anxiety. Instead she finds herself in a throttling, suffocating battle for domination and her life becomes completely absorbed by a mixture of fear and hatred and by the desire for escape by any means. Gliding on his yacht in the Mediterranean her whole world is reduced to a 'tiny plank island' encircled by the sea, cutting her off from human contact. Between her and the wide horizon looms the figure of Grandcourt – he not only blocks her view but becomes the very medium through which she sees, clouding all her judgements like a miasma.

Eliot makes us actually feel the way that personal experience affects physical and moral perception. Objectivity vanishes, for the world is seen always from *within*, from the opening moment when the reader is made to share the questions which dart through Daniel's mind as he watches Gwendolen at the roulette table. Nothing, not even physical objects, remain untouched by the distorting perspective of individual feeling; the necklace which Grandcourt's mistress Lydia Glasher returns to Gwendolen on her wedding night seems to swarm with the venom of her accompanying curse. When Gwendolen tries desperately *not* to think constantly about how she can escape from her marriage we are told that the effort is

like trying to talk down the singing in her own ears. The thought that is bound up with our passion is as penetrative as air – everything is porous to it; bows, smiles, conversation, repartee, are mere honeycombs, where such thought rushes freely, not always with a taste of honey.

(*Daniel Deronda*, Chap. 48, p. 664)

But although feeling can thus flood through material reality and daily life, paradoxically, because we all feel differently we each still live in different and separate worlds. In *Daniel Deronda*, as in *Middlemarch*, we are forced to confront the variability and loneliness of experience, even in the closest relationships; we experience time differently, we think at different speeds, even our consciences 'are the voice of sensibilities as various as our memories (which also have their kinship and likeness)' (Chap. 41, p. 570). Daniel puts it at its simplest when he tells Gwendolen, 'experience differs for different people. We don't all wince at the same things' (Chap. 45, p. 624).

At times the reiteration seems a statement of the obvious, but in due course the repeated patterns of kinship and diversity (which are expressed in the story itself by family and racial groupings of characters) lead to greater and greater complexity. When all experience is acknowledged to be relative the problem becomes one of moral distinction: how can one impose standards of judgement which will enable one to take the right actions?

The issue becomes more complex still when Eliot turns her attention to the feelings which shape the outlines of our subjective worlds. For these too begin to shift and slide, evading definition by simple labels such as 'love', 'jealousy', 'anger' or 'fear'. In *Middlemarch* she had lamented the lack of a vocabulary subtle enough to evoke the whole spectrum of emotions of love and desire. We continue to feel this lack in *Daniel Deronda*, with its subtle variety of emotional groupings, as intense between men (Deronda and Mordecai, Grandcourt and Lush) and between women (Lydia and Gwendolen) as between the sexes. The forms love takes are unpredictable. Even the jousting for power between Gwendolen and Grandcourt, we are told, has such magnetism that in its early stages it might be called a kind of love. But is it doomed to decline into a repetition of the intense, lingering feeling between Grandcourt and Lydia, circling each other with 'caressing signs of mutual fear'.

Lydia Glasher is torn between her desire for revenge and her need to keep Grandcourt sweet so that their son may remain his heir: 'The two dominant passions were at struggle. She must satisfy them both' (Chap. 30, p. 397). Like all the principal characters in this novel, with the exception of the 'stagnant', monolithic Grandcourt, Lydia feels mixed passions rather than a single cut-and-dried emotion. Grandcourt's one weakness, which leads to his downfall, is his inability to appreciate the multiple strands in Lydia's feeling, or later in Gwendolen's; for, says Eliot, 'there is no escaping the fact that want of sympathy condemns us to a corresponding stupidity. Mephistopheles thrown upon real life, and obliged to manage his own plots, would inevitably make blunders' (Chap. 48, p. 658). Openness to complexity is openness to the essence of life and it is the story-teller's duty to make plots which avoid the blunders of over-simplification. But too much openness can swamp one complete-ly – this is the fate described in *The Lifted Veil* and in the famous lines from *Middlemarch*:

That element of tragedy which lies in the very fact of frequency has not yet wrought itself into the coarse emotions of mankind; and perhaps our frames could hardly bear much of it. If we had a keen vision and feeling of all ordinary human life, it would be like hearing the grass grow and the squirrel's heart beat, and we should die of that roar which lies on the other side of silence. As it is, the quickest of us walk about well wadded with stupidity.

(*Middlemarch*, Chap. 20, p. 226)

While sympathy is essential for fine distinction of judgement, we need to protect ourselves, to balance autonomy against the threat of engulfment.

Daniel Deronda recognises the security as well as the oppression given by clear definitions of self – the lines drawn by family or sexual relationships, by social rank and wealth, the stereo-types of nationality and religion. But it also shows how illusory these clear lines are, as they shade into the less direct links of adopted son and step-daughter, into landed gentry with a background in trade, or families like the Davilows who exist 'in that border-territory of rank where annexation is a burning topic'. Eliot is fascinated by the models which western society uses to impose order upon these shifting sands, and she focuses here on what one might call vertical structures, where people claim a 'natural' power over others which implies not only control but actual possession – the total right to rule. The narration draws continual analogies between social institutions such as the landed estate, the colony or the slave plantation, and the way individuals behave in private and family life – Grandcourt would have 'made a good governor of a colony'; Gwendolen, whose forebears got their wealth from the West Indies, finds herself a slave. In the background to the story echo political struggles which widen the references still further – Bismarck's campaigns, 'affairs in the South Seas', the American Civil War. We are reminded that (whether in public or in private life) the story told by the conqueror, the trader or the master will be very different from that of the people they colonise, exploit or enslave.

In a book which abounds with images of fetters, chains, handcuffs and bonds, the most powerful controlling force turns out not to be that of direct political or territorial rule but that of the indirect domination of the market. Notions of property and natural divisions into buyers and sellers link all the different groups in the book: Genoese merchants, East End pawnbrokers, landed gentry, professional artists. Furthermore the marketplace and patriarchy go hand in hand, for it is men who buy and sell, while women – like slaves – are disposable assets. This is the truth Mirah Lapidoth learns when she hears someone speculating about her father: 'I wonder what market he means the daughter for?'. Lapidoth not only exploits her gifts ('his wishing me to sing the greatest music and parts in grand operas was only wishing for what would fetch the highest price'), but even tries to sell Mirah herself, offering her as repayment to a count who has settled his gambling debts and secured his release from prison.

This sexual barter is cruder, but not in essence very different from the attitude of Mr Gascoigne – a 'gentleman' and clergyman – when he sizes up his daughter Anna and his niece Gwendolen to see if they will compete or complement each other in the county marriage stakes. George Eliot makes the point explicit in the epigraph to Chapter 10, which leads up to Gwendolen's meeting with Grandcourt:

> 1st gent: 'What woman should be? Sir, consult the taste
> Of marriageable men. This planet's store
> In iron, cotton, wool, or chemicals –
> All matter rendered to our plastic skill,
> Is wrought in shapes responsive to demand:
> The market's pulse makes index high or low,
> By rule sublime. Our daughters must be wives,
> And to be wives must be what men will choose:
> Men's taste is woman's test.'
>
> (*Daniel Deronda*, Chap. 10, p. 132)

Gwendolen, high with exhilaration, deludes herself that *she* will be the one to choose, but Eliot presses the point home in a cruel aside: 'perhaps it is not quite mythical that a slave has been proud to be bought first.' The harsh fact is that all women have to sell is themselves – either their bodies, like Gwendolen, or their art, like Mirah – and consequently they risk all in the transaction.

No wonder they long to escape. And the reader is allowed to feel that they can, for against these narrow vertical hierarchies of rank, rule and ownership George Eliot sets wide horizontal sweeps of time and space. Thus the houses of England which so often confine or entrap the womenfolk within are set against broad natural vistas. Like the Meyricks' cottage with its view of the stars, Offendene, where Gwendolen's mother Mrs Davilow settles with her daughters, suggests contrasting visions of constriction and escape:

The old oblong red-brick house, rather too anxiously ornamented with stone at every line, not excepting the double row of narrow windows and the large square portico . . . But though standing thus behind a screen amid flat pastures, it had on one side a glimpse of the wider world in the lofty curve of the chalk downs, grand steadfast forms played over by the changing days.

(*Daniel Deronda*, Chap. 3, p. 51)

The action of the story (which begins in the gaming room where all European races are represented) and the stories within the story told by 'wandering Jews' like Klesmer, Mirah and Mordecai provide a different kind of widening of the horizon, carrying the reader away from the nervous, rigid, English background to the edge of Europe itself. Both hero and heroine are forced to define themselves against the limitless background of the wider world and of historical change. This is something which is hard, even painful, to do for we are all, Eliot says, so used from birth to see the horizon only from our own perspective – as if we stood on a flat plain and marked the boundaries of the universe we inhabit by the range of our own eyes. Only very occasionally does anyone see their life in relation to the rolling movement of history, as Mordecai does when he hands on his mission to Daniel: 'The generations are crowding on my narrow life as on a bridge: what has been and what is to be are meeting there; and the bridge is breaking. But I have found you.'

But some people are more aware of their historical and cultural position than others, particularly artists and musicians whose life is spent reinterpreting tradition and yet adding to it. Deronda's artistic receptivity, which diminishes in a strange way his sense of self, makes him sensitive both to individual need and to historical flow. This is one of the key differences between him and Gwendolen, with her self-reflecting, self-referring way of judging outward events. Deronda reads Sismondi's *History of the Italian Republics* at the age of thirteen and grows up with a passion for history. But he wants to be an actor in the historical drama, and assumes that he can be, because he is a boy. Gwendolen, on the other hand, with her meagre girl's education, only a step above that of Rosamund Vincy or Esther Lyon, is entirely uninterested in history. She consistently, deliberately, closes her eyes to the wider view. Even her cultural vision is narrow, and Klesmer when he hears her sing has to urge her to leave trivia behind and find music with 'wider horizons'.

Yet Gwendolen too is obsessed with boundaries. Her early banter is larded with reference to explorers and discoverers. She sees her impotence, as Deronda sees his power, as 'natural' to her sex:

We women can't go in search of adventures – to find out the North-West Passage or the source of the Nile, or to hunt tigers in the East. We must stay where we grow, or where the gardeners like to transplant us. We are brought up like the flowers, to look as pretty as we can, and be dull without complaining. That is my notion about the plants: they are often bored, and that is the reason why some of them have got poisonous.

(*Daniel Deronda*, Chap. 13, p. 171)

Her horticultural conclusion brings her without knowing it to the conclusion of Mary Wollstonecraft and J.S. Mill. But because she lacks historical awareness she is unable to relate her personal restlessness to the rebelliousness of her contemporaries who actually want to change the position of women. She is in danger of thinking that this vegetable existence, at the mercy of male gardeners, is a 'natural state'. She is in danger, too, of accepting Grandcourt's reply, with its suggestion that there is only one kind of adventure possible: 'But a woman can be married.' It is, of course, a marvellous irony that her marriage, the most outwardly conventional step she takes, should be – as she knows so well – such a foolhardy and virtually immoral act.

Gwendolen's marriage to Grandcourt is a step of such magnitude and danger that, like Maggie Tulliver, she can only jump by abandoning her will. She drifts, is caught by currents and propelled towards the brink. Her fall is a sexual trespass, just as Maggie's desire for Stephen was; it is, if anything, less 'moral' than Lydia Glasher's relationship with the same man. For it is not impelled by love but by self-interest. It is a gamble. And Eliot shows us repeatedly that gambling – whether sexual or monetary – is always likely to have worse consequences for a woman than for a man. The risk is total, whereas for men, as we are told in relation to Grandcourt's 'youthful folly' with Lydia, 'All accounts can be suitably wound up when a man has not ruined himself, and the expense may be taken as an insurance against future error' (Chap. 13, p. 177). Women get no such second chance from a kind accountant.

Gambling, the image with which *Daniel Deronda* opens, is a surrender to chance. It is one way (a key way in a novel so linked to the rules of the market) that people feel they can fling aside the overt rules which govern their existence. Like drink or drugs – with which it is frequently linked – it is an intoxicating defiance of a dominant order. On a grander scale, as in the collapse of Grapnell and Co. which ruins Gwendolen's family fortunes, it threatens the solidity of the whole civilised, cultured social world.

Other elements in *Daniel Deronda* keep us alert to the way this social world may be only a façade. One is the insistence that our imaginations may be inhabiting another realm, often at the same time as we appear to be behaving 'normally'. Dreams, second sight, waking fantasies and all the sensational and melodramatic elements show how the ordinary world may fall apart, to reveal mysterious currents beneath. In Gwendolen's terror at the prophetic 'dead face' and fleeing girl painted on the hidden panel at Offendene, and in the fear of the dark which drives her to share her mother's bed, we see the same panic at crossing the threshold of the known and unknown which makes her recoil from the touch of men and shudder at the murderous fantasies lurking in the depths of her mind. The most brilliant touch is the way that the Gothic 'ghosts' whom she fears turn out to be real people like Lydia Glasher, who steps forth from Grandcourt's past to haunt his future bride. In the end it is the *reality* which is so terrifying: 'Gwendolen, watching Mrs Glasher's face while she spoke, felt a sort of terror: it was as if some ghastly vision had come to her in a dream and said, "I am a woman's life" ' (Chap. 14, p. 190).

Eventually she must face this fearful reality within herself. Eliot forces us to enter the undersea world of the mind, where feelings take on a life of their own, 'dim and clashing as a crowd of ghosts'. The petrifying vision of Lydia with her Medusa face drives Gwendolen nearer and nearer a different kind of forbidden threshold, where the figures of Grandcourt and herself change places in an unending dance of murderer and victim:

Fantasies moved within her like ghosts, making no break in her more acknowledged consciousness and finding no obstruction in it: dark rays doing their work invisibly in the broad light.

(Daniel Deronda, Chap. 48, p. 669)

By the time she reaches that Mediterranean sea these fantasies have taken on so vivid a life that they exist almost independent of herself:

In Gwendolen's consciousness Temptation and Dread met and stared like two pale phantoms, each seeing itself in the other – each obstructed by its own image; and all the while her fuller self beheld the apparitions and sobbed for deliverance from them.

(Daniel Deronda, Chap. 54, p. 738)

Her inner feelings parody the way she has watched and kissed her outer reflection in a series of mirrors in the past. At the terrible climax we experience her inner division directly, through the fractured words in which she describes the paralysis of her 'fuller self' when Grandcourt, knocked from the sailing boat by a swinging spar, cries out for help. Chance has played out her fantasy for her but she is now her own victim and destroyer: 'I was leaping away from myself – I would have saved him then. I was leaping from my crime' (Chap. 56, p. 761).

Daniel Deronda, a work supreme in conveying the sparkle and lush appeal of an over-sophisticated society, is thus also supreme in conveying the panic of individuals desperate to escape from their own fate, succumbing to the vertiginous lure of madness or death. Gwendolen is pulled back from the edge by Deronda, the perpetual rescuer, just as Mirah was pulled back by him from her suicidal leap into the dark waters of the Thames. The two women could not be more different – the key note of

Gwendolen's nature is the desire to dominate, that of Mirah's the urge to submit and trust. Yet Eliot gives them the same images to express the seductive appeal of death and the longing to wash away personality and memory: 'The more I thought', says Mirah, 'the wearier I got, till it seemed I was not thinking at all, but only the sky and the river and the Eternal God were in my soul. And what was it whether I died or lived? If I lay down to die in the river, was it more than lying down to sleep? – for there too I committed my soul – I gave myself up' (Chap. 20, p. 264).

What both women describe, with a mixture of longing and terror, is that melting of the self which all Eliot heroines feel at their darkest hour and which recurs so often that one cannot help feeling it must have been a crucial experience for the author herself. In her work this total self-loss often precedes a process of healing and self-discovery, and in *Daniel Deronda* Eliot attempts to explain how this might be. The impulse to surrender, she suggests, so destructive when turned inwards, is closely akin to the artist's abnegation of self. But the latter is positive because it is turned outwards, into communication with others. Shortly before he rescues Mirah, Daniel himself is drifting on the Thames:

He used his oars little, satisfied to go with the tide and be taken back by it. It was his habit to indulge himself in that solemn passivity which easily comes with the lengthening shadows and mellowing light, when thinking and desiring melt together imperceptibly, and what in other hours may have seemed argument takes the quality of passionate vision. . . . He chose a spot in the bend of the river just opposite Kew Gardens, where he had a great breadth of water before him reflecting the glory of the sky, while he himself was in shadow. He lay with his hands behind his head propped on a level with the boat's edge, so that he could see all around him, but could not be seen by any one at a few yards distance; and for a long while he never turned his eyes from the view right in front of him. He was forgetting everything else in a half-speculative, half-involuntary identification of himself with the objects he was looking at, thinking how far it might be possible habitually to shift his centre till his own personality would be no less outside him than the landscape.

(*Daniel Deronda*, Chap. 17, p. 229)

It is at this moment that he catches sight of Mirah, and rushes to her rescue.

The passage makes it clear that there is a way in which mortals can escape the bounds of self. Daniel's receptivity is extremely close both to what Keats described as the negative capability of the artist's imagination and to what George Eliot in all her earlier novels described as the essentially 'feminine' capacity to suppress the self in a relationship with another.[4] Daniel is not an artist but he and Mordecai are described as having a 'poetic yearning' in relation to their large political visions (if poets are indirect legislators then legislators may be hidden poets).

On a more direct level the novel presents art, and particularly music, as the one human activity which can transcend the boundaries of space and time. But there is a problem in raising culture to the level of salvation in this way. For Eliot is really writing only about a refined tradition of art, literature and music – Sophocles, Dante, Mozart – which is not accessible to those common people she set out at the start of her career to celebrate in her work. And even in elite circles the consolation of art is not open to all. For she insists that artistic talent, at the highest level, is a gift – backed up by training and hard work to be sure – but ultimately a quality of soul. The musicians and poetic visionaries in *Daniel Deronda* are the equivalent of the 'great souls' in *Middlemarch* and it is hard to apply their experience to the lot of common humanity – Gwendolen is excluded from this vocation just as certainly as she is excluded from Daniel's Jewish destiny. Every attempt she makes to act, to sing, to study, turns to disaster – she is warned off from the artist's life with the same sort of vehemence George Eliot had used thirty years before when she railed against amateur, second-rate writers (of the kind of books which Gwendolen enjoys as a girl) in 'Silly Novels by Lady Novelists'.

The privileges and pains of the true artist are shown in a trio of Jewish musicians, in whom the artist's status as permanent outsider is heightened by their race. There is Klesmer, the fiery composer and teacher based on Liszt and Rubinstein; Mirah, whose talent fits her for small, intimate performances; and Princess Halm-Eberstein, Daniel's mother, formerly the great opera singer Alchirisi. These three are shadowed, as it were, by talented amateurs like Catherine Arrowpoint and the Meyrick sisters, and by artists who work in different fields, like the painter Hans Meyrick. In a different rank again are those who wish to be considered as a part of the fellowship of artists but who lack real understanding or talent: Mrs Arrowpoint, with her foolish studies of Tasso's divine madness, and Gwendolen herself.

Gwendolen is attracted to the artist's life because it seems to offer the only escape from financial need which will satisfy her natural exhibitionism and which is compatible with her status as a 'lady' – for art defies social boundaries as well. In the Arrowpoint family the thought of romance between Klesmer and their daughter Catherine never arises, principally because of the unspoken hierarchy of the market-place: 'The large cheque that Mrs Arrowpoint was to draw in Klesmer's name seemed to make him as safe an inmate as a footman.' Once this is swept aside by Catherine's championship of different, non-material values (like Eppie, Esther and Dorothea before her), then nothing can separate the lovers. Klesmer himself claims the highest rank for the artist, that of Shelley's unacknowledged legislators of mankind: 'We help to rule the nations and make the age as much as any other public man. We count ourselves on level benches with legislators.' His retort to the accusation that he is not a gentleman rings with a pride his creator may also have felt when considering the 'respectability' of her own position: 'My rank as an artist is of my own winning, and I would exchange it for no other' (Chap. 22, p. 292).

But it is a rank won with pain, and as with all the gambles in this novel, the risks are far greater for a woman than for a man. Alchirisi (like George Eliot and in contrast to Klesmer) has to achieve triumph as an artist by defying the normal expectations of what a woman from her background should do. She turns her back first on the role laid down for her by her father and her race, and then on the conventional female destiny of motherhood, sending her son Daniel to be brought up as an English gentleman by Hugo Mallinger. She is like Armgart, the great opera singer in Eliot's poem of the same name, who claims that she was born an artist as much as she was born a woman and declares:

> I need not crush myself within a mould
> Of theory called Nature.
>
> *(Poems,* p. 98)[5]

Alchirisi speaks out clearly her sense of artistic vocation and her 'natural right' to escape from the narrow pattern of the good Jewish daughter (which is not so different from the pattern approved by the Pearson aunts which so oppresses poor Maggie Tulliver):

'I cared for the wide world, and all that I could represent in it. I hated living under the shadow of my father's strictness – "this you must be", "that you must not be" – pressed on me like a frame that got tighter and tighter as I grew. I wanted to live a large life, with freedom to do what every one else did, and be carried along in a great current, not obliged to care.'

> *(Daniel Deronda,* Chap. 51, p. 693)

Like Maggie, Romola, Mirah, Gwendolen and all the Eliot women who long to abandon themselves to a great current of irresponsibility she finds she cannot, eventually, escape the obligation of all people to care – 'the pressure of the common yoke of humanity'. Although she is absolutely right to see in art, however governed it is by the network of buyers and sellers, a 'chance for escaping from bondage' and a route to high status, she finds that the rank alone is insufficient, for it is lonely and impermanent. Like Armgart, Alchirisi loses her voice. Unable to bear the idea of remaining in the theatre as a mere actress, she retires from the stage into a loveless marriage, only to find that her voice returns, too late. Even in her last retirement, wasted by illness and haunted by dreams, she embodies the almost supernatural power of the woman artist caught by the world – evoked by the images of Erinna, the poet forced to sit and spin, or Melusina, half-woman, half-snake. Such power seems able even to cross that final boundary, which separates the living from the dead. This is our parting view of her:

> With the last words she raised her arms till they were bare to the elbow, her brow was contracted in one deep fold, her eyes were closed, her voice was smothered: in her dusky, flame-coloured garment, she looked like a dreamed visitant from some region of departed mortals.
>
> (*Daniel Deronda*, Chap. 53, p. 730)

She is the woman artist as sybil and prophetess, endowed with 'uncanny' power. The portrait of Alchirisi burns with energy, expressing the same feelings we encounter in George Eliot's own letters – her resistance to restrictions, her sense of destiny, her defiant yet pained awareness of what she lost in cutting herself off from her family and her background and in deciding not to have children, and her fear that her gift would vanish, never to return. But what Alchirisi lacked – and what George Eliot so joyfully seized and possessed – was the capacity to love, and the knowledge that she was loved in return.

In that parting image of the great singer the historical theme merges, suddenly and dramatically, with the theme of the re- demptive power of the passive imagination. Alchirisi's immense gift allows her to be at once a forceful individual performer and a vehicle for something greater and more resonant than herself which comes from the past and flows on into the future. Her son shares this gift, as we know, and on occasions that 'not other' – loss of self in fantasy or in identification with others – threatens to overwhelm his individuality altogether. He eventually becomes a vehicle for a different kind of music which will allow him too to inspire others. The idea is a difficult one to accept because of its elitism, and also the dangerous implications of notions of racial memory, a notion Eliot does not explore to the full. She is content to see in Daniel a model of the way that the 'feminine' capacity for fruitful sacrifice can channel historical currents and thus empower leadership as well as submission. Daniel speaks to

Mordecai of his life's task in language almost identical to that used by Eliot herself when she described how it felt when she was writing at full stretch, as if controlled by something outside herself:

It is you who have given shape to what, I believe, was an inherited yearning – the effect of brooding, passionate thoughts in many ancestors – thoughts that seem to have been intensely present in my grandfather. Suppose the stolen offspring of some mountain tribe brought up in a city of the plain, or one with an inherited genius for painting, and born blind – the ancestral life would lie within them as a dim longing for unknown objects and sensations, and the spell-bound habit of their inherited frames would be like a cunningly-wrought musical instrument, never played on, but quivering throughout in uneasy mysterious moanings of its intricate structure that, under the right touch, gives music. Something like that, I think, has been my experience.

(*Daniel Deronda*, Chap. 63, p. 819)

Gwendolen too crosses the boundaries of the self, but in a different way. She returns to England after plumbing the depths of her own anger, hatred, need and looking 'like one who had visited the spirit world and was full to the lips of an unutterable experience'. But hers is a sterner lot; she still has to see that she is not the centre of a special universe, and she is offered no vision of artistic or political greatness. The uncertain future which faces this dazzling, anguished heroine is hard for her, and hard for those generations of readers who have felt for her. But in leaving Gwendolen thus, George Eliot wrote the more truthful and courageous ending for the women of her day. It is an ending which asserts that while men are carried more swiftly by the currents of history, it is possible for women without a special mission or vocation to work for a better life for others without suffocating their sense of self. It is an ending which asks for boldness: we must stand alone but we must also be prepared to cross the boundaries into the unmapped territories which lie within us, as well as those without, and welcome without fear the wide horizons of the future.

CHAPTER FOURTEEN

WINTER AND SPRING

After the publication of *Daniel Deronda* life seemed to close in slightly around the Leweses – incredible though it seemed, it looked as if they might be moving into a mellow late middle age. But instead of calm came storm: the illness and death of George in 1878. Disabled for a time by grief and weakened by her own recurring renal illness, Marian could have declined into invalidism or gracious widowhood at the age of sixty. Instead she defied expectations and eighteen months later took a step which shocked her contemporaries almost as much as her early elopement – she married Johnny Cross, twenty years her junior.

John Cross was a constant visitor at The Priory in that winter of 1876–7. The Leweses cherished their friendship with him, his mother and his sister Eleanor. They often stayed with Cross's brother-in-law, Henry Bullock Hall, at his house at Six Mile Bottom near Cambridge. Johnny, who lived with his mother at Weybridge, had been set the task of looking out for a country house for them and in November 1876 he found one – The Heights at Witley, looking across the woods and fields of Surrey to the South Downs and the Sussex border. George and Marian were delighted and, taking Cross's shrewd financial advice, they made a cautious offer which was immediately accepted.

The Heights, they found, needed much alteration and they could not think of moving in until the following summer. So, after spending Christmas with the Cross family at Weybridge, they settled back into London life. They still read and studied together; when Marian was ill Lewes read aloud Harriet Martineau's *Autobiography* (written thirty years before but only just published), which prompted her to write tartly to Cara, the only friend to whom she always said just what she felt even if she took it back immediately afterwards:

One regrets continually that she felt it necessary not only to tell of her intercourse with many more or less distinguished persons – which would have been quite pleasant to everybody – but also to pronounce upon their entire merits and demerits, especially when, if she had died as soon as she expected, these persons would nearly all have been living to read her gratuitous rudenesses.

(*Letters*, Vol. VI, p. 353)

She kept her own ruthless analysis of people's 'entire merits and demerits' for her fiction.

In London the Leweses were seeing plenty of distinguished persons themselves; one party at the Lehmanns' included not only George and Marian and the Benzons, but Browning, Frederick Leighton and Clara Schumann – an extravagant display of Victorian culture. Music was a vital part of the pleasure of this circle and the Leweses were seen at private recitals and public concerts. (As it was at these concerts that many of the later sketches of Marian were made, including one by Princess Louise, it is not surprising that they show her looking formal and preoccupied.) In the spring Cosima Wagner arrived, bringing with her a letter of introduction to Lewes from Liszt, her father. While the Wagners were in England they saw the Leweses constantly and Marian arranged dinner parties and excursions for the dynamic young Cosima – not so tyrannical then as in later life. There were other, now annual, dates on their calendar such as visits to Oxford as the guests of Benjamin Jowett and to Cambridge where, in 1877, Marian visited Girton. Still unconfident despite her fame, she wrote to her young friend Georgie Burne Jones: 'I wonder what I ought to have for a morning dress to wear at breakfasts and walk out at Oxford and

Cambridge?', for she felt that her black silk 'of the robe species' would do for dinner, but wanted something 'less heavy and dust-showing for the daytime'. Then come the joking disclaimers: 'These remarks are to give you a faint idea of my heavy private anxieties – not to urge you into taking the trouble to write me advice' (*Letters*, Vol. VI, pp. 364–5).

But by the end of May they were longing to escape to The Heights and despite the usual plumbing problems they moved in, in 'camp style', in June. The summer passed in walks and talks with friends, and the good weather allowed them to indulge a craze for the new game of lawn tennis. It was Johnny who pushed Marian and George into playing, and even when they returned to London he kept them at work, sending a new badminton set for The Priory lawn, a gift which prompted one of several flirtatious notes to her 'dear nephew', as Marian called him. She wrote that really they were quite happy playing battledore and shuttlecock in their entrance hall, and continued:

Still – which would you choose? An aunt who lost headaches and gained flesh by spending her time on tennis and Badminton, or an aunt who remained sickly and beckoned death by writing more books? Behold yourself in a dilemma! If you choose the plump and idle aunt, she will declare that you don't mind about her writing. If you choose the pallid and productive aunt she will declare that you have no real affection for her. It is impossible to satisfy an author.

(*Letters*, Vol. VI, p. 415)

Maybe, but either way she is fishing for reassuring declarations of some sort. During these years I think she felt towards Johnny (who sent her, for example, large bunches of pansies – *pensées* – when she was ill) very much as she felt towards Edith, Elma, Georgie Burne Jones and the many passionate younger women who assuaged her deep insecurities. She was greedy for their affection – she said so openly – and was afraid to let them go, but she kept them at arm's length by a bantering, distancing tone.

She also simply enjoyed the company of people younger than herself, which is partly why she got on so well with Charles

Lewes, who had come to feel like her own son. In London that winter they often saw him and his family with their new baby Elinor. They liked this family life, but they were still very much in the public eye and could not avoid a round of social engagements. Some they enjoyed very much, for example a visit to the Bullock Halls where they met Turgenev, not only one of their favourite authors but a great admirer of Marian's novels. By now they were accepted into the very highest society. George Eliot's novels were admired by Queen Victoria, whose daughters were quick to show their favour. In May the previous year Princess Louise had asked the banker George Goschen to give a dinner party so that she could meet Marian; and now Lewes, at a concert, was summoned to the box of Princess Christiana of Schleswig-Holstein to 'talk about Polly's works'. Then in May the Goschens were asked to invite the Leweses to another dinner, this time to meet the Princess Royal, Crown Princess of Germany. Cara received a wry, pleased account:

The royalties did themselves much credit. The Crown Prince is really a grand looking man, whose name you would have asked for with expectation if you imagined him no royalty. He is like a grand antique bust – cordial and simple in manners withal, shaking hands and insisting that I should let him know when we next came to Berlin, just as if he had been a Professor Gruppe, living *au troisième*. *She* is less distinguished in physique, but equally good-natured and unpretending, liking best to talk of nursing soldiers and of what her Father's taste was in literature. She opened the talk by saying, 'You knew my sister Louise' – just as any other slightly embarrassed mortal might have done.

(*Letters*, Vol. VII, pp. 29–30)

Marian's only complaint was that 'she never sat down till quite late in the evening – a sore trial to plebeian legs and backs'.

In June, after their usual summer visit to Oxford, they turned their backs on society and fled to The Heights where they spent a quiet summer, punctuated only by visits from friends such as Edith Simcox and neighbours like Tennyson (to whom they had become very close), the Cross family, the artist Helen Allingham and her husband, and the Tom Trollopes, their hosts in

Florence, whom they had not seen for the last nine years. But work was never far from their minds. Marian was finishing the essays which were included in *Impressions of Theophrastus Such*. These essays throw interesting sidelights on her life: the portrait of Theophrastus's conservative father could be Robert Evans, and George Bernard Shaw was absolutely convinced he caught a glimpse of Lewes in 'a certain passage . . . about an amateur vocalist who would persist in wrecking himself on O Ruddier than the Cherry'.[1] And it also shows her continued intolerance towards lesser women writers. This time her target was not the lady novelist but the non-fiction writer, satirised in the pretentious 'Vorticella' from the Channel Islands who could toss off a book on history, geography or any other subject in each island she stopped at. No wonder hard-working writers like Eliza Lynn Linton resented her, or that Mrs Oliphant, who admired her work greatly, said it was impossible to compare the life of a burdened professional woman with that of such a figure, 'kept in a mental greenhouse and taken care of' by G.H. Lewes.[2]

In addition to his careful tending of Marian's genius ('proving conclusively in his own person', said Shaw, 'that "womanly self-sacrifice" is an essentially manly weakness'), George was deep in his own work, another volume of *Problems of Life and Mind*. But he was not well: he had cramp, gout and rheumatism, was unable to sleep or concentrate. Although he still told his famous stories, played tennis and 'sang the major part of the Barber of Seville' with Marian accompanying him, he was often noticeably quiet and withdrawn, avoiding all discussions on the subject of death. As they lingered on at Witley, trying to prolong the summer into November, their mood became increasingly sombre. In hopes of improving Lewes's health they went to Brighton for a week, but as soon as they got back to London he collapsed with severe enteritis. He was, Marian told Georgie, 'grievously ailing'. He himself thought that 'the storm had passed' and was still able to send off the manuscript of *Theophrastus* to Blackwood. But, unknown to him, he was dying from cancer. Despite their doctor Sir James Paget's ambiguous words that 'the actual trouble will soon be allayed', neither

Marian nor George himself realised that he was going to die so soon. The shock of his final decline, when it began on 28 November, was unbearable. Charles was summoned and Johnny Cross was told to take care of Marian's investments – and given a box of cigars for his brother. The next day, in the evening, Lewes died.

It was like a physical blow, which left her maimed, retreating into grief as into a dark cave. She could not go out without George who had been, for so many years, the outgoing part of herself. Deprived of his presence she clung to his absence and made her very grief a replacement for him. As she had written of Gwendolen, a great passion makes everything seem porous, and for the next few weeks all she did or touched seemed penetrated by her sense of loss. For the first week she stayed in her room, brooding on death, copying stanzas of *In Memoriam* and other meditations on bereavement; her cries of pain were heard throughout the house. She did not go to his funeral. But eventually she came down, and then steadily, for the next few weeks, seeing no one, she worked on the manuscript of the last part of *Problems of Life and Mind*. Not until she was satisfied with this did she go out into the garden or reply to a single note. Her first letter was to Barbara, on 2 January:

I bless you for all your goodness to me, but I am a bruised creature, and shrink even from the tenderest touch. As soon as I feel able to see anybody I will see *you*.

(*Letters*, Vol. VII, p. 93)

Others wanted to see her. In the grim winter weather Johnny Cross and Edith Simcox met at the gate, hovering, waiting for news. But she would not see them, putting Johnny off until the end of February.[3] Gradually she emerged, brought back into the world by the need to see the men whose help she wanted to set up a George Henry Lewes Studentship at Cambridge. She began to write to Blackwood, who was ill himself and would die the following September, about the business details which Lewes had always dealt with, and in March she started to see her friends – Herbert Spencer, Elma Stuart, Bessie Belloc.

It turned out that Bessie wanted to ask for a loan of £500. This was another aspect of life George had always handled and a matter with which Marian seems to have felt unable to cope. She summoned her financial adviser, her dear 'nephew':

Dearest.
I am in dreadful need of your counsel. Pray come to me when you can – morning, afternoon or evening. I shall dismiss anyone else.

(*Letters*, Vol. VII, p. 138)

From then on they saw each other often. She valued Johnny's advice, but also his company and his shared determination to recover from grief, for his mother had died just a week after Lewes. They began to spend time together, and to read Dante, which Johnny had been stumbling through with the help of Carlyle's translation. In his biography he wrote that when he told Marian she exclaimed, '"Oh I must read that with you." And so it was.' In the next year they read the *Inferno* and the *Paradiso* with minute attention to each grammatical point: 'The divine poet took us into a new world. It was a renovation of life.'[4]

When Barbara saw her in July she had recently been ill again and was wasted away, not the giantess we imagine somehow (perhaps because the portraits always concentrate on her large head), but a tiny woman of seven stone, 'a black shadow of herself'. She did, however, seem to have a new vivacity and to be determined to recover because, she told Barbara, 'the world was so *intensely interesting*'. Although her kidney illness brought acute pain her letters show her emerging into vivid life, like the breaking of a chrysalis.

During these months, Cross wrote later, his feeling for Marian 'engrossed me completely'. People had often been fascinated with her, she was used to that; and she was even used to Johnny being in love with her. What was difficult was to allow herself to *accept* this love, to return it, to be dependent again and perhaps shock her friends and admiring public by doing so. There were precedents: when Annie Thackeray married Richmond Ritchie in 1877 Marian said she felt that 'the nearly twenty years' difference between them was bridged hopefully by his solidarity and gravity. This is one of several instances that I have known of lately, showing that young men with even brilliant advantages will often choose as their life's companion a woman whose attractions are wholly of the spiritual order' (*Letters*, Vol. VI, p. 398). But there was still bound to be gossip about the kind of relationship that could exist between an ill, sixty-year-old intellectual woman and a young, strong, red-bearded city financier. She had to say, yet again, that she did not care for the opinion of the world and his wife.

Johnny was in many ways the opposite of Lewes: steady where he had been mercurial, slow where he was quick, physical where he was intellectual. His physical energy may have been part of his appeal, for Marian had lived so much with illness. She and Lewes, as Phyllis Rose perceptively suggests in *Parallel Lives*, almost made their ill health a hostage to fortune, as if it was the price they had to pay for their happiness together.[5] Cross asked her to marry him three times before she accepted. Although she poured out sentiment in her letters ('Best loved and loving one – the sun it shines so cold, so cold when there are no eyes to look love on one'), her correspondence also shows how intensely nervous she was at the thought of such a step. The winter passed before she said yes, on 9 April 1880, after taking the advice of her doctor Sir James Paget – which makes Johnny seem even more like a physical cure.

They at once chose a house, at 4 Cheyne Row, and within a month they were married, having told virtually no one except the close family. The wedding, on 6 May, was at St George's, Hanover Square, a further blow to her free-thinking and Unitarian friends, while her Positivist friends, like the Congreves, were distressed at her breaching the doctrine of 'perpetual widowhood'. At once, as so often, Marian was off across the Channel, this time not to escape reviews of a new book but, as in 1854, to evade shocked exclamations of her friends, many of whom she had left only with cryptic notes about her intentions. Poor Charles had to break the news to some of the closest – Edith, Elma and Georgie – and although he did his best to make it all sound quite reasonable the town buzzed with rumour. Annie Thackeray Ritchie, whom he probably expected to be sympathetic, was agog with excitement: 'I am still thrrrrrrilling over a conversation I had yesterday with Charles Lewes', she wrote. 'Lionel Tennyson was here; he declared that his hair stood on end as he listened' (*Letters*, Vol. VII, p. 284).

One person Marian wrote a full explanation to was Barbara, only to leave the letter 'accidentally' in a drawer, not to be discovered for seven weeks. But Barbara needed no explanations; when the news reached her she wrote with characteristic warmth and open-mindedness:

> My dear I hope and I think you will be happy. Tell Johnny Cross I should have done exactly what he has done if you would have let me and I had been a man.
>
> You see I know all love is so different that I do not see it unnatural to love in new ways – not to be unfaithful to any memory. If I knew Mr Lewes he would be glad as I am that you have a new friend.
>
> I was glad to hear you were going to Italy but I did not guess this.
>
> My love to your friend if you will.
>
> Your loving
>
> Barbara
>
> (*Letters*, Vol. VII, p. 273)

They were indeed off to Italy, travelling via Paris and Grenoble to Milan. In Milan she wrote to her brother Isaac who had written to congratulate her, his first communication for over twenty years, a marvellous irony given that this marriage was almost more unconventional than her life with Lewes. True to the Pearson spirit, pinned down for ever in the Dodsons of *The Mill on the Floss*, he proved again that it was the form he valued, not the content. But Marian was delighted and Isaac's note added to her happiness. She looked better every moment and, said Cross, 'She began at once to look many years younger'. But, as if relieved of the responsibility of caring for her, Johnny himself snapped – he jumped from the window of their hotel in Venice into the Grand Canal below, whether under the influence of fever or of an acute depression no one knows, though many continue to speculate. Fished out by gondoliers, sedated with chloral, his brother summoned from England – here was food for more club-land rumours. Had he tried to commit suicide? All the old myths of Eliot's sexual voracity, dating from the time of her elopement with Lewes when Carlyle dubbed her 'a strong-minded woman' and others called her simply 'a harlot', suddenly surfaced. Were they expressions of the fear of inadequacy many men seem to feel when faced by a woman of unconventional power and strength?[6]

Untroubled by rumours, the Crosses limped homewards, allowing Johnny to recuperate in the Black Forest spa of Wildebad. Then, once they crossed the Channel back again to the damp English climate, Marian herself gave way. It is sad to read her letters, where determined cheerfulness fights against an emptiness beneath. The relationship, though a good one, was *not* like that with Lewes after all, and perhaps she did feel out of her depth, surrounded by Johnny's friends. The cruel comments of Mrs Jebb may have some truth in them:

She adores her husband, and it seemed to me it hurt her a little to have him talk so much to me. It made her, in her pain, slightly irritated and snappish, which I did not mind, feeling what troubled them was beyond remedy. He may forget the twenty years' difference between them, but she never can . . .[7]

Marian was also troubled by the planned move to Cheyne Walk which meant that in November she had to spend days going through all her papers, deciding what she should shed of her past and what she should keep. Her poor health meant, as she wrote to Elma Stuart, that she was 'obliged to be passive and useless'. Johnny organised everything, the shelves of books were arranged exactly in the order they had been in at The Priory, and on 3 December they moved in. At once they started the kind of London life they planned to have: going to a Greek production of the *Agamemnon*, attending a concert, asking friends round. But when Herbert Spencer visited them on Sunday 19 November Marian was complaining of 'a slight throat'. After he left she sat down to write to Mrs Strachey about her sister, recently widowed, consoling her: 'One great comfort I believe she has – that of a sister's affection.' They were her last written words.

No one suspected the illness was serious, just a touch of laryngitis. But her pulse was racing and by Wednesday, after a day's reprieve, she was in severe pain. That evening, while she dozed, Johnny said, 'I listened to her breathing, hoping it was coming sleep – but it was death coming on'. Her face was ashen, her hands cold; her heart had been fatally weakened and, complaining briefly of a great pain in her left side, she slipped into unconsciousness. Cross wrote to Elma Stuart that she:

passed away quite painlessly at 10 last night. And I am left alone in this new house we meant to be so happy in. And your heart too will know the void there is no filling.

(*Letters*, Vol. VII, p. 351)

George Eliot was buried in Highgate cemetery, the corner of her grave just touching that of George Lewes, on 29 December 1880. In driving sleet and snow a crowd of mourners watched. Among them were Charles Lewes, Spencer, William Blackwood, Robert Browning – and Isaac Evans, tall and stooping, bearing a clear resemblance to Marian. As with Tom and Maggie Tulliver it had taken death to bring brother and sister close again, but too late, and with no reconciling embrace. The names listed in the papers were almost all of men but, writes Gordon Haight, 'from other accounts we know that there were as many women as men at the ceremony'.

Right into this century George Eliot, and her reputation, seemed to be the property of men, from five years after her death when Cross wrote her life, to 1902 when Leslie Stephen pronounced upon her achievement, and up into the '40s when Leavis aligned her with the 'great tradition' of Dickens and Lawrence. But, as Virginia Woolf's essay should remind us, and as the wealth of recent feminist criticism has confirmed, there have always been as many women as men at the ceremony. It is because of Eliot's own awareness of their exclusion and her depiction of the complex relations of power between men and women that her fiction is so rich. And it is because of her exploration of the complementary nature of masculine and feminine qualities (within individuals of both sexes as well as within societies), and her subtle re-working of the images of the good daughter, sister, wife and mother, that her novels remain so suggestive and disturbing, particularly to women readers. She uses the metaphors of separate spheres, not to justify women's restriction to the realm of 'feeling' and domesticity, but to argue that the sympathy and sense of responsibility for others traditionally associated with 'maternity', and the passion and intuitive vision associated with 'female irrationality' should be brought to bear in the 'masculine' spheres of action and judgement. While women will be better able to achieve their full potential if they are given access to good education and to professional work, so men will grow if they are free to nurture and care – like Silas, Rufus Lyon and Daniel Deronda. If this could be achieved, society might replace a repressive, rule-bound ethic with one that is flexible, imaginative, and able to cater for humanity in its infinite variety.

Her fiction does not realise this vision, for the novels are firmly rooted in the existing world, a world which demonstrates the difficulty of achieving utopias. Its very obstacles, however, make such guiding visions more important. Although the fate of her heroines may make us uncomfortable, George Eliot's art, like her life, shirks very little and questions much. She shows us a world where biological destiny, patriarchal law and ingrained social assumptions seem to combine in a web of constraint, where it may not be possible to reach all our goals, and where people are separated from each other and divided within themselves. But her daring lies in her acceptance of difficulty and doubt, and her insistence that if we combine anger with humour and analysis with sympathy (as she does in her writing) both women and men *can* reach the higher ground and achieve a vantage point from which we can see clearly, make choices, and create our own futures in defiance of our vast uncertainties.

NOTES

Introduction

1. For persuasive readings, which also relate Eliot's work to contemporary women's writing, see Sandra M. Gilbert and Susan Gubar, *The Madwoman in the Attic* (New Haven and London, Yale University Press, 1979); Nancy Miller, *The Heroine's Text: Readings in the French and English Novel* (New York, Columbia University, 1980); Nina Auerbach, *Woman and the Demon: The Life of a Victorian Myth* (Cambridge, Mass. and London, Harvard University Press, 1982), and Gillian Beer, *George Eliot* (Brighton, Harvester Press, 1986).

2. This element is very clearly brought out by Gilbert and Gubar in 'George Eliot as the Angel of Destruction' in *The Madwoman in the Attic*, pp. 478–535; Carol Christ, 'Aggression and Providential Death in George Eliot's Fiction' (*Novel*, 9, 1976, pp. 130–40) also discusses the 'magical connection' between the victim and the person who desires his or her death.

3. After 1850 she never deviated from this stance, which is made most explicit in 'The Natural History of German Life', *Essays of George Eliot*, ed. Thomas Pinney (London, Routledge & Kegan Paul, 1963), and the 'Address to working men by Felix Holt' (appendix to *Felix Holt*, Harmondsworth, Penguin, pp. 607–27).

4. Compare Virginia Woolf, 'Thought of my own power of writing with veneration, as something incredible, belonging to someone else; never again to be enjoyed by me' (*A Writer's Diary*, London, The Hogarth Press, 1954).

5. George Eliot's influence and incorporation into the work of later women writers is demonstrated in Elaine Showalter's 'The Greening of Sister George', *Nineteenth Century Fiction* 35, 1980, pp. 292–311. That the novels do repay reading in the light of the politics of 'women's writing' is shown by Mary Jacobus's essay 'The Question of Language: Men of Maxims and *The Mill on the Floss*' in *Writing and Sexual Difference*, ed. Elizabeth Abel (Brighton, Harvester Press, 1982). The theoretical and polemical basis of this approach is that of Luce Iragaray's essay 'This sex which is not one' in *New French Feminisms: An Anthology* ed. Elaine Marks and Isabelle de Courtivron (Brighton, Harvester Press, 1981), pp. 245–64. See also the essays by Hélène Cixous, 'The Laugh of the Medusa', and those by Xavier Gautier and Julia Kristeva in the same anthology.
6. Virginia Woolf, 'George Eliot', *The Times Literary Supplement*, 20 November 1919, reprinted in *The Common Reader I* (London, The Hogarth Press, 1984), pp. 171–2.

Chapter One: Growing Up at Griff

1. J.W. Cross, *George Eliot's Life as related in her Letters and Journals* (Edinburgh, Blackwood, 3 vols., 1885).
2. Her relationship with Isaac and its transformation in the sonnet sequence are suggestively linked by Ruby Redinger in *George Eliot: The Emergent Self* (New York, Knopf and London, The Bodley Head, 1976), pp. 45–65.
3. See Gordon S. Haight, *George Eliot: A Biography* (Oxford, The Clarendon Press, 1968), p. 6; Blanche Bolton Williams, *George Eliot* (New York, Macmillan, 1936), p. 10; Redinger, op. cit., pp. 39–43. It is noticeable that in Eliot's novels the realistic, often critical, portraits of mothers are balanced by the tendency of motherless children, like Eppie, Romola, Esther, Dorothea, Daniel and Mirah, to idealise their image of their mother.
4. Cross, op. cit., p. 19.
5. See Ellen Moers, 'Performing Heroism: The Myth of Corinne' in *Literary Women* (London, The Women's Press, 1978, pp. 173–210) for an impression of the impact of de Staël on nineteenth-century women writers.
6. Cross, op. cit., p. 26.

7. See 'Evangelicalism and the Power of Women' in Jane Rendall, *The Origins of Modern Feminism* (London, Macmillan, 1985). Eliot read Sarah Lewis's *Women's Mission*, with its emphasis on power through renunciation, in 1838 and was 'electrified' by it.

Chapter Two: From Coventry to Geneva

1. J.A. Froude, *Thomas Carlyle: Life in London* (London, Longmans, 1884), pp. 290–1.
2. 'Thomas Carlyle', *Leader* VI, 27 October 1855, pp. 1034–5.
3. Although the context usually shows that she no longer took it seriously, see, for example, *The Lifted Veil*, p. 6 and *Felix Holt*, p. 148. For the relation between *Felix Holt* and phrenology see Sally Shuttleworth, *George Eliot and Nineteenth Century Science* (Cambridge, Cambridge University Press, 1984), pp. 123–32.
4. Charles Bray, *Phases of Opinion and Experience during a Long Life: An Autobiography* (London, Longman, 1884), p. 23.
5. Mathilde Blind, *George Eliot* (London, W.H. Allen, 1883), p. 25.
6. Sara Hennell, *A Memoir of Charles Hennell* (printed for private circulation, 1899).
7. Charles Hennell, *An Inquiry into the Origins of Christianity* (1838), Preface VIII.
8. Haight, op. cit., p. 186.
9. The facts about the Bray household were only recently discovered; see 'George Eliot's Bastards' in *George Eliot: A Centenary Tribute*, ed. Gordon Haight and Rosemary T. Van Arsdel (London, Macmillan, 1982).
10. *Diaries and Letters of Marie Belloc Lowndes*, ed. Susan Lowndes (London, Chatto & Windus, 1971).
11. Patricia Thomson, *George Sand and the Victorians* (London, Macmillan, 1977, p. 3): a fascinating account of Sand's influence.
12. Blind, op. cit., p. 87.

Chapter Three: The Westminster Review

1. See G. Haight, *George Eliot and John Chapman* (New Haven and London, Yale University Press, 1940) for a full account, and also Haight, op. cit., pp. 80–95.

2. Eliza Lynn Linton, *My Literary Life* (London, Hodder & Stoughton, 1899). This opinion is quoted by Elaine Showalter, as evidence of the way the Eliot legend made other women writers feel inadequate, in *A Literature of Their Own* (London, Virago, 1978, pp. 107–8).

3. Chapman's diary for 28 May 1851, in Haight, op. cit., p. 90.

4. For a history and detailed contents list of *The Westminster Review* see *The Wellesley Index to Victorian Periodicals*, ed. Walter Houghton, Vol. III (London, Routledge & Kegan Paul, 1979), pp. 525–705.

5. William Hale White, *Athenaeum*, 28 November 1885, p. 702. See also his portrait of Teresa in *The Autobiography of Mark Rutheford*, 1885.

6. Bessie R. Belloc, 'Dorothea Casaubon and George Eliot', *Contemporary Review*, 65, February 1894, p. 213, quoted by Haight, op. cit., p. 103. For Bessie's own account of their first meeting and long friendship see her essays, *In a Walled Garden* (London, Ward & Downey, 1895).

7. Ludwig Feuerbach, *The Essence of Christianity*, trans. Marian Evans (London, John Chapman, 1854), p. 271.

8. Haight, op. cit., p. 148.

9. It was at Tenby, in July, that Marian allegedly told Barbara, who had come to visit them, how tender and satisfying the sexual side of her relationship with Lewes was and said that they had definitely decided not to have children. See Haight, op. cit., p. 205.

10. 'The Morality of Wilhelm Meister', *Leader* VI, 21 July 1855, p. 703; reprinted in *Essays*, pp. 146–7.

11. 'Evangelical teaching: Dr Cumming', *Westminster Review* 64, October 1855, pp. 436–62; reprinted in *Essays*, pp. 187, 188.

12. See Gillian Beer, *Darwin's Plots: Evolutionary Narrative in Darwin, Eliot and Nineteenth-Century Fiction* (Brighton, Harvester Press, 1983).

13. 'The Natural History of German Life', *Westminster Review* 66, July 1856, pp. 51–79.

Chapter Four: 'George Eliot' and the Woman Question in the 1850s

1. The three essays which I use as the basis for discussion in this chapter are: 'Woman in France: Madame de Sablé', *The Westminster Review* 62, October 1854, pp. 448–73; 'Margaret Fuller and Mary Wollstonecraft', *Leader* VI, October 1855, pp. 988–9, and 'Silly Novels by Lady Novelists', *The Westminster Review* 66, July 1856, pp. 51–79; they are reprinted in *Essays*, ed. Pinney, pp. 52–81, 199–206 and 300–24. Karen McCormack argues that Marian's reading of Wollstonecraft strongly influenced 'Silly Novels by Lady Novelists', in 'George Eliot and Mary Wollstonecraft', *English Language Notes*, September 1981.

2. For useful surveys of published debates as they appeared in contemporary journalism, books and fiction, see Barbara Kanner's bibliographies in *Suffer and Be Still: Women in the Victorian Age* and *A Widening Sphere: Changing Roles of Victorian Women*, both ed. Martha Vicinus (Bloomington and London, Indiana University Press, 1972 and 1977); *Women in Britain from Anglo-Saxon Time to the Present*, ed. Barbara S. Kanner, and Elizabeth Helsinger, Robin Sheets and William Veeder, *The Woman Question: Society and Literature in Britain and America, 1837–1883*, (3 vols., New York and London, Garland, 1983), Vol. 3: *Literary Issues*.

3. Florence Nightingale, 'A Note of Interrogation', *Fraser's Magazine* 87, 1873, p. 567, quoted in Shirley Foster, *Victorian Women's Fiction* (London, Croom Helm, 1985), p. 194.

4. These quotations, listed in the order used, are taken from *Letters*, Vol. I, p. 366; Vol. II, pp. 39–40, 31, 27, 104.

5. For this vital friendship see Hester Burton, *Barbara Bodichon, 1827–1891* (London, John Murray, 1949); Muriel Bradbrook, 'Barbara Bodichon, George Eliot and the Limits of Feminism', *Women and Literature, 1779–1982* (Brighton, Harvester Press, 1982), and Sheila Herstein, *A Mid-Victorian Feminist: Barbara Leigh-Smith Bodichon* (Cambridge, Mass. and London, Yale University Press, 1986).

6. 'A Gentle Hint to Writing Women', *Leader* I, 1850, p. 189, quoted at length in Helsinger, op. cit., pp. 5–6.

7. 'The Lady Novelists', *The Westminster Review* 58, July 1852, pp. 129–41.

8. 'Ruth and Villette', *The Westminster Review* 59, October 1853, pp. 474–91.
9. Gillian Beer, 'Marian Evans: Reading Women Writers', op. cit., pp. 31–50.

Chapter Five: Scenes of Clerical Life: Fruitful Sacrifice

1. Cheverel Manor was closely based on Newdigate Hall, which Eliot remembered from a child and which, she told Blackwood, had been similarly remodelled in Gothic fashion with beautiful ceilings. For photographs see Marghanita Laski, *George Eliot and her World* (London, Thames & Hudson, 1973).
2. On the physical scale and grandeur, the flowing hair and large hands of Eliot's women, compared to other contemporary heroines, and their relation to an iconography of female power, see Auerbach, *Woman and the Demon*, op. cit.

Chapter Six: Adam Bede: The Mystery Beneath the Real

1. Haight, op. cit., p. 247.
2. See Shuttleworth, op. cit., pp. 68–9 for an analysis of the conceptual link between *The Physiology of Common Life* and *The Mill on the Floss*.
3. See G.A. Davis, 'Ruskin's *Modern Painters* and George Eliot's Idea of Realism', *English Language Notes*, March 1981, and Eliot's review of Vol. III of *Modern Painters*, *Westminster Review* 65, April 1856, p. 626.
4. Haight, op. cit., p. 278.
5. See 'The History of Adam Bede', *Letters*, Vol. II, pp. 502–5, and the Nottingham Journal account, 20 March 1802, both reprinted as appendices to the Penguin edition. John Purkis in *A Preface to George Eliot* (London, Longman, 1985), p. 77, refers to a detailed version of this story in a book by Elizabeth Evans's great-nephew William Mottram, *The True Story of George Eliot*, and quotes the 'Ballad of Mary Voce':

> When Mary from the Prison came
> A crowd had gathered round
> But she was not dismayed, for now
> Her heart true peace had found.

Chapter Seven: The Lifted Veil: The Limits of Vision

1. This self-searching aspect has been noted by several critics. Two interesting examples are U.C. Knoepflmacher, in *George Eliot's Early Novels: the Limits of Realism* (Berkeley, Los Angeles and London, University of California Press, 1968), and Gilbert and Gubar in 'Made Keen by Loss: George Eliot's Veiled Vision', op. cit., p. 445, who write: 'Indeed Eliot's identification with the "half-womanish, half-ghostly" Latimer's powerlessness, his silence, his secondary status, his weak body and his wounded soul significantly illuminates her own attitudes toward her art and her gender. Driven by an intense need to be loved, motherless in a world of coercive fathers, a female is in a sense a paradigmatic second-born child who must resort to passivity and invalidism to survive.' But, at the same time, they also see Eliot as identifying with Bertha's elemental power and rage.

2. The image must have seemed particularly apt to a Victorian woman artist posing as a man; compare Elizabeth Gaskell's description of Charlotte Brontë: 'henceforward Charlotte Brontë's existence became divided into two parallel currents – her life as Currer Bell, the author, her life as Charlotte Brontë, the woman. There were separate duties belonging to each character, not opposing each other, not impossible, but difficult to be reconciled.' Elizabeth Gaskell, *The Life of Charlotte Brontë* (Harmondsworth, Penguin Books, 1985), p. 334; quoted in Jane Miller, *Women Writing about Men* (London, Virago, 1986), p. 273, n. 58. I am struck by the coincidence that Eliot read Mrs Gaskell's *Life* and found it 'deeply affecting' in April 1857 (*Letters*, Vol. II, pp. 318–20).

Chapter Eight: The Mill on the Floss: The Search for a Key

1. Maria Congreve later told Edith Simcox that she 'had loved my Darling lover-wise' in these early days (Haight, op. cit., p. 495).

2. Simone de Beauvoir, *Memoirs of a Dutiful Daughter*, trans. J. Kirkup (Harmondsworth, Penguin Books, 1963), p. 140.

3. Maggie's inability to plot, and her desire for vengeance have been read as both a personal and literary critique of conventional femininity. Ellen Moers sees it as the spite of Eliot herself, a plain

adolescent dreaming of fame, stamping on the notion that only love brings happiness, and taking 'her ugly revenge on blondes' (Moers, op. cit., pp. 174–5); but for a different reading see Nancy Miller's influential essay 'Emphasis Added: Plots and Implausibilities in Women's Fiction', *PMLA* 96, January 1981 (reprinted in *New Feminist Criticism*, ed. Elaine Showalter, London, Virago, 1986), and Margaret Homans, 'Eliot and Wordsworth' in *Writing and Sexual Difference*, ed. Abel, op. cit., pp. 53–71. Homans suggests that here 'Maggie discovers the inexorable laws of feminine plotting . . . her endeavour to depart from convention only underscores for her both the heroine's and her own entrapment'.

4. And see Mary Jacobus, 'Men of Maxims and *The Mill on the Floss*', *Writing and Sexual Difference*, ed. Abel, op. cit., pp. 37–52.

5. A similar example occurs when Mrs Tulliver meets Wakem. Of course, says the narrator, no one could tell he was a rogue just by looking at him: 'But it is really impossible to decide this question by a glance at his person; the lines and lights of the human countenance are like other symbols — not always easy to read without a key' (*Mill*, Book III, Chap. 7, p. 334).

6. See Barbara Hardy, 'The Mill on The Floss', in *Critical Essays on George Eliot* (London, Athlone Press, 1970); Gillian Beer, 'Beyond Determinism: George Eliot and Virginia Woolf' in *Women Writing and Writing about Women*, ed. Mary Jacobus (London, Croom Helm, 1979), p. 88; Carol Christ, op. cit., pp. 130–40. Nina Auerbach sees Maggie's death as not related to Isaac, but as vicarious punishment and payment for Eliot's own transformation into a 'fallen woman' through her union with Lewes, which had brought her such happiness and artistic power (Auerbach, op. cit., p. 94), while Tony Tanner suggests the orgasmic ending is a replacement for the forbidden sexual trespass with Stephen: 'There are cases when the bourgeois novel avoids adultery only by presenting and even pursuing something very close to incest', *Adultery and the Novel* (Baltimore and London, Johns Hopkins University Press, 1979).

Chapter Nine: Silas Marner: Springs of Renewal

1. We should not underestimate Eliot's fear of the 'degradation' which accompanied industrialism, and which underlies her alarm at the prospect of speedy democratic reforms in *Felix Holt*. In 1868 after she had visited Clifford Allbutt's new infirmary in Leeds she wrote to Barbara that 'the Leeds work-people we are told, are sadly coarse beer-soaked bodies, with pleasures, mostly of the brutal sort, and the mill-girls "epicene" creatures that make one shudder' (*Letters*, Vol. IV, p. 476).

2. Alexander Welsh, in his ingenious and detailed study *George Eliot and Blackmail* (Cambridge, Mass. and London, Harvard University Press, 1985), argues that all Eliot's later novels are structured on the idea of a discontinuous past, on hidden knowledge and on the 'culture of information'.

3. Carol Gilligan takes *The Mill on the Floss* rather than *Silas Marner* to illustrate the legal and moral difficulty, for Victorian women, of reconciling the 'feminine' ethic of responsibility and the 'masculine' ethic of individual rights. See *In a Different Voice: Psychological Theory and Women's Development* (Cambridge, Mass. and London, Harvard University Press, 1982).

Chapter Ten: Romola: Daughter to Mother

1. For the extraordinary hidden levels of symbolism in *Romola* see Joseph Wiesenfarth, 'Antique Gems from *Romola* to *Daniel Deronda*' in Haight and von Arsdel, op. cit., pp. 55–63.

2. See Hugh Witemeyer, *George Eliot and the Visual Arts* (New Haven and London, Yale University Press, 1979), pp. 58–60.

3. See Coral Ann Howells, 'Dreams and Visions in George Eliot's fiction', *AUMLA* 56, November 1981, pp. 167–72.

4. But Romola's search has been read as an expression of duty, in relation to Eliot's own life, by Susan M. Greenstein, 'The Question of Vocation: from Romola to Middlemarch', *Nineteenth Century Fiction* 35, 1980–1, p. 501: 'Surely, however, George Eliot's situation with respect to Agnes Lewes, despite obvious differences, bears an unmistakable resemblance to Romola's relation to the childish and innocent Tessa, Tito's unwitting concubine.' More interesting is that the motif of the adopted child as

compensation for the blasted life runs through her work from the *Scenes of Clerical Life* to *Daniel Deronda*.

5. Rosemary Ashton, *George Eliot* (Oxford, Oxford University Press, 1984), p. 57; she notes that Eliot was reading the early part of the *Philosophie positive* while working on *Romola* in 1861.

6. Louis Aimé Martin, *De l'Education des mères de famille, ou de la civilisation du genre humain par les femmes*, trans. Edwin Lee, 1842.

7. Kenneth Thompson, *Auguste Comte* (London, Nelson, 1976), p. 66. Thompson quotes a salient passage from the *Philosophie positive* on the role of women to soften and transform the egotism of men: 'Comme mère d'abord, et bientôt comme soeur, puis comme épouse surtout, et enfin comme fille, accessoirement comme domestique, sous chacun de ces quatre aspects naturels, la femme est destinée à préserver l'homme de la corruption inhérente à son existence pratique et théoretique.'

Chapter Eleven: Felix Holt, the Radical:
Personal and Political

1. For this and other extracts from the notes on *The Spanish Gypsy*, see Cross, op. cit., Vol. III, pp. 30–5.

2. Sally Shuttleworth (op. cit., pp. 28–31) links *Felix Holt* with Charlotte Brontë's *Shirley* (1848): both are novels about earlier uprisings written in a time of debate about possible revolution, and both draw analogies between women and workers. Shuttleworth sees *Felix Holt* as a regression to a more conservative position than that of *Romola* (as I do) but follows F.T. Myers in reading it in terms of Comte's 'concept of an ideal union between philosophers, who represent Intellect, the working class, who furnish Activity, and women, who embody Feeling'. On the other hand Bonnie Zimmerman in '*Felix Holt* and the true Power of Womanhood' (*ELH* 46, 1979) also links the feminist and radical strands in the novel, but relates them to Eliot's interest in the contemporary debate on women's suffrage.

3. See Florence Sandler, 'The Unity of Felix Holt' in Haight and von Arsdel, op. cit., pp. 132–52, but compare David Craig, 'Fiction and the Rising Industrial Classes', *Essays in Criticism* 17 (1967), pp. 64–75.

4. For a view of the influence of Greek drama see F.C. Thomson, '*Felix Holt* and Classical Tragedy', *Nineteenth Century Fiction*

(1966), pp. 47–58.

5. I discuss the subversive nature of sensation novels in my Introduction to M.E. Braddon's *Lady Audley's Secret* (London, Virago Press, 1985).

6. This strikes a familiar note in relation to mid-twentieth-century feminist rhetoric. Compare, for example, Hélène Cixous: 'Woman must put herself into the text – and into the world and into history – by her own movement', Marks and de Courtivron, *New French Feminisms*, p. 254.

Chapter Twelve: Middlemarch: Against Simplicity

1. Haight, op. cit., pp. 409–11.

2. Ibid., p. 417.

3. In addition to those mentioned below see her letters to Emily Davies, *Letters*, Vol. IV, pp. 437–8, Clementia Taylor, Vol. IV, p. 366, Sara Hennell, Vol. IV, p. 390 and Barbara Bodichon, Vol. IV, pp. 399, 425. Beer, *George Eliot*, Chap. 6, relates *Middlemarch* closely to this context as does Kathleen Blake in '*Middlemarch* and the Woman Question', *Nineteenth Century Fiction* 31 (1976), pp. 285–312.

4. Oscar Browning, *Life of George Eliot* (London, Walter Scott Ltd, 1899), p. 99.

5. Haight, op. cit., p. 445, *Letters of Emily Dickinson*, ed. T.H. Johnson (Cambridge, Mass., Harvard University Press, 1958), Vol. II, p. 506.

6. 'Middlemarch and the Passions' in Barbara Hardy, *Particularities: Readings in George Eliot* (London, Peter Owen, 1982), pp. 86–103; she is especially good on Will's false romanticism.

7. See Beer, *Darwin's Plots* (London, Routledge & Kegan Paul, 1983), pp. 176–9 for a different reading of the Ariadne–Antigone myth and of Dorothea as 'martyr and spiritual bride'.

8. For this nineteenth-century obsession see George Steiner, *Antigones: the Antigone Myth in Western Art, Literature and Thought* (Oxford and New York, Oxford University Press, 1986). Eliot's own review is 'The Antigone and its Moral', *Leader* VI, 27 October 1855, pp. 1034–5.

9. For the way the metaphor of obstructions and waves links the scene with Rosamund to that of Will I am indebted to Karen Chase, *Eros and Psyche: the Representation of Personality in*

Charlotte Brontë, Charles Dickens and George Eliot (London, Methuen, 1984).

10. Cross, op. cit., Vol. III, p. 306: 'she told me that in all her best writing there was a "not herself" which took possession of her, and that she felt her own personality to be merely the instrument through which this spirit, as it were, was acting. Particularly she dwelt on this in regard to the scene in 'Middlemarch' between Dorothea and Rosamund, saying that, although she always knew they had, sooner or later, to come together, she kept the idea resolutely out of her mind until Dorothea was in Rosamund's drawing-room. Then, abandoning herself to the inspiration of the moment, she wrote the whole scene exactly as it stands, without alteration or erasure, in an intense state of excitement and agitation, feeling herself entirely possessed by the feelings of the two women.'

Chapter Thirteen: Daniel Deronda: The Frontiers of Self

1. Haight, op. cit., p. 492.
2. But see Deirdre David, *Fictions of Resolution in Three Victorian Novels* (London, Macmillan, 1981), pp. 191—4 for a more psychoanalytical reading of Gwendolen. David also gives an excellent analysis of the Jewish element in *Daniel Deronda*.
3. K.A. Mackenzie, *Edith Simcox and George Eliot* (London, Oxford University Press, 1961), pp. 96—7.
4. One of the most suggestive discussions of Daniel's feminine 'priest-like' nature, his relation to his artist mother and to George Eliot herself ('He is both her son, and herself in the role of son'), is given by Jane Miller, op. cit., pp. 129—31.
5. See Kathleen Blake, who relates the dilemma to Eliot's own life, in 'Armgart — George Eliot on the Woman Artist', *Victorian Poetry* 18 (1980), pp. 75—80.

Chapter Fourteen: Winter and Spring

1. Moers, op. cit., p. 43.
2. Margaret Oliphant, *Autobiography* (W. Blackwood & Sons, Edinburgh & London, 1899), p. 5.
3. There has been speculation, based chiefly on her writing of the word 'Crisis' in her journal, that Eliot discovered while reading through Lewes's papers that he had been unfaithful to her, but this has never been confirmed. See M. Laski, op. cit., and John Bayley, *Times Literary Supplement*, 23 July 1982.
4. Cross, op. cit., Vol. III, p. 359.
5. Phyllis Rose, *Parallel Lives: Five Victorian Marriages* (London, Chatto & Windus, 1984), p. 228.
6. The latest in this tradition is David Williams in *Mr George Eliot: A Biography of George Henry Lewes* (London, Hodder & Stoughton, 1983). Williams suggests that Marian exhausted Lewes sexually, and says of Cross that although custom decreed that the man propose, 'There can be no doubt that it was she who made the running − he was tactful, reverent and scared out of his mind' (p. 286).
7. Lady Jebb, *With Dearest Love to All* (London, Faber & Faber, 1960), pp. 163−4, quoted in Haight, op. cit., p. 545.

SHORT BIBLIOGRAPHY

Works by George Eliot

First editions in book form
Note: all the following editions were published by William Blackwood
and Sons, Edinburgh and London, apart from the first edition of *Romola*, which appeared under the imprint of Smith, Elder and Co., London.

Scenes of Clerical Life, 2 vols., 1858
Adam Bede, 3 vols., 1859
The Mill on the Floss, 3 vols., 1860
Silas Marner: the Weaver of Raveloe, 1861
Romola, 3 vols., 1863
Felix Holt: the Radical, 3 vols., 1866
The Spanish Gypsy: a Poem, 1868
Middlemarch: a Study of Provincial Life, 4 vols. (published in 8 books),
    1871
The Legend of Jubal and Other Poems, 1874
Daniel Deronda, 4 vols. (published in 8 books), 1876
Impressions of Theophrastus Such, 1879

The most authoritative collected edition published in George Eliot's
own lifetime, corrected by herself, is the Cabinet Edition, published
by William Blackwood and Sons, 20 vols., 1878–80.

Translations and Essays

Strauss, David Friedrich, *The Life of Jesus, Critically Examined*, trans. from the 4th German edn. by Marian Evans, London (no pub.), 1846. Reprint of 1860 edn., St. Clair Shores, Minn., Scholarly Press, 1970.

Feuerbach, Ludwig, *The Essence of Christianity*, trans. Marian Evans, London, John Chapman, 1854. Reprint edn., Magnolia, Mass., Peter Smith, 1958.

Pinney, Thomas ed., *Essays of George Eliot*, London, Routledge & Kegan Paul, 1963. New York, Columbia University Press, 1963.

Critical and Biographical Works

Note: this list refers to books only. Individual articles, where relevant, have been listed in the notes.

Abel, Elizabeth, ed., *Writing and Sexual Difference*, Brighton, Harvester Press, 1982. Chicago, University of Chicago Press, 1983.

Adams, Ian, ed., *This Particular Web: Essays on Middlemarch*, Toronto, University of Toronto Press, 1975.

Ashton, Rosemary, *George Eliot*, Oxford and New York, Oxford University Press, 1983.

Auerbach, Nina, *Woman and the Demon: the Life of a Victorian Myth*, Cambridge, Mass. and London, Harvard University Press, 1982.

Basch, François, *Relative Creatures: Victorian Women in Society and the Novel, 1837–67*, London, Allen Lane, 1974. New York, Schocken Books, 1975.

Beer, Gillian, *Darwin's Plots: Evolutionary Narrative in Darwin, George Eliot and Nineteenth Century Fiction*, London, Routledge & Kegan Paul, 1983. New York, Methuen, 1983.

Beer, Gillian, *George Eliot*, Brighton, Harvester Press, 1986. Bloomington, Indiana University Press, 1986.

Blind, Mathilde, *George Eliot*, London, W.H. Allen, 1883. Reprint of 1888 edn., Brooklyn, N.Y., Haskell House, 1972.

Browning, Oscar, *George Eliot*, London, Walter Scott, 1890. Reprint of 1892 edn., ed. Eric S. Robertson, Philadelphia, Century Bookbindery, 1982.

Carroll, David, ed., *George Eliot: the Critical Heritage*, London, Routledge & Kegan Paul, 1971. New York, Barnes & Noble, 1971.

Chase, Karen, *Eros and Psyche: the Representation of Personality in Charlotte Brontë, Charles Dickens and George Eliot*, London and New York, Methuen, 1984.

Cross, J.W., *George Eliot's Life as Related in Her Letters and Journals*, 3 vols., Edinburgh, Blackwood, 1885. Reprint edn., Philadelphia, Richard West, 1973.

David, Deirdre, *Fictions of Resolution in Three Victorian Novels: 'North and South', 'Our Mutual Friend', 'Daniel Deronda'*, London, Macmillan, 1981. New York, Columbia University Press, 1981.

Davidson, C.M. and Broner, E.M., eds., *The Lost Tradition: Mothers and Daughters in Literature*, New York, Frederick Ungar Publishing Co., 1980.

Foster, Shirley, *Victorian Women's Fiction: Marriage, Freedom and the Individual*, Beckenham, Croom Helm, 1985. New York, Barnes & Noble Imports, 1985.

Gilbert, Sandra and Gubar, Susan, *The Madwoman in the Attic: the Woman Writer and the Nineteenth-Century Literary Imagination*, New Haven and London, Yale University Press, 1979.

Haight, G.S., *George Eliot and John Chapman*, New Haven and London, Yale University Press, 1940.

Haight, G.S., ed., *The George Eliot Letters*, 9 vols., New Haven and London, Yale University Press, 1954–6, 1978.

Haight, G.S., ed., *A Century of George Eliot Criticism*, London, Methuen, 1986. Boston, Houghton Mifflin, 1965.

Haight, G.S., *George Eliot: a Biography*, Oxford and New York, Oxford University Press, 1968; reprinted, Harmondsworth, Penguin Books, 1986. Paperback edn., New York, Oxford University Press, 1976.

Haight, G.S. and von Arsdel, R.T., eds., *George Eliot: a Centenary Tribute*, London, Macmillan, 1982. New York, Barnes & Noble Imports, 1982.

Hardy, Barbara, *The Novels of George Eliot: a Study in Form*, London, Athlone Press, 1950. Paperback edn., New York, Oxford University Press, 1959.

Hardy, Barbara, *Critical Essays on George Eliot*, London, Athlone Press, 1970. Boston, Routledge & Kegan Paul, 1970.

Hardy, Barbara, *Particularities: Readings in George Eliot*, London, Peter Owen, 1982. Athens, Ohio University Press, 1983.

Hardy, Barbara, *Forms of Feeling in the Victorian Novel*, London, Methuen, 1985. *Forms of Feeling in Victorian Fiction*, Athens, Ohio University Press, 1985.

Helsinger, E.K., Sheets, R.L., and Veeder, W., *The Woman Question: Society and Literature in Britain and America, 1837–1883*, 3 vols., New York, Garland, 1983.

Jacobus, Mary, ed., *Women Writing and Writing about Women*, London, Croom Helm with Oxford University Women's Studies Committee, 1979. New York, Barnes & Noble Imports, 1979.

Knoepflmacher, U.C., *Religious Humanism and the Victorian Novel*, Princeton, N.J., Princeton University Press, 1965.

Knoepflmacher, U.C., *George Eliot's Early Novels: the Limits of Realism*, Berkeley, Los Angeles and London, University of California Press, 1968.

Laski, Marghanita, *George Eliot and Her World*, London, Thames & Hudson, 1973. Levittown, N.Y., Transatlantic Arts, 1974.

Leavis, F.R., *The Great Tradition*, London, Chatto & Windus, 1948. Paperback edn., New York, New York University Press, 1963.

MacKenzie, K.A., *Edith Simcox and George Eliot*, London, Oxford University Press, 1961. Reprint edn., Westport, Conn., Greenwood Press, 1978.

Marks, Elaine and de Courtivron, Isabelle, *New French Feminisms: an Anthology*, Brighton, Harvester Press, 1982. New York, Schocken Books, 1981.

Miller, Jane, *Women Writing about Men*, London, Virago, 1986. New York, Pantheon Books, 1986.

Miller, Nancy, *The Heroine's Text: Readings in the French and English Novel*, New York, Columbia University Press, 1980.

Millett, Kate, *Sexual Politics*, London, Abacus, 1972; reprinted London, Virago, 1977. Garden City, N.Y., Doubleday, 1970.

Moers, Ellen, *Literary Women: the Great Writers*, London, The Women's Press, 1978. Garden City, N.Y., Doubleday, 1976.

Moers, Ellen, *Nineteenth Century Fiction*, Special Issue, 'George Eliot 1880–1980', 35, December 1980.

Newton, Judith, *Women, Power and Subversion: Social Strategies in British Fiction, 1778–1860*, London, Methuen, 1983. Athens, University of Georgia Press, 1981.

Newton, Judith and Rosenfelt, Deborah, *Feminist Criticism and Social Change*, London and New York, Methuen, 1985.

Paris, Bernard, *Experiments in Life: George Eliot's Quest for Values*, Detroit, Mich., Wayne University Press, 1965.

Pinney, Thomas, ed., *The Essays of George Eliot*, London, Routledge & Kegan Paul, 1963. New York, Columbia University Press, 1963.

Purkis, John, *A Preface to George Eliot*, London and New York, Longman, 1985.

Redinger, Ruby, *George Eliot: the Emergent Self*, London, The Bodley Head, 1976. New York, Alfred A. Knopf, 1975.

Sadoff, Dianne, *Monsters of Affection: Dickens, Eliot, and Brontë on Fatherhood*, Baltimore and London, Johns Hopkins University Press, 1982.

Showalter, Elaine, *A Literature of Their Own: British Women Novelists from Brontë to Lessing*, Princeton, N.J., Princeton University Press, 1977; reprinted London, Virago, 1978.

Shuttleworth, Sally, *George Eliot and Nineteenth Century Science: the Make-Believe of a Beginning*, Cambridge and New York, Cambridge University Press, 1984.

Spacks, Patricia Meyer, *The Female Imagination: a Literary and Psychological Investigation of Women's Writing*, London, George Allen & Unwin, 1976. New York, Alfred A. Knopf, 1975.

Stephen, Leslie, *George Eliot*, London, Macmillan, 1902. Reprint edn., ed. John Morley, New York, AMS Press, 1971.

Tanner, Tony, *Adultery in the Novel: Contract and Transgression*, Baltimore and London, John Hopkins University Press, 1979.

Thomson, Patricia, *The Victorian Heroine: a Changing Ideal 1837–1873*, London, Oxford University Press, 1951. Reprint edn., Westport, Conn., Greenwood Press, 1978.

Thomson, Patricia, *George Sand and the Victorians: Her Influence and Reputation in Nineteenth-Century England*, London and Basingstoke, Macmillan, 1977. New York, Columbia University Press, 1976.

Willey, Basil, *Nineteenth Century Studies: Coleridge to Matthew Arnold*, London, Chatto & Windus, 1949. New York, Cambridge University Press, 1981.

Witmeyer, Hugh, *George Eliot and the Visual Arts*, New Haven and London, Yale University Press, 1979.

Woolf, Virginia, *The Common Reader I*, London, The Hogarth Press, 1925; repr. 1984. New York, Harcourt Brace Jovanovich, 1955; annotated edn., 1985.

INDEX

JENNIFER UGLOW was born in 1947, grew up in Cumbria and Dorset, and was educated at Cheltenham and Oxford. After finishing her research she began work in publishing and is now the editor of The Hogarth Press. She is the compiler of the *International Dictionary of Women's Biography*, has written for *The Times Literary Supplement*, *Literary Review*, *Guardian* and *Vogue* and has taught literature and women's studies in adult education over several years. Her great interest is Victorian literature, and she has edited works by Pater, George Eliot, Trollope and Meredith. She is married to a lecturer in law at the University of Kent, and they live in Canterbury with their four children.